COMPANY TOWNS
of the Pacific Northwest

Linda Carlson

Nov

04

COMPANY TOWNS
of the Pacific Northwest

LINDA CARLSON

UNIVERSITY OF WASHINGTON PRESS

Seattle and London

University of Washington Press
P.O. Box 50096, Seattle, WA 98145
www.washington.edu/uwpress

Library of Congress Cataloging-in-Publication Data
can be found at the back of the book.

The paper used in this publication is acid-free and recycled from 10 percent
post-consumer and at least 50 percent pre-consumer waste. It meets the
minimum requirements of American National Standard for Information
Sciences-Permanence of Paper for Printed Library Materials,
ANSI Z39.48–1984.⊗ ☺

CONTENTS

Contents

ACKNOWLEDGMENTS

MANY OF THE PEOPLE who lived in company towns and labor camps shared their memories, helping create a sense of what life was like in these unique communities during the twentieth century. Curators, archivists, public affairs directors, and museum staff have also provided invaluable help. Without the following, it would have been impossible to understand how daily life in company towns compared—and contrasted—to how other Americans lived during the same period: Mary Daheim (Alpine); Kate Krafft (Black Diamond); Marian Thompson Arlin, Roger Kiers, Ron and Mary Young McDivitt, Dave Parker, Marie Ruby, and Jack Young (Cedar Falls and the Cedar River watershed towns); Deanna Ammons (Clear Lake); Isabelle Fletcher Anderson, Mary Gilchrist Ernst, Charles Hale, Gary Poole, Art Sherman, and Joan Lockhart Snider (Gilchrist); Patti Case, Lou and Ann Messmer, and Peter Replinger (Grisdale); H. A. (Andy) Solberg and Michael D. Sullivan (Headquarters); Sandy Wigbers Adam, John Bley, Mike Brogan, Brenda Getty Clark, Betty Bickford Christianson, Gayle Rodgers Davidson, Elbert Hubbard, Sr., Linda Powell Jensen, Wilma Johnson, Mary Ellen Field Lacy, Joye Hamm Malmstrom, Jim Marr, the family of Larry Penberthy, Bill Phillips, Elmer Smith, Marge Haddon Stansfield, Patty Haddon Tappan, Vivien Weaver, Janet Adams Westom, and Harriet Wilbour (Holden); Marilyn Garcia, Gene Grant, and Max Woods (Kinzua); Louise Schmidt Robertson (Klickitat); Myrtle Beckwith Alexander and Florence Beckwith Pistilli (Kosmos); Steve Willis (McCleary);

Acknowledgments

Jack Coyner, John Hartman, and Erika Kulhman (Potlatch, Idaho); Ruth Redden Cole and Lee Maker (Shevlin); Megan Moholt and Frank W. Telewski (Vail); Donald Denno, Stacey Graham, and John Heffley (Valsetz); and Ted Rakoski (Whites). For information on railroads, I am indebted to John Phillips and Peter Replinger. For his enthusiastic assistance with photographs, special thanks to Daniel Kerlee.

The following also provided material of particular value: Washington State Historical Society; Washington State Library; Washington State Regional Archives, Bellevue and Ellensburg; Tacoma Public Library's Northwest Room and Special Collections; University of Washington Libraries, including Special Collections and Forest Resources; Forest History Society; Mason County Historical Society; McCleary Museum and the McCleary branch, Timberland Regional Library; Seattle Public Library; Seattle Public Utilities, Cedar River Watershed Education Center; Diocese of Olympia, the Episcopal Church in Western Washington; Synod of Alaska Northwest, Presbyterian Church (U.S.A.); the Milwaukee Road Collection of the Milwaukee, Wisconsin, Public Library; Deschutes County Historical Society; Polk County Historical Society; and the Potlatch, Idaho, Historical Society.

A project of this scope also requires the continuing support and discerning eyes of a publisher, and for that, my appreciation to Pat Soden and other staff members at the University of Washington Press.

For all the friends who encouraged me, even when the revising and footnoting and verifying were daunting, and for my husband and children, who claim they cannot remember when I wasn't writing a book, my thanks for your patience and forbearance.

Finally, for my parents and late grandparents, whom I remember standing on the porch at their lakeside cabin, watching the plume of smoke in the nearby hills and saying, "They're working at Clay City today," thank you for that childhood introduction to company towns.

COMPANY TOWNS
of the Pacific Northwest

1 / When the Boss Built the Town

Holden. McCleary. Clay City. Kinzua. Coulee Dam. DuPont. Diablo. Ryderwood. Richland. Potlatch. Port Gamble. Grisdale. Valsetz. Vanport. Black Diamond. Brookings. Shevlin. Taylor. They were all towns that the boss built.

Between the last decades of the nineteenth century and the middle of the twentieth century, employers in Washington, Oregon, and Idaho built thousands of communities. The houses and stores and schools, the mines and mills and factories went up on company land, for company employees. The first were built on the rivers, where there were salmon to be canned, and in the mountains, where there were coal deposits to fuel locomotive steam engines. Entrepreneurs built towns near copper outcroppings, near clay mines, and near quarries. Government agencies moved in where there were rivers to be dammed. Much later there would be communities for war workers. But most of the towns were built by timbermen, driven west by the railroad and its unprecedented consumption of wood and by the depleted lumber supplies in the eastern and Great Lakes states.

Some settlements were nothing more than stag camps for laborers, who were mostly male and mostly transient. By the U.S. Army's estimate, there were some 1,500 logging camps alone in the Pacific Northwest as World War I began. In addition, there were scores of company-dominated towns. These communities were not founded by an employer, but they soon came to depend on a company's payroll and largesse. In many, the employer

Some of the company-built communities that existed in Washington, Oregon, and Idaho in the twentieth century. Employers began building company towns in the Northwest in the mid-1800s; some operated as late as the 1990s. A few communities are still privately owned. (Map compiled by author; drawn by Barry Levely)

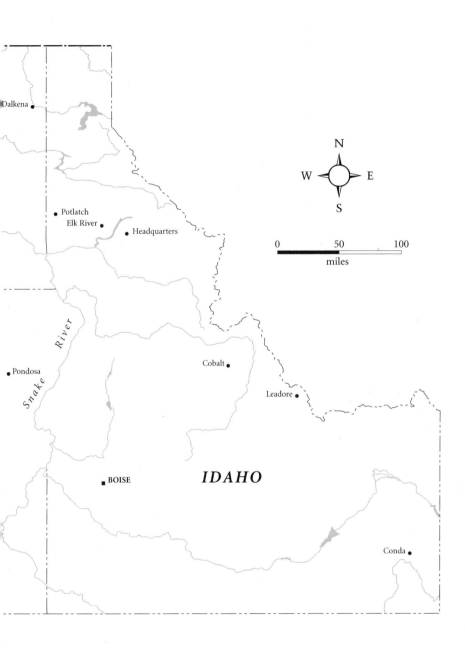

Dalkena •

N
W ←→ E
S

0   50   100
miles

Potlatch •
Elk River •
• Headquarters

Snake River

• Pondosa

Cobalt •

Leadore •

BOISE ■   *IDAHO*

Conda •

Hundreds of loggers settled at Vail, Washington, shown here shortly after it opened in 1927. At left center near the railroad tracks is the railway depot; at far right, the company store and general offices. Eventually Vail boasted several bunkhouses, a staff guest house, meeting hall, tennis courts, ballpark, dining hall, and sixty-one houses. By 1969, however, there were only ten houses left. (MSCUA, University of Washington Libraries, Kinsey 4859)

influence was short-lived. Or the settlement itself was short-lived, never developing past a temporary camp that was relocated or closed down altogether when the trees were cut or the ore exhausted.

Of these thousands of villages, only a small percentage truly could be called company owned, and only a few were incorporated towns. In some cases, the boss bought or built—and continued to own—the entire town. In others, lots were platted so that homes and businesses could be privately owned. Without exception, however, the company provided almost every job in a company town. Even government jobs like postmaster usually went to a relative of the boss. Teachers were hired—and fired—at the will of the company managers who served as school board directors.

The villages that are the focus of this book, those that were built or sur-

ation Hall   Dining Hall   Dormitories   Staff Houses

Larry Penberthy climbed a tree in 1939 to photograph Holden, Washington. At left is the recreation hall and "fountain lunch." After World War II a grocery store was built in the north dorm on the left side of the road. The building with the covered loading dock and dormers housed the post office and shops on the lower level, the dining hall on the main level, and the community hotel on the third level. Professional staff lived in the houses on the right, with the three-story house on the far right reserved for the superintendent. (Courtesy of the Penberthy family)

vived into the twentieth century, seldom had local government, at least during the period of company ownership, and some were always referred to as "camps." But they meet the definition of "town" in one important way: they developed into cohesive communities, with Boy Scouts and Bible study, baby showers and baseball teams, card clubs, volunteer fire departments, and many of the other characteristics of small towns. These villages endured as company entities for decades, sometimes a half-century or longer. People came and stayed—some for a few years, some long enough to raise their children to adulthood, some for the town's entire life.

When we hear "company town," we often think of the distant past, of a centuries-old way of life. In the Pacific Northwest states of Washington,

Oregon, and Idaho, however, company towns were being established as late as the 1950s. More than a hundred company towns in the region existed well into the twentieth century. A few survived into the 1990s.

The words "company town" evoke images of control, of paternalistic managers who hand-picked everything from house design and paint colors to the weekly movies and sometimes even the state legislators. Often control is equated with exploitation: dawn-to-dusk labor; tarpapered shanties; trainloads of strikebreakers imported at any hint of labor unrest; wages paid in scrip good only at a monopolistic company store; locations so remote that the only way in—or out—was by company train.

We'd like to think that these are outdated stereotypes, never applicable in the Washington, Oregon, and Idaho company towns that flourished for decades. After all, these communities were planned to attract and retain families despite work that was dangerous, sites that were usually isolated, and weather that could be unrelentingly severe. Unlike the West's earliest logging and mining camps, these towns had to attract skilled craftsmen as well as laborers, experienced managers and professionals as well as transients. Undeniably, the stereotypes sometimes did apply. Most settlements were built by entrepreneurs or small companies; the company owner or his son or a trusted lieutenant usually lived in town and monitored both morals and manufacturing output. In those towns built by the government, there was often a strong-willed administrator who dictated policy on even pets and parking. In some towns, the boss (or the bureaucracy) owned every inch of land and every building. He (and very occasionally she) ran the bunkhouse, the cookhouse, the store, the saloon, and the theater. The employers built the houses, the recreation hall, and the hotel, selected the school board members who hired the teachers, and decided which denomination the church would serve. In towns like these, if you didn't work for the company or the school, you were unlikely to have a job or a place to live. You might not have even had a place to eat.

Why was this control so important to employers? Some were smitten with the concept of model towns, where bosses could impose their standards on workers. At least a few Northwest employers were influenced by the railroad train car manufacturer George Pullman. In the city he built outside Chicago in 1881, Pullman was determined to create beauty and order for his employees. He hired architects to design spacious houses and apartments,

In bachelor camps, even as late as the 1950s, loggers and miners sometimes lived in crowded bunkhouses and tent houses. The only heat came from a large stove in the center of the structure. Wet clothes hung from haywire strung along the walls. (Courtesy of Potlatch Corp./forestphoto.com)

he restricted the sale of liquor and tobacco, and he imposed curfews. He even selected the plays to be performed. Not incidentally, Pullman believed that this emphasis on housing, health, and morals would make workers less likely to strike. His town was soon judged a failure—it was dilapidated and being sold off by court order within twenty years—but it remained a model for at least two employers who built communities in Washington and Idaho in the first years of the twentieth century, the Delaware-based E. I. du Pont de Nemours and Company and the Weyerhaeuser-affiliated timber syndicate that founded the Potlatch Lumber Company.

Ownership created other opportunities for bosses. Three decades after the construction of DuPont and Potlatch, when Mason City was built by

BEAUTY, ORDER—AND A 6 PERCENT PROFIT

George Pullman, who had founded the Pullman Palace Car Company to manufacture, operate, and lease railway cars, wanted to build a town that would be distinguished for its beauty and order—and that also would return a 6 percent profit on his investment. Opened in 1881, the Chicago suburb of Pullman, Illinois, offered better-quality housing than any other company town, but at premium prices. Even when their paychecks were bolstered with overtime, most skilled workers spent at least a third of their wages on rent. When the overtime ended or men were laid off, George Pullman refused to reduce rents. In 1898 the Illinois Supreme Court ordered the Pullman Palace Car Company to sell the town. Sales prices were set at 100 times the rental fees, so a modest row house was $2,000. Properties sold slowly, and by 1930, Pullman's once-admired model town was rundown and "pocketed with blight." (For more information, see Stanley Buder, Pullman: An Experiment in Industrial Order and Community Planning, 1880–1930 *[1967].)*

the private contractors working on the Grand Coulee Dam, the emphasis was on an experiment of enormous scale. Every single one of the original 280 houses, in addition to every bunkhouse, cafe, store, church, library, and school, was heated with electricity. The federal government was financing this huge hydroelectric project partly as a Depression work-relief project, and it was researching how much of a payback it could expect. It wanted to know if farm homes, which would finally have access to power with the dam's completion, could be made comfortable with electric furnaces and stoves despite eastern Washington's winter blizzards.

Some employers felt that their position gave them the right and the responsibility to be paternalistic, that it was their mission to lead laborers to a better life. Often this better life meant keeping the town dry. Controlling both the sale and the use of liquor was probably one of the most important reasons that employers built towns. As logging camp operators had learned early, a dry camp had fewer fights and fewer accidents in an industry that was then the most dangerous in the United States. Some company towns had no taverns and did not permit liquor to be sold in the local store, even if it was privately operated. A few communities worked hard to keep liquor from being sold within any reasonable distance. Before Potlatch was built, the timber company's owners quietly bought up miles of property along the town's railroad route to ensure that saloons couldn't be constructed a short ride away. At Port Gamble, Washington, the mill owners eventually acquired the hotel in order to make liquor harder to buy. A laborer intent on a drink could still get one, but he might have had to row across Gamble Bay to an Indian settlement. Not every employer forbade liquor. The coal-mining towns established in western Washington in the late 1800s frequently had saloons—but sometimes the company permitted only one per town. Other employers were less rigid: the timber baron Henry McCleary is remembered for permitting open drinking, unrestricted gambling, and "the other bits of tinsel and spangle" that kept single men content in his southwestern Washington town.[1]

Some bosses built towns for more practical reasons: the communities provided a means of keeping employees productive and stable. Towns weren't built as philanthropies, but many clearly were an employee benefit operated with a significant company subsidy. Some companies had assumed that they could fill their work force with bachelors who would live in spartan bunkhouses, but these laborers frequently turned out to be unreliable and transient. "We've got three crews," early bosses were heard to say, "One coming, one going, and one working." Even economic recession did little to stem the turnover. To recruit the more stable married workers, companies built towns with schools, stores, recreation halls, and sometimes even churches.

Company towns often resulted from the fear of unions. Timber companies, determined to avoid labor unrest like that caused by the Industrial Workers of the World (Wobblies) in the early 1900s, often offered workers economical housing and convenient schools. They also supported an industry-backed association, the Loyal Legion of Loggers and Lumbermen, or Four L. Coal-mine executives took the opposite tack and used their towns to try to legislate out unions. Workers had to sign leases that prohibited union meetings in homes and that allowed the company to immediately evict striking miners. Businesses operating in coal-company–owned buildings had to agree not to serve striking miners.

There's no question that employers often saw the company-founded town as a profit center and as a means of recovering most of the wages paid out. Especially in Northwest coal towns, bosses wanted to control all possible sources of income: housing, hotel, store, and tavern. They shared George Pullman's belief that company towns should contribute to corporate profits. In towns where the company owned all the land, workers had little choice but to live in company housing and have rent deducted from their paychecks. Though some employers allowed bachelors to board with families, turn-of-the-century coal-mine managers occasionally demanded that single workers pay rent to no one other than the company. The company store was usually the only grocery and general store in town; in a few communities, mail orders, buying from peddlers, and shopping in the nearest city were discouraged.

Finally, there were towns that existed because the company owners yearned for their own little empires. As the founder of McCleary, Washington, was well known to say, "A good kingdom is better than a poor democracy."

Not every employer owned everything. A few town founders, eager to reap the rewards of real estate speculation, platted Main Streets and parks, neighborhoods and schoolyards, and welcomed other businesses, both small and large. In towns long owned by the company, the boss eventually may have rented out storefronts, but he determined who could operate businesses and what those businesses could offer. If the company leased land to a worker who wanted to build his own house, the rental agreement spelled out who could live there, what the house could be sold for, and when the house would revert to company ownership. Some employers insisted on retaining ownership of all the land because that guaranteed them complete freedom in exploiting the resources; if a mine or a mill needed to be expanded, houses or schools could simply be moved. Some employers did not have the option of selling land because their communities were built on land leased from the United States Forest Service or the railroad.

Many of the Pacific Northwest's company towns are gone now. So are the men and women who built them. The museums and corporate histories show off old equipment and describe the mine or mill or factory's out-put; the tattered newspaper clippings and yellowing snapshots tell about accidents and strikes, record snowfalls and school graduations. They say little, however, about the people who worked in these company towns, the men and women who produced the ore, the lumber, the Liberty ships, the gunpowder, and the clay pipe, the people who made electric lights and irri-gation and atomic power possible. The historical exhibits give us little of the flavor of everyday life: the kind of people who came to these villages, where they lived, and how they reared their children. How did these people shop and play and pray? Most important, what kind of life did they create in the shadow of the company? How similar was it to life in other small western towns? Were people in company towns happy—or just marking time until they could afford to move on? It is that spirit of community that this history attempts to capture, that sense of how the townspeople lived their daily lives, both in ordinary times and in periods of war and Depression and corporate conglomeration.

2 / Bunkhouses, Tent Houses
and Silk Stocking Row

What defines a company town? Housing provided by the boss and a store run by the company, most people will say. Not every community had a company store, but it's hard to think of a company town or camp where at least some of the houses weren't built by the employer. In the Pacific Northwest's company towns and remote camps, the lodging sometimes was more luxurious than anything available in the closest towns—or no better than a camp site. As late as the 1940s, some families lived in tent houses with outdoor privies. Others, even before World War I, had running water, leaded-glass windows, and rose gardens.

Towns like DuPont, Washington, were thoughtfully designed by well-known architects. They featured carefully spaced trees that eventually created leafy canopies over broad streets lined with Craftsman bungalows. Most small villages were laid out by the camp boss, the mine manager, or the owner himself. The best town to come from a boss's design is undeniably Port Gamble, Washington, reminiscent of the Maine hometown of the founding Popes and Talbots. But few owners designed towns that would grow into such pristine landmarks as Port Gamble. More often the communities were monotonous grids of look-alike small houses crowded together on denuded slopes, or shacks thrown up between giant stumps.

It is difficult to generalize about town-site plans. However, bunkhouses often were separated from family houses, and managers' homes often were built atop hills or on larger lots. Ethnic minorities usually were isolated,

14

"Accommodations equal to the best hotel!" enthused newspaper reporters when Holden, Washington, opened in the late 1930s. Rooms above the dining hall housed both visitors, such as traveling sales representatives, and dining hall workers. They were similar to rooms shared by miners. Each had a sink; bathrooms were down the hall. (Courtesy of the family of Larry Penberthy)

sometimes in the town's only worker-built housing. Geography occasionally dictated plans: in Holden, Washington, avalanche fields created a natural division between worker and management housing. In Brookings, Oregon, the architect Bernard Maybeck originally conceived of a town following the contours of the hills above the harbor. Newhalem and Diablo, the two Washington towns built high in the Cascade Mountains by Seattle City Light, were strung out on the narrow strips of level terrain between mountainside and the Skagit River.

Few early towns had street signs, but some had street names. In DuPont, Washington, some people lived on Hercules or Atlas Streets, named for other company operations. Richland, Washington, "the atomic city," gave its streets names like Ion, Proton, and Electron Lanes. In Holden, Washington, managers lived in the "circle," and miners lived on the "upper," "middle," or "lower" rows. In other towns, houses were simply numbered.[1]

When a company provided housing, it usually expected single men to

Single men who worked in Ryderwood, Washington, in the 1920s and 1930s lived in the Tavern, a dorm that despite its name did not sell liquor. Nor did any other business in the town built by the Long-Bell Lumber Company, which was headed by a teetotaler, R. A. Long. (Courtesy of the Longview Public Library)

live communally in bunkhouses and boarding houses or in hotels that were nothing more than tiny rooms above a dining hall. The bunkhouse rooms at Holden, described by 1930s newspaper reporters as luxurious, were wide enough for two single beds and a bedside table. Amenities included reading lamps, electrical outlets for radios, and a sink below a medicine cabinet and mirror. Some employers allowed bachelors to rent rooms from families. Others, especially the owners of western Washington coal towns, forbade boarding. This guaranteed that any money a miner paid out for room and board came back to the company. It also ensured that a worker's wife couldn't contribute to the household income and reduce the family's dependence on the husband's paycheck.[2]

Among the first buildings constructed in the mid-1930s in Mason City,

Washington, for employees of the Grand Coulee Dam contractor were forty-five bunkhouses, each one housing two dozen laborers. Professional employees of the federal Bureau of Reclamation lived across the Columbia River in more comfortable quarters. At Grisdale, Washington, built in 1946 by the Simpson Timber Company, eight loggers shared each two-room bunkhouse just a short walk away from the wash house and cookhouse. At Newhalem, Washington, Seattle City Light built bunkhouses and a cookhouse at the Skagit River Gorge Dam and power plant in 1920. But once the initial dam construction was complete, single men had to live in tent houses during the summer so that their bunkhouses could be used by tourists.[3]

Especially when a town was operating at peak capacity, accommodations might be crowded: "hot sheets" were common. During the busiest years in McCleary, Washington, the door plant and sawmill ran three shifts, so the hotel assigned four men to every two-bed room. When Holden, Washington, started up, copper miners working days shared their bunks with those on the night shift.[4]

Companies usually provided separate quarters for single professionals and managers. Some were more comfortable than the laborers' bunkhouses; others offered nothing extra except privacy. At Holden, the staff house, set between managers' homes, housed the bachelors on the professional staff and those married managers whose families had not yet arrived in camp.[5]

Teachers frequently were the only single women in town. Often their accommodations seem to have been an afterthought, even though some towns required teachers to live in the community. Though maids and waitresses were usually provided rooms in the hotel, a teacher occasionally slept behind a curtain at one end of the schoolroom. In some towns, teachers shared a company-owned cabin or house; at Cedar Falls, Washington, the two women who ran the Seattle City Light elementary school had a two-bedroom house. In other communities, teachers roomed with one family and boarded with another. Some communities provided nothing for their teachers. Gertrude Murphy, who came to the Northern Pacific railroad town of Lester, Washington, in 1932, remembered that there was no teacher's cottage and no family with space to lodge her. She spent her first few nights in the NP hotel, which was used primarily by the railroad engineers and firemen, but that was embarrassing for both her and the men. "They'd run out in their underwear to the bathroom and meet me in the hall," she recalled.[6]

At Holden, built in the 1930s, the Howe Sound Company didn't expect to have unmarried women in its mining town. Nor did it anticipate women vendors: when one supplier sent in a woman auditor for a lengthy stint, Howe Sound had to lodge her in the staff house, surprising those who regarded the house as an all-male bastion. The first teacher was a man who lived in the staff house. When he decided that mining paid better than teaching, he was replaced by two women whose husbands were company employees, allowing Howe Sound to avoid housing county school district employees. When teacher shortages after World War II forced the company to accept teachers who were single or who lived at Holden without their husbands, the women stayed in two-room apartments that had been created in a bunkhouse.[7]

Teachers were often protected from contact with laborers, at least in housing and at mealtime. They were, after all, professional women, and many were also very young, away from home on their first or second jobs. In Taylor, Washington, in the years before World War I, teachers walked to the hotel for their meals; sometimes still teenagers themselves, they were seated at their own table and served by the hotel manager herself. Even a couple of decades later it took courage for a young single woman to walk into a mess hall. While in fifth grade, Dorothy Anne Hobson, who chronicled everyday life in an Oregon timber town in the *Valsetz Star,* reported in a 1939 issue of her newspaper that "Miss Virginia Leyton, our pretty new teacher, ate in the dining room with one hundred and sixty loggers. She was very calm."[8]

Mason City, the town erected in the mid-1930s by the Grand Coulee Dam contractor, was unusual in that it had a dorm built specifically for women. Richland, Washington, established in the middle of World War II to produce plutonium for the atomic bomb, started out with more women's dorms than men's. The women's barracks also had the protection of a six-foot-high fence and a guarded entrance. But these were for single women without children: there was no housing provided for those women workers who had children but no husbands. Not until mid-1949, more than six years after the government took over Richland, were houses allocated to women with families. Then, despite the community's thousands of residents, only twelve houses—each with only one bedroom—were made available to working mothers. By 1952, housing for women in Richland was so scarce that some managers admitted that they had to discriminate in hiring, recruiting only from among married women who already lived in the community.[9]

Family housing was usually intended as a means of recruiting and retaining employees, so those homes were sometimes better designed than houses that rented for similar prices in metropolitan areas. For Potlatch, Idaho, sawmill workers, the Spokane architect C. Ferris White in 1906 designed houses with three to seven rooms: a six-room house had a kitchen, parlor, dining room, and three bedrooms. Each laborer's house had two cold-water faucets, one in the kitchen and one outside. Because of the cost of installing sewers, workers' homes had backyard privies, which the company kept clean with its own honey bucket service.[10]

The Pacific States Lumber Company added bathrooms to all its Selleck, Washington, houses within ten years of building the town in 1908. Each white millworker's home had a garden surrounded by a picket fence, but no basement or foundation. Japanese workers lived some distance away, most in houses they built for themselves. Even in coal-mining towns, employers sometimes built comfortable houses for laborers as well as supervisors. As World War I began, three dozen new four- and five-room houses for workers were being finished in Carbonado, Washington.[11]

Some lumbermen hired noted architects like Bernard Maybeck of the San Francisco Bay area and Carl F. Gould of Seattle to design entire communities. For John Brookings's Oregon coast town, Maybeck's plans were modest, providing bedrooms, a living room, and a large kitchen in houses that could be built with simple carpentry and the products of the Brookings mill. Gould, who had designed a mansion for the timberman R. D. Merrill and buildings for Merrill & Ring's Pysht, Washington, logging operations, was commissioned during World War I (probably through Merrill's influence) to design a 3,000-worker community on Washington's Olympic Peninsula for the U.S. Army's Spruce Production Division. With his partner, Charles Herbert Bebb, Gould laid out a half-mile-square town site with bunkhouses and dining and recreation halls reminiscent of Adirondack lodges but designed for construction by unskilled workers. (Few of

Maybeck's designs were built before Brookings was forced to sell out; the armistice came before Gould and Bebb's Lake Pleasant community ever got off the drafting boards.)[12]

Most housing for government projects was designed to be built cheaply and quickly. For the Grand Coulee contractor's community at Mason City, the first several hundred houses were three-room structures measuring twenty-eight by twenty feet. A Spokane architect was hired to design the buildings for Richland during World War II, but he was pressured to keep costs down. Garages were unnecessary, the government decreed; so were fireplaces and porches. Entry closets were a luxury; bathtubs were almost unknown.[13]

Richland's utilitarian, government-issue appearance endured for years; even in 1955, when the city was preparing for incorporation and private ownership, the buildings were still being described as barracks-like. Building names suffered from the military influence, too: Richland's local hotel was officially named Transient Quarters, and the dorms still were identified by nothing more than numbers in 1949.

More spartan yet was the housing at Vanport, the war-worker project Henry Kaiser built near Portland, Oregon, in the early 1940s. Despite being the largest wartime housing project in the nation and Oregon's second-largest community at the time, it had landscaping only because Kaiser insisted; the Housing Authority of Portland, which operated the project, believed that trees and shrubs were a waste of money. Unlike most employer-provided family housing, Vanport offered only tiny apartments. A couple was eligible for a one-room apartment that cost $7 a week, while a family could rent a slightly larger one-bedroom apartment. None of the units had refrigerators, which weren't manufactured during World War II. The kitchens were so tiny that a community group organized a meeting to demonstrate how to cook a turkey in an oven that measured only ten by ten by seven inches. (Vanport also shared one of the worst characteristics of early logging camps: within a year of its opening, tenants were making thousands of complaints a month about bedbugs, cockroaches, and rodents.)[14]

At Newhalem and Diablo, the two Seattle City Light villages more than one hundred miles from Seattle, there never was enough family housing, and the few houses that did exist were allocated in ways that frustrated employees. Obtaining housing required both seniority with City Light and seniority in class of employment; new hires, especially laborers, could not expect to ever bring their families to the community. By 1939, the Skagit projects employed 151 people, but only 67 had been able to rent houses. When nine new houses were finished that year, there were 29 men vying for them. The situation never improved significantly; a man who retired in late 1959 after working on the Skagit since 1928 was one of many who had spent decades commuting home to Seattle for a four-day break every two weeks.

Houses at the Skagit dam projects were uncomfortable as well as scarce; uninsulated, they were hard to heat, and snow sometimes drifted inside through exterior siding. When early employees asked for improvements, the City Light superintendent, J. D. Ross, responded by complaining that workers were wasteful with the electricity provided free with housing. Unlike employers who provided materials or rental credits for tenant improvements, City Light officials expected their employees to maintain and improve their houses on their own time and at their own expense.[15]

In logging communities where structures were designed to be moved, houses were small. The Shevlin-Hixon Company's earliest family houses were little more than boxcars without wheels. They had no power; they had no plumbing. By the late 1920s, they still had no power or plumbing, but the houses were larger and more comfortable, and each had a covered porch that folded against the building on moving day. To make the houses easy to relocate, each was built with special grooved channels on walls and sills so that cables could be attached to the bottom and the house hoisted by crane or log loader onto a rail car.

Shevlin-Hixon's community of Shevlin was the most famous of the portable towns. Although it sometimes had as many people as permanent Gilchrist, Shevlin could be moved—all 600 people and more than 400 structures—in a few days. After roads were bulldozed, holes were dug, and an outhouse plucked from a flatcar and dropped over each hole. Finally, a house was lifted off the train and onto its new site between the road and the outhouse. To reduce the risk to household goods, loggers and their families packed towels around dishes in the cupboards, laid dressers flat on floors, and nailed screen doors and windows to the side of the house. But the crane operators had a reputation for a smooth operation; the longtime

Shevlin postmistress, Lois Maker Gumpert, insisted that they could lift a house onto a flatcar without breaking an egg. When her own house was moved twenty miles in the mid-1930s, she claimed that a bucket of water forgotten on the floor arrived at the new location without a drop spilled.[16]

At Cedar Falls, the City of Seattle laid out a tiny town site in the Cascade Mountain foothills and built comfortable homes for its power plant staff. People who grew up at Cedar Falls remember how visitors, after struggling up a steep, rough road, seemed surprised by the manicured little community. At night it was an island of light, with street lamps aglow and every house bright with electricity provided by City Light. Adjacent to the City Light town site were camps for employees of the Pacific States Lumber Company and the Milwaukee Road, where housing in the 1920s was sometimes boxcars. The rent and electricity were free. So was water—but it came from a faucet out in the yard. The toilets flushed, but they were in a row behind the boxcars. Families did laundry with a wash boiler on the range, a No. 3 metal tub, and a washboard.[17]

Few of the people who lived in company towns and camps in the early 1900s had electricity, running water, or decent sanitation—but they were no different than those who lived in other small towns, on farms, or even in the region's largest cities. Soon after World War I ended, when Tacoma, Washington, had nearly 25,000 homes, only 600 kitchens had electric ranges. In the late 1920s, Polk County, Oregon, appliance dealers advertised Maytag washing machines with the customer's choice of motors: for housewives with limited or no access to electricity, the washers still came with gasoline motors. These washing machines were true luxuries, but their motors sometimes didn't start—and occasionally even exploded. In smaller communities that did have electricity, power was often available for only a few hours a day. In McCleary, Washington, lights went off at 10 P.M. (after five minutes of flickering as a warning) until a new mill and power plant were completed in 1912.[18]

A far more serious problem, wherever people lived, was typhoid, which broke out every year because privies and cesspools contaminated well water. In Seattle in 1909, the health department reported a record number of 501 typhoid cases, 51 of them fatal. During World War I, flooding rivers in the City of Tacoma's watershed swept sewage from company settlements like

Lester, Nagrom, and Baldi into the City's water supply; for months afterward, local residents were instructed to boil their drinking water.[19]

Especially outside metropolitan areas, the lack of plumbing continued to be a problem into the 1930s and 1940s. In logging communities like Shevlin-Hixon's, three or four families often shared a standpipe; in coal-mining towns the faucets sometimes were so far apart that women carried drinking and wash water for blocks. Even by 1940, the Census Bureau found that almost two-thirds of Idaho homes lacked what the government called "complete facilities": a flush toilet, a tub or shower, and both hot and cold running water.[20]

It was 1936 before Shevlin, Oregon, homes had electric power. In the meantime, loggers and their families heated water in wood stove boilers and read by Aladdin lamps or Coleman lanterns. They stored their food in root cellars and in the company-provided coolers, two-by-three-foot cupboards with screened backs. The Cobbs & Mitchell camps in the Oregon Coast Range in the same era didn't have plumbing or electricity, either, but the homes built in Valsetz, the company's nearby mill town, had bathrooms and power from the mill's generator.[21]

McCleary was criticized for the sewage that was still running in its streets in 1941, but the problem was common. In Taylor, a western Washington clay-mining village, the stream flowing through town was familiarly known as Shit Creek. In Potlatch, because there were no sewers to carry away wastewater from kitchens, it was simply dumped outside, often to stream downhill through alleys and yards. The Vanport housing project for workers in World War II shipyards near Portland was built with secondhand sewer pipe that frequently broke, allowing sewage to ooze up between buildings. The project was more than a year old before permanent repairs cured the problem.[22]

As rare as electric power, plumbing, and sewers were as late as the 1930s and 1940s, it's easy to understand why people were impressed with the central Oregon community built by the Gilchrist Timber Company in 1939. The houses weren't large—700 square feet for a two-bedroom cottage— but every single one had indoor plumbing and electricity. The company paid for the power, built the sewers, and provided all the maintenance. At Grisdale, Washington, the Simpson Timber logging camp built in 1946, houses had two conveniences unusual for the era: oil heat and mud rooms.

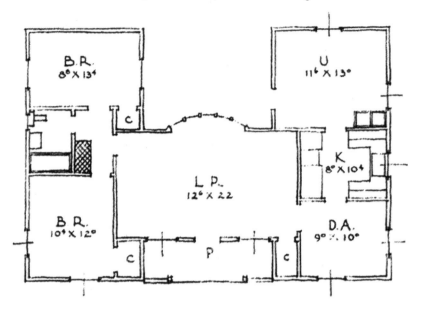

Designed by Hollis Johnston, a Portland architect, the compact houses that Frank Gilchrist built in the late 1930s in isolated central Oregon for his lumber company employees offered full plumbing and spacious laundry rooms. (Gilchrist Real Estate Company brochure)

Oil heat meant that housewives didn't have to split their own kindling—and it also mean that the company wasn't wasting precious virgin timber on stove wood. (Oil, even hauled in on the company railroad, was a less expensive fuel than top-quality timber.) And because Grisdale was in the foothills of the Olympic Mountains, where 150 inches of rain a year was common, each of these houses was built with an enclosed porch where a logger could strip off wet work clothes before stepping into his kitchen.[23]

Housing costs in most Northwest company towns were modest in contrast to prices in corporate towns like Pullman, Illinois. Just before the turn of the century, new seven-room houses in Port Gamble, Washington, complete with bathrooms and free electricity, rented for $6.00 or $7.00 a month. In Carbonado, a western Washington coal town, rents in 1918 ranged from $7.50 a month for a four-room house to $16.50 for a six-room house with bath. In nearby Black Diamond, where the coal miners owned their houses

When Vail, Washington, opened in 1927, loggers paid from $13 to $23 a month to rent houses ranging in size from four rooms to five- and six-room bungalows with large yards and access to shared garages. A two-story Dutch colonial was built for the manager, R. A. McDonald. (Courtesy of the Weyerhaeuser Company Archives)

but not their land, the company charged $1.00 a month for land rent in the early days, with an extra monthly charge of $1.00 for each boarder. About the same time, before World War I housing shortages drove prices up, a "modern" five-room house, complete with furniture, cost $30.00 a month in Tacoma. In the mid-1930s, a worker at Grand Coulee Dam paid $32.00 a month for an all-electric, fully plumbed three-bedroom house in Mason City. In Grisdale, the houses rented for $20.00 to $30.00 a month in the 1940s and 1950s, including garage, water, electricity, garbage service, and maintenance. Most rents stayed modest: when Gilchrist sold in 1991, rents ranged from $67.00 to $125.00.[24]

Even if a company owned only one town, the boss may not have lived there. Especially when settlements had small schools or no schools at all, company executives often maintained homes in larger communities for their families and stayed in camp only a few days at a time. Where senior managers did live in town full-time, their homes usually were more impressive than workers' quarters. In DuPont, Washington, designed in the early 1900s, the manager had a fifteen-room house with two and a half acres of gardens, and the assistant manager a ten-room house on a one-acre lot. When the Cedar Falls power plant superintendent married in 1917, the Seattle city architect designed the newlyweds a Craftsman bungalow that included spacious living and dining rooms, a library, and a sleeping porch. In Selleck, just a few miles away, the Pacific States Lumber Company superintendent also had a Craftsman house with leaded glass cabinet doors, wainscoting, and picture molding. When the Neils family took over the sawmill town of Klickitat, Washington, the general manager built himself a Dutch colonial with ample accommodations for visitors from company headquarters, including the only guest bathroom in town. His brother-in-law, the sales manager, lived next door in an English Tudor-style house. At Holden's town site, the Howe Sound Company in 1937 built a three-story, four-bedroom, three-bath house with fireplace, den, and formal living and dining rooms for its general manager.[25]

In some communities, owners and managers, despite their status, chose modest homes. At McCleary, the company president and his brothers lived side-by-side in simple bungalows. At Shevlin, where every house started out as a two-room structure that could be lifted onto a rail car, the camp manager, who returned home to his family most weekends, had nothing fancier. (In early camps, even the boss's relatives roughed it: Gertie Simpson, sister-in-law to the founder of Simpson Timber, remembered living in a tent house for three years as she accompanied her husband from one Simpson camp to another in the late 1800s.)[26]

Some companies provided separate—although not necessarily more luxurious—housing for those employees who couldn't be labeled either management or laborer: the teachers, preachers, doctors, and cookhouse managers. Most often, these quarters allowed the employees and their families to live close to where they worked. At Grisdale, teachers were often hired as a husband-and-wife team that lived not in the neat rows of logger housing but in a teacherage near the school. For its married teachers, Potlatch built an eight-room family house. It also supplied the materials for the parsonage built by the high school manual arts students. At Holden, the mess hall steward had an apartment near the kitchen, and the first grocer lived with his family in a two-room suite behind the store. The company doctor usually lived in an apartment adjoining the medical clinic.[27]

There's no denying that company-town houses were sometimes just shacks. The miners' cottages built in western Washington's coal towns around the turn of the twentieth century often were designed for neither comfort nor appearance. Some were built on slag piles that continued to burn, filling nearby homes with fumes and smoke. Few had toilets. Electricity was uncommon. Water came from a common tap that might be blocks away. The miners who owned their houses were sometimes reluctant to paint and landscape, because the company continued to own the land and might reclaim it at any time. Mill towns could be as primitive. Although Henry McCleary's village had been described as a "model town with all modern conveniences" in a 1910 newspaper article, it deteriorated quickly. As a child arriving in 1913 from an impoverished Italian village, Angelo Pellegrini was struck by McCleary's shabbiness: "The houses were rectangular insecurities of wood, unpainted, in various stages of dilapidation." Decades later, some communities were no better constructed or maintained. When she arrived in Wilark in 1930, Grace Brandt Martin described the teacherage, like the other houses in the Oregon lumber camp, as a weather-beaten shack.[28]

Especially in the early years of the century, employers often owned all the land in their towns. This was common when the company had acquired the property through land grants made to the railroads. These bosses usually required that workers live in company housing or build homes on company-owned land. Although rent payments, whether for houses or for land alone, were often modest, the company still recovered some of the wages it paid out. Requiring employees to live in town also guaranteed business for the company store. The most important advantage of company-owned housing, however, was the control management wielded, especially over union activities. A worker tempted to strike had to anticipate not only the loss of his job but also the eviction of his family.

Some communities always included privately owned homes. In towns like Wilkeson, Washington, the coal company's land grant extended only part of the way into the community, and the adjoining land had been home-steaded before the employer's arrival. In other towns, companies built the houses and sold them to employees. Many workers in timber communi-ties built or remodeled existing homes with reject lumber from the mill. Some employees built their own homes even when supplies had to be shipped into remote locations.

In Holden, Washington, the Howe Sound Company built a dozen chalet-style houses for married mine managers. But these houses, along with apart-ments for the doctor and hotel steward, provided for only about fifty adults and children. Hundreds of other Holden residents lived a half-mile or so west, in a community that eventually included more than a hundred houses constructed by employees on land leased from the Forest Service. Platted by Howe Sound into 50-by-100-foot lots with a septic-tank system, water mains, and electricity, these home sites rented for $20 a year. Miners paid an additional penny per kilowatt for power. Many houses were small: a liv-ing room, kitchen, bedroom, and finished attic for children's bedrooms. The more spacious had basement shops, mother-in-law apartments, and room for home businesses. Lumber came from the mine's sawmill; other building materials were barged north on Lake Chelan. (Supplies such as dynamite for blasting out the bedrock in a basement were occasionally filched from the company and carried home in a lunchpail.) Howe Sound financed the construction of many of these houses and regulated the sales price of all of them; to ensure that miners did not speculate in real estate, the com-pany mandated that houses could be sold for no more than the original cost plus the value of any improvements. For the first several years of the mine's operation, some employees lived three-quarters of a mile up toward the mine portal at a neighborhood named Honeymoon Heights, because it was newlyweds who had converted the original camp site's rustic struc-tures to tiny cabins. For those who preferred rental cabins at Lucerne, twelve miles away on the shore of Lake Chelan, Howe Sound ran a commuter bus from the 3,262-foot-elevation town site down the nine-switchback road to the waterfront.[29]

During the same era, many of the seasonal employees at the Deschutes Lumber Company logging camp at Mowich, Oregon, also built their own houses. They used the generous supply of mill scraps and reject lumber, supplemented with building materials shipped in from Bend hardware stores

LAUNDRY HUNG HIGH, ABOVE SNOW

Housewives in Holden climbed up high to hang out their laun-
dry. Because the central Washington mining town received
hundreds of inches of snow each winter, clothes lines were sus-
pended between a pulley attached high on the house to a nearby
tree. Drying clothes meant leaning out a second-story bedroom
window to reach the line. In the winter, laundry was hung out
until it froze; then, with most of the moisture gone, it dried
quickly on wooden racks set inside near the floor furnace.

via the Southern Pacific or ordered from the Montgomery Ward catalog.
Despite the snowy weather typical at the beginning and end of each work
season, most of these homes started as canvas tents stretched over wood
platforms and half-walls. Families used the showers built for men's
bunkhouses during warmer months. When freezing weather closed these
bath houses, people scrubbed up at basins or in folding rubber bathtubs.[30]
Company-owned housing was often assigned by professional and marital status as well as by ethnic and racial group. In Potlatch the residential
areas were laid out to ensure that managers lived high on the hill, where
smoke from the mill wouldn't blow into their homes; laborers lived within
walking distance of their jobs. In general, the higher someone's professional
level, the higher elevation house he was assigned. Company officials also used
housing to reward the best workers and as a tool to reduce turnover among
the most desirable employees. But regardless of what jobs they held or their
performance, Greek, Italian, and Japanese employees lived farthest down
the hill and in the smallest houses. In McCleary, another timber town, there
were few such distinctions: company owners and mill bosses, the doctor,
the minister, and the merchants all lived in modest homes. In Grisdale, families lived in the lower camp, closer to the school and away from the single
men's bunkhouses. Near Grand Coulee, Bureau of Reclamation engineers—
the top of the hierarchical dam site community—lived in a pristine, federally financed neighborhood complete with grass and trees planted in
topsoil trucked in by the government; contractors' crews lived across the

Elsa Phillips, who spent the first nineteen years of her marriage at Holden, Washington, was one of the brides to set up housekeeping in a tent house at the mining community's ballpark. The snow was knee-deep before she and her husband, Wellington, moved to a cabin in late 1937. The top photo shows the dining area of the one-room wood and canvas structure; the bottom photo shows the extended shelf that served as the kitchen counter. (Courtesy of Bill Phillips)

river in Mason City, less attractive and less prestigious. Minorities and those who couldn't wrangle housing in the contractors' town had to struggle to find their own homes in boom towns like Grand Coulee.[31]

Minorities also had difficulty finding housing when World War II work brought thousands of blacks to the Portland and Seattle areas. In Portland, Oregon's largest city, although the African-American population increased from 1,900 in 1940 to about 18,000 by 1945, blacks were allowed to rent in only two of the city's twenty-five wartime housing projects. As a result, they occupied more than a third of the units at Vanport, the Columbia River defense-worker community that has been compared to a company town.[32]

In communities like Potlatch and Holden, at least a few houses were assigned by position. An executive's promotion or departure for another job could trigger a series of moves within the community. During the twenty years that Howe Sound operated in Holden, some couples lived in several homes and in three different neighborhoods. Many mine employees started out as bachelors living in bunkhouses and then, when they married, spent a hundred dollars or so for a cabin in Honeymoon Heights. They moved closer in when one of the miner-built homes in the Winston family neighborhood became available. When a promotion meant someone was eligible for the circle of company-owned management houses, a home in Winston would be freed up. The Phillips family, in its stay of nineteen years, made even more moves: as newlyweds, the couple camped the summer of 1937 at the local baseball park and then moved to a lakeside cabin for the winter. They came back up the mountain when they found space at Honeymoon Heights. Their next home was in Winston, and then, with the husband's promotion, they moved to the circle, where they lived in two different houses.[33]

In some communities, housing was assigned based on seniority and family size. In others, any employee—regardless of job title—could get on a waiting list for a larger house. In Gilchrist, unlike in most company towns, everyone who worked in town was eligible for the low-priced company rentals; this meant the Gilchrist Timber Company subsidized housing for teachers, state police officers, postal clerks, and the merchants who leased space in the company shopping center. Across the state in Valsetz, most houses were also assigned on a first-come, first-served basis. At Shevlin, employees were allowed to select their home sites when houses were being moved. In Richland, Washington, built by the federal government during World War II, there was little choice, and waiting lists were sometimes 700 families long. Residents complained that neighborhoods were "unnatural," with scientists housed next to unskilled laborers.[34]

When the company owned the town site, it usually assumed the responsibility for house and street maintenance, but the quality of the maintenance varied. In Potlatch, the company crew painted, installed furnaces, replaced window screens, built sidewalks, and poisoned rats. In the days of outhouses, the company even provided the honey bucket service to clean out privies. But house colors, as in most company towns, were the boss's choice. Sometimes the company bought in bulk and painted every house the same color: white in Grisdale and Port Gamble, brown in Gilchrist and Kinzua, Oregon, grey in Shevlin, and red in Coal Creek, Washington. At Mason City, the contractors' town at the Grand Coulee Dam site, a house's color indicated how large it was: one-room houses were painted green, one- and two-bedroom houses cream, gray, or sand. In some towns, employers handled interior painting and wallpapering—with the company's choice of colors and patterns. Other bosses expected residents to maintain house interiors. In Richland, Washington, built in 1943, every room in every house was painted buff unless a worker was willing to wield his own paintbrush. Then he and his wife could select from the seven colors approved and provided by the boss.

Occasionally, maintenance extended far beyond painting and exterminating. In Richland, houses were rented with furniture until 1948; until 1949, the government contractors handled all maintenance, including the replacement of light bulbs, fuses, and faucet washers. At Vanport, another wartime settlement, tenants were prohibited from handling any repair or maintenance, even of the furniture. In some communities, services and maintenance depended on where employees lived. In Newhalem, which attracted thousands of visitors each summer, the Seattle City Light superintendent installed attractive five-globe street lamps on ornamental iron poles on Silk Stocking Row, the street where managers lived, along Main Street, and near the railroad depot and bunkhouses where tourists walked. But there were no similar street lamps outside the tourist areas or in the neighborhoods where most workers lived.[35]

Some companies did virtually no maintenance, even when times were good. Old pictures of Barneston, a logging community outside Seattle, show swampy patches between the houses; those who lived there during World War I remembered that walking at night was risky, especially for those heading toward the Japanese village, because of the giant stumps and logging debris. When the boom went bust—because of a miners' strike or the Depression or a mill running out of trees to cut—companies were even less likely to spend any money on town site upkeep.[36]

Besides maintenance, monthly rental fees sometimes included street maintenance and snow removal, water, sewer, and garbage pickup. In timber towns where the sawmill power plant was fueled with sawdust and scrap lumber, electricity was occasionally free. One Port Gamble old-timer claimed that when the company wired the houses it didn't even bother to install switches for the porch lights because the power was so cheap. Free firewood was typical, especially in timber communities. In Simpson Timber's early family camps, the company provided firewood—but in the form of peeler logs dropped in a logger's yard, ready to be cut and split by the logger. In the explosives village of DuPont, as long as there were wood-burning stoves, stove wood and kindling could be cut for free on company land. At Holden, the copper-mining town built on Forest Service land, foresters marked the trees that could be cut and assigned each one to a miner. Men cut their wood into stove-length logs and stacked it by the road; a company laborer would pick up the wood and truck it to the right home. At Shevlin-Hixon camps, employees excavated their own slop holes for dumping table scraps; the company provided wood platforms to cover each hole for safety and to keep out rats. Like the outhouses, these platforms were hoisted onto rail cars and moved when the community relocated.[37]

Employees, except for those senior enough to have company-provided gardeners, almost always were expected to maintain their own yards. To ensure that lawns and gardens were attractive, some companies used incentives and others punishment. Some used both: in Potlatch, the company sponsored spring clean-up days, gave occasional prizes for well-kept yards . . . and threatened eviction to those workers who didn't meet company standards. In Grisdale, county extension agents judged the annual home improvement awards; to encourage loggers to keep up their yards year after year, there were cash prizes for both the most improved and the consistently best maintained yards. The company also waived a month's rent for families making major yard improvements. One town where employees didn't have to keep up their own yards, at least in the earliest days, was Richland. When the federal government created the town during World War II, it gave tenants grass and flower seeds and sapling trees for their yards and then provided a free lawn-mowing service every Saturday—regardless of workers' rank.[38]

How families chose to furnish their homes depended, just as it did elsewhere, on people's income, professional level, and family size. Especially in the period before World War II, it also depended on whether a village had electricity. The permanence of the camp and the remoteness of the location determined whether employees arrived with pianos and sterling silver or fold-up beds and a few pots and pans. The instant communities constructed for World War II workers assumed that tenants might arrive with little more than their clothes. In Vanport, the war-worker community near Portland, a one-room apartment came with a fold-out couch, table and chairs, miniature icebox, hot plate, and small oven. Like at Richland, all a worker needed to bring were linens, dishes, and cooking utensils. In Mowich, Oregon, where work was seasonal and many employees built their own houses, most furnishings were limited: a fold-out bed, a cheap kerosene stove from Sears, Roebuck or Montgomery Ward, and a few boxes and shelves in the kitchen. Some homes were never more than sparsely furnished. The Hamms, one of the first couples to arrive at the Holden mine in 1937, bedded down their two young daughters on a mattress and box spring that had come west with them in their car. For four years, the parents slept on a fold-out couch ordered from the Sears catalog. The kitchen was furnished with a table hinged to the wall and flanked by benches, all built by Leonard Hamm himself.[39]

In some homes, even in remote locations, even during the Depression, there were a few household luxuries. Trula Hamm spent what she considered a significant sum of money for a sewing machine soon after arrival in Holden. Patty Haddon Tappan, whose family moved to Holden from a British Columbia mining town the same time as the Hamms, remembered being lulled to sleep by Chopin played on her mother's piano, which had been shipped down the Pacific coast from Canada and then up Lake Chelan. A door or two away, other managers' wives poured from silver teapots and set their tables with bone china and crystal, especially when Howe Sound executives came to visit.[40]

Few generalizations can be made about company-town housing. Some homes were comfortable, even luxurious. Others in the same community were spartan or ramshackle. However, almost without exception, company-provided housing in the Pacific Northwest was inexpensive. When the boss was the landlord, rents were low and some were explicitly subsidized. This employee benefit is part of what helped drive company towns out of existence. As the towns aged, even the most carefully constructed buildings and utility systems demanded increasingly expensive and complicated maintenance. The town site costs increased far faster than rents did. What had originally been a benefit for both employee and employer now ballooned into a financial burden for the town owners. The landlord business cost too much, took too much time, and carried too many liabilities. Company owners wanted out—and they got out. Some closed down all the operations and let the town die; some razed the houses and turned the land to more remunerative uses. Others kept their mills or mines or factories or dams going, but they sold off the houses, either as a group or one at a time, to tenants and retirees and city folk seeking second homes. Now many of the remaining company-built houses are historic landmarks, their features carefully documented as remnants of a way of life that is almost entirely lost.

3 / Who Lived in Company Towns?

W ho lived in the Northwest's company towns? Men—most of
them young, strong, single, and white. Even as the twentieth
century began and war in Europe threatened the supply of
cheap immigrant labor, most company towns in the Northwest continued
to recruit no one other than immigrant men from northern Europe or their
American-born sons. Many towns didn't have a single black; some wouldn't
let Japanese and Chinese step off when the train chugged into the depot.
Few women were recruited for the corporate offices of timber and mining
firms—or for the cookhouses, company stores, or medical clinics.[1]

Although early logging and mining camps seldom provided accommodations for single women, family housing was more common after 1900 as
employers discovered that married men were more reliable employees than
bachelors. (Families also spent more at the company store.) Despite family housing, timber communities remained predominantly male settlements
and for good reason: most loggers were single. In 1918, only 14 percent of
western Washington loggers—and a slightly higher percentage of mill
workers—were married. Many early logging communities offered bunks
for a hundred or more men and houses for only a dozen. At Grisdale, Washington, built in the 1940s, there were about fifty houses for families and
bunkhouses for three hundred. Other towns were little different: DuPont,
Washington, eventually housed a hundred families, but another hundred
men lived in the bunkhouse, and the hotel had forty more rooms. At the

In company towns, bunkhouses were full of single young men and employee houses were full of young families. Children's Christmas parties at Holden, Washington, were often attended by more than 200. At one party soon after the mining community opened in the late 1930s, Santa Claus visited and Marcella Brooke's dance class (including the costumed Patty Haddon, left, and Barbara Brooke, right center) entertained. (Courtesy of the family of Larry Penberthy)

Howe Sound mine in Holden, Washington, half the employees in 1941 were single. Of the men who were married, half bunked with the bachelors because their families lived too far away for the miners to commute home daily.[2]

Some company towns and logging camps had no more than one or two single women: the schoolteachers and occasionally a nurse. Many communities recruited no single women, partly because of the difficulty in providing housing. In Holden, several teachers came to the village when their husbands were also offered jobs by the mine. One of the first nurses was married to a geologist; most other nurses were hired with their doctor husbands.

Company towns were also different in that they didn't have elderly people. Most jobs were so physically demanding that laborers tended to be young. In Mason City and Coulee Dam, the Washington towns built by contractors and the government for Grand Coulee Dam, the population remained young long after construction was complete; in 1953, only 4 percent of the residents were older than sixty. In towns like Richland, Washington, where the federal government's atomic bomb research and plutonium production required less brawn, employees still were younger than average, with correspondingly low death rates and high birth rates. When towns were long-lived, the work force—and thus the population—did age along with the town site and company operations. In Holden, the professionals and managers who arrived in the late 1930s as recent college graduates were middle-aged when the mine closed in 1957. Several towns existed long enough for employees and their children—and sometimes even their grandchildren—to retire from the company.[3]

Company towns often had no retirees. Sometimes laborers kept their jobs because they needed the income; others worked to guarantee roofs over their heads. When housing was employer owned, the company was more likely to require that a retiree or someone too disabled to work leave town and free up a house for his replacement. In many western Washington coal towns in the first part of the century, those who did not work simply could not stay. Only in a few communities did companies provide free or low-cost housing for widows and the elderly.[4]

If you hadn't worked in a company town, you were unlikely to settle there in old age or widowhood. Seldom did an elderly parent move to a company town to live with an adult child. Where all housing was company owned, few single people were allowed to rent houses; it was unusual for a bachelor worker to maintain a home with his widowed mother and unmarried sisters as he might have in other towns. A widowed father occasionally came to help out a newly widowed daughter, but these men usually had jobs of some sort. Henry Jones, a Black Diamond native, remembered his grandfather moving in after Henry's father died; he took a job sorting coal in the bunker, the kind of low-paying job usually reserved for men too old to work underground. If companies did permit unemployed people to live in town, it was difficult for a widowed or disabled parent to move in with grown children and their families: a miner's four-room cottage didn't easily accommodate extended families and neither did the two-room houses provided in some logging camps. Even if there was adequate space for grand-parents, the company-town locations were often remote, making visits to other children and friends difficult. Medical care, especially in early days, was provided only for company employees. Weather could be severe, and social activities were oriented to the employees and their families.[5]

Company towns were distinguished by full employment. Except during such economic crises as the Depression and strikes, every man in a company town worked. Most people worked in company operations: in the mine, mill, cannery, or dam or in its offices. Some worked in the town site department, handling building construction and repair, the cookhouse and bunkhouse, landscaping, snow removal, or the company store and post office. Almost every town had at least a few professionals: the doctor and nurse, the teachers, and maybe a minister.

Many company-town employees had more than one job. Some men worked a couple of jobs at a time or ran small businesses after hours. Several moonlighted as local reporters for the closest daily papers or published community newsletters. Ted Goodwin, the Ryderwood, Washington, chaplain, also wrote and worked part-time in the woods with his parishioners. His weekly newspaper column was well enough respected that the *Longview Daily News* sent Goodwin in the press car that accompanied Franklin D. Roosevelt on the president's 1937 trip through Washington state. One Holden geologist repaired his neighbors' televisions after hours; a neighbor did shoe repair. The Shevlin, Oregon, camp clerk supplemented his salary by raising hogs that were later butchered and sold to the logging camp cookhouse. Mill workers at Mowich, Oregon, and several other timber communities worked nights for the company and drove school buses during the day. Vic Parker, who worked at the Seattle City Light power plant in Cedar Falls, ran a little printing company, and during World War II, he held a third job as a railroad night watchman. A few after-hours businesses were less savory; at a Kosmos Timber Company camp in western Washington's Cascades, one logger ran a tattoo parlor in his corner of the bunkhouse. Especially during Prohibition, many loggers and miners moonlighted with moonshine.[6]

Some couples worked together to generate additional income. When the company permitted employees to take boarders, married workers and their wives often provided rooms and meals for bachelors. In Holden, a few couples built small apartments in their basements for newlyweds or new arrivals waiting for houses to become available. Other couples ran village concessions like the movie theater.[7]

Women also worked, although opportunities outside the home were limited, and almost no women worked in mills, mines, factories, or on construction sites except during wartime. The most common professional opening in company towns and logging camps was in the schoolhouse. Except for the few towns that bused their children away to school, each community had at least one teacher. The one- and two-room schools that were typical often attracted inexperienced young women who left after a year or two. Nurses often arrived in company towns with doctors as part of a husband-and-wife team. Other "women's work" was almost always done by those who didn't have to be recruited—the wives, widows, and grown daughters of workers. Until the labor shortages caused by war created more variety, most of these women clerked in the company store, staffed the telephone switchboard, or sorted mail in the post office. A few worked as secretaries and bookkeepers. Although most larger cookhouses hired only men as cooks, women sometimes waitressed or served as the kitchen assistants, called flunkies. Some women were waitresses and maids in the company hotel and, if women employees were allowed in bunkhouses, worked as bed makers and janitors. In the largest towns, there was occasionally a paid part-time librarian.

Early logging-camp bosses could be quick to claim that women were bad luck, and this superstition carried over into other industries, especially when the Depression made jobs scarce. When Grand Coulee Dam was under construction in desolate central Washington in the mid-1930s, men insisted that having women on the dam site—if only at telephone switchboards—would jinx the project. Although thousands of men eventually worked on the dam, only about seventy-five women held jobs in offices or in the construction area, mostly working as operators, secretaries, and clerks. And they had to fight for those jobs: the first local bureaucrats initially refused to hire women even as stenographers, claiming that there was no housing for them. The only dam-site jobs for women in Mason City and Coulee Dam were intended to be in the mess halls: an early bureaucrat had bragged to his boss that the contractors "are going to give the women a break" by offer-ing them kitchen assistant and waitress positions.[8]

Women's job opportunities were also limited if their husbands held man-agement positions in a closed-shop operation. At Holden, Washington, all mining jobs required union membership, but managers' wives could not join the union. This ruled out jobs in the dining hall and kitchen, although wives could work in the offices, the school, the stores, and the post office.[9]

The most enterprising women ran their own businesses: they taught piano and dance or set up one-chair beauty shops in their homes. Others did laundry and mending. In the portable Oregon logging camp of Shevlin, the camp clerk's wife started a store in a rail car to sell fabric and sewing notions. Each time Shevlin moved, the store took over more space; within a dozen years, Florence Olson's "gift shoppe" offered work clothes, sport-ing goods, toys, gifts, a soda fountain with jukebox, and even slot machines so women could gamble in privacy. At Holden, Helene Bell started a dress shop in her home. By the early 1950s, the shop had expanded to a company-owned space next door to the post office, and she was running fashion shows for the community.[10]

Some companies guaranteed employees' children summer jobs. This may have been paternalistic, but it kept kids busy during vacations and sent col-lege students back to school with healthy bank balances. At Holden, boys couldn't work in the mines until they were eighteen, but many went to work at sixteen in jobs like road maintenance and camp clean-up, gardening and garbage pickup. Girls cashiered in the grocery, sorted mail in the post office, and "slung hash." Unlike their mothers, the children of Holden managers sometimes took union jobs for the summer, but they were never allowed to attend union meetings. At Gilchrist, Oregon, the company didn't prom-ise a job to every teenager, but it did ensure an opening for any employee's child enrolled in college. DuPont managers also gave students an oppor-tunity to work their way through school. In Valsetz, employees' children could work in the mill during college vacations and when they needed to take a quarter off to accumulate tuition money.[11]

Bosses occasionally found other ways to encourage ambitious kids. In McCleary, Washington, one of the McClearys helped persuade Angelo Pellegrini's parents when the boy wanted to take the unexpected (and, for his immigrant family, unprecedented) step of attending high school. The company also made sure Pellegrini had a weekend and vacation job in the sawmill. A few years later, when three teenagers wanted to establish a local newspaper, Henry McCleary offered a building lot as a prize in the new paper's subscription drive. At Ryderwood, Washington, one teenager worked as the night operator on the community switchboard; with only 200 telephones in the village, he had time for homework and catnaps between calls. Some teenage boys in logging camps had more traditional jobs like bull cook: they split the wood that fed the mammoth cookhouse stoves.[12]

Younger children earned spending money with projects that, though not unique to company towns or camps, were made easier by the predominantly bachelor population or the towns' locations. Whether or not a camp was officially dry, kids usually could collect and redeem beer bottles. Others trapped; near Grand Coulee Dam, one dam site employee's son sold muskrat skins to Sears, Roebuck for a dollar each. In many logging areas, kids peeled bark from the cascara buckthorn, which was sold for use in laxatives like Fletcher's Castoria, and dug the roots of Oregon grape, used for an antiseptic. Like in every other town and city, boys carried newspapers: in a company town or camp, however, some of the routes were shorter— up and down the bunkhouse halls instead of up and down streets. In Valsetz, Oregon, a nine-year-old started her own newspaper; Dorothy Anne Hobson's *Valsetz Star,* published on the timber company's mimeograph from 1937 to 1941, probably didn't make much money for her or the assistant editor, but it got them written up in newspapers across the country and invited to press luncheons and radio shows. At Cedar Falls, Washington, where a longtime teacher was an enthusiastic supporter of 4-H, children earned pocket money by winning awards at the state fair for their projects. Kids received fifty cents for a prize squash or a few dollars for a first-place cooking or sewing project. One boy continued his beekeeping into high school, earning $150 one year from selling tons of honey to his neighbors and the lumber camp cookhouses. Another, short of cash for an upcoming 4-H trip, sold hot dogs at his own concession stand at water's edge when a unexpected freeze brought the Cedar Falls community out to skate on Rattlesnake Lake.[13]

Even the few disabled and elderly people in company towns worked. At Holden, Washington, a miner blinded on the job ran a variety store. A miner who had lost a leg went to work in the dining hall. When the mine closed, it was he and his wife who served as caretakers, helping the mine superintendents close up and families move out the last of their belongings. When Allan Teagle was crippled in a sawmill accident, he was hired as a bookkeeper for the Henry McCleary Timber Company. At Grisdale, a man who started with Simpson Timber in 1899 retired in 1952 after a final job serving as the community's "camp engineer," blowing the morning whistle, lighting the cookhouse stove, tending the lawns and the roses, and turning out the camp lights each evening. At Cedar Falls, a one-legged janitor the kids called "Pegleg" lived in a shack near the school and kept the restrooms clean and the coal furnace fired.[14]

Most company towns in the Pacific Northwest were run by whites for whites and it's no surprise, when you look at early census figures for the region. In 1910, Washington and Oregon were more than 97 percent white. In Idaho, out of a total of 325,594 people, only 651 were black and 1,363 Asian. In Washington, the most populated and most ethnically diverse state of the three, 40 percent of the blacks lived in Seattle; several other cities had only a handful of minorities, or none at all.[15]

Especially in the beginning of the twentieth century, company-town bosses often recruited workers from other branches of the company and from affiliated companies. This ensured new employees had the necessary skills, experience, and work ethic. It also perpetuated the company's existing ethnic mix. In Potlatch, Idaho, many of the first employees came from Great Lakes states operations of the Potlatch Lumber Company founders, Weyerhaeuser, Musser, and Laird-Norton. Years later, the Long-Bell Lumber Company moved key executives from Missouri when it established Longview and Ryderwood. The Gilchrist Timber Company brought so many of its Mississippi employees along when it came to Oregon that southerners made up more than half the new town in 1939. The Howe Sound Company opened Holden, Washington, with executives from its mine at Britannia Beach, British Columbia, and then, as the Holden mine neared closure, moved some managers to Cobalt, Idaho.[16]

Workers also came from similar operations that shut down. When the lumber mill at Brookings, Oregon, closed in 1925, the town emptied almost overnight, with workers heading east to Shevlin-Hixon and Brooks-Scanlon operations in Bend and nearby logging camps. In 1939, when the southern Oregon company town of Pine Ridge burned, some mill workers took jobs in newly built Gilchrist. When Port Blakely, Washington, closed, Japanese laborers moved across Puget Sound to the Kent Lumber Company town of Barneston.[17]

Workers also followed family members—at both entry and management levels. Crowded into old Fords with their children and in-laws, Mowich loggers bumped along the back roads of central Oregon to camps where relatives had found work. The operations in company towns were also the proving grounds for company scions. Potlatch employed several young Weyerhaeuser sons and cousins during summer vacations and soon after college graduation. At Holden, sons of New York City–based Howe Sound executives spent their summer vacations from Princeton and Yale in Washington's North Cascades, working alongside local managers' sons and longtime miners.[18]

Potlatch Lumber Company instructions to employment agencies make clear the company's original preference for workers of Nordic heritage. Many other employers must have had similar policies: in two of the Washington counties where logging and sawmilling were important, the largest groups of foreign-born workers came from Norway and Sweden. Few employers recruited immigrants from other countries, especially before World War I, except for exhausting unskilled labor on the railroad and in factories. As Angelo Pellegrini wrote, "The immigrants from southern Europe were not in a friendly and sympathetic atmosphere before World War I." The 1910 census showed that there were 250 Italian immigrants in the southwestern Washington county where Pellegrini's family lived. Some were mill workers, but most worked as unskilled railroad section hands. In the same era, almost 300 Italians lived in Washington's Skagit County, where the Superior

Potlatch Lumber Company tag, front (top) and back. (Courtesy of David Ownbey)

Portland Concrete Company offered menial jobs like bagging and stacking cement. Shevlin, isolated in central Oregon, had no Italians or Greeks, even by 1950. Nor did Shevlin have blacks, Asians, Hispanics, or Native Americans. DuPont, Washington, was no different. In 1940, the explosives town had about 500 people, but only seven were classified as nonwhite by census workers. By contrast, as early as the turn of the century the little schoolhouse in Port Blakely, Washington, had children of more than twenty-five nationalities. In Kittitas County, Washington, where the coal towns of Roslyn and Cle Elum were built, more than three-quarters of the 1910 work force was foreign-born; the two largest immigrant groups were from Austria and Italy.[19]

Coal-mining bosses also brought in workers from other company mines in the eastern United States and in California, but there's no evidence that this was done for ethnic homogeneity. In fact, the opposite was probably true: some coal-mining executives deliberately hired from a wide variety of ethnic and racial groups, assuming that cultural differences would keep workers from assimilating enough to oppose management.[20]

It was because of labor issues that a few Northwest company towns did have significant black populations. In the late 1800s, determined to break unions formed by white miners, both the Northern Pacific Coal Company and the Oregon Improvement Company brought a thousand black miners to the western Washington coal towns of Roslyn, Cle Elum, Franklin, and Newcastle. Many stayed, despite discrimination and harassment, because the mines offered black men one of the few respectable means of supporting their families. As one African-American miner wrote the *Seattle Post-Intelligencer,* "We are aware that prejudice is against us here; but where can we go? It is against us everywhere. . . . Let them call us scabs if they want to. We have concluded that half a loaf is better than none." The black miners significantly—although only temporarily—changed the look of towns like Roslyn. By 1900, a decade or so after the strikebreakers arrived, Kittitas County had 401 blacks; by comparison, King County, where Seattle is located, then had only 600 blacks among its 110,000 residents. Familiarity did not eliminate prejudice, however: a history of Kittitas County published in 1904 claims that "the first Negroes imported were such a corrupt lot that they were replaced with white workers . . . as soon as it was possible." Census

Kerriston, Washington, like nearby Barneston and Selleck, was one of the timber communities with a significant Japanese population. Most Japanese workers built their own homes, usually at some distance from the company-built houses for white employees. Some Japanese communities also had their own bathhouses and recreation halls. (Allen & Perkins photo, courtesy of Michael Maslan Historic Photographs)

data show that by 1910, the county was again almost completely white; of its 9,700 people, only 247 were identified as minorities. By 1940, when the population had almost doubled, there were a few hundred nonwhites total.[21]

At Grand Coulee Dam, despite federal mandates that black men were to be offered at least messenger positions, both Bureau of Reclamation and dam-site contractors had to be badgered into hiring African Americans. In response to complaints from the Urban League, the acting commissioner of the Bureau said that such hiring was unwarranted because African Americans constituted an insignificant proportion of Washington state's population. His count was accurate: blacks made up less than half a percent of the state's population in 1930. There were barely a dozen black men total in the three counties that Grand Coulee spanned. (Despite the numbers, the Bureau of Reclamation finally did agree to offer blacks a small number of laborer positions.)[22]

Besides being reluctant to hire blacks, Asians, and southern Europeans, many employers were quick to lay them off. In the coal-mining town of Franklin, Washington, where blacks had come in as strikebreakers, the mine superintendent later accused them of inefficiency and arbitrarily replaced them with nonunion whites. At Grand Coulee, an occasional foreman was suspected of replacing laid-off blacks with white men. For some bosses, however, loyalty and quality of work were more important than race and ethnic background. When the Depression brought cutbacks and mill closures, the Potlatch Lumber Company general manager was one of those who refused to force out faithful Greek, Italian, and Japanese employees to create openings for American-born job applicants. Similarly, Angelo Pellegrini remembered how the Henry McCleary Timber Company almost always seemed to find work for his father, regardless of the economy.[23]

The color of a worker's skin and where he came from had a lot to do with what jobs he was offered. At Roche Harbor, Washington, the Japanese worked not in the lime quarries but as domestic servants for the McMillin family and as hotel staff. Legend says it was they who painstakingly hand-picked the weeds out of the turf on John McMillin's private golf course. In timber towns, ethnic groups sometimes clustered in certain jobs. In a few mill towns the Japanese population was unusually large. At Selleck, east of Seattle, white men may have had the best jobs in the 1920s, but most of the workers were Japanese. In nearby Barneston, shortly before the timber town closed in the early 1920s, a third of the 231 residents were Japanese. Here the Asians had more job opportunities: besides working as railroad or mill laborers, some held jobs as cooks and assistant foremen. A few worked as foremen of the Japanese sawmill crews, a position also called bookman. (Bookmen usually received a monthly fee from each worker— sometimes fifty cents—and a 5 percent commission from Seattle's Asian merchants on all Japanese foods and novelties purchased by workers.)[24]

Hierarchies in company towns were defined by more than race or ethnicity. Some who grew up in these communities remember that it was impossible to ignore who were the bosses' sons and daughters. Laborers' children assumed that managers' children were condescending; managers' children recall the stigma of being the boss's kids. Others say few economic and ethnic differences existed in the schoolroom and on the playground. With just one school in a company town, children could not be segregated. Angelo Pellegrini, writing about his boyhood in McCleary just before World War I, was impressed by the equitable treatment. All the McCleary "bigwigs," as Pellegrini called them, sent their children to the same school as the laborers, where children were seated in alphabetical order. The ten-year-old Pellegrini sat next to the executive William McCleary's daughter, who became a lifelong friend. After eighth-grade graduation, however, many children were separated. Few small towns or logging camps had high schools, so most laborers' children went to work, while managers often moved to cities or sent their children away to school.[25]

In certain towns, and on certain occasions, class lines were seldom drawn. In Gilchrist, Oregon, when the company head's daughter married, mill workers mingled with management at the wedding reception. In little Cedar Falls, children of Seattle City Light employees dated—and some eventually married—children of those who worked at the Milwaukee Road railroad camp. In Coulee Dam, the wife of the top federal employee was known to go Halloween trick-or-treating in costume. Angelo Pellegrini recalled how he as a child delivered milk to the McClearys and then walked to school with their children. When his mother died decades later, her coffin was carried by the last surviving McCleary brother, by executives of the McCleary and Simpson Timber companies—and by the laborers who had boarded at her table for decades.[26]

Because most company towns in the Northwest were remote communities built for loggers, miners, and construction crews, it would be easy to stereotype the people as rough-and-tumble laborers. Brute strength was undeniably an important characteristic in early days, and many employees had little formal education and few social graces. But skilled workers and professionals played an important role in many company operations. At Holden, where the staff included engineers, geologists, and metallurgists, mine employees were encouraged to pursue research, publish articles in professional journals, and make presentations at industry conferences. Many of the first employees were recruited from the mining and engineering programs at the University of Washington and what was then Washington State College. Some, including the general manager, continued their education while working, earning degrees despite Holden's remote location. A "great place to cut your teeth [professionally]," recalled the historian Nigel Adams, who lived there his entire boyhood.[27]

Some of the men who worked in company towns came to stay; others, typical of the wanderers who characterized early-day mining and logging camps, were quick to move on after a couple of paychecks. Turnover in Washington logging camps averaged 55 percent a month—660 percent a year—just before World War I. Even during the worst of the Depression, when families camped in caves and packing cartons near Grand Coulee, waiting for the chance of a job, laborers didn't always stay long. By the World War II years, when the defense plants in the Pacific Northwest were chronically short of labor, workers were quick to abandon jobs in isolated Richland. Turning bachelor camps into towns for families helped stem the turnover, but in the late 1940s, the timber industry reported that a quarter of the men hired for logging crews stayed only two weeks. Although Grisdale, Washington, was notable for its stability—some employees stayed almost all forty years of the logging camp's life—Simpson Timber reported that it still took 700 hires in 1947 to keep the camp's 350 positions filled.[28]

Why did people stay in company towns? Some couldn't afford to move. When the Depression began, most married men in a company town could count on at least a few days of work a month, and the boss tended to be lenient about arrears in rent payments or the balance due at the company store. In the late 1940s and early 1950s, when the postwar boom had faded, many workers welcomed any employment. "I was 61 and it was a job," explained a teacher who was delighted by an offer from the Holden school in the early 1950s—despite her dreary two-room apartment and a seemingly endless winter. Others stayed because the beauty and safety of the rural settings compensated for the isolation. And still others remained because the remoteness created a sense of community. For some company towns, that sense of community continued to live on decades after the towns closed and the people scattered around the country.[29]

4 / When the Dinner Bell Clanged

B urned johnnycakes and greasy salt pork may have been staples in early logging- and mining-camp cookhouses, but by the early 1900s most employers were striving to provide good quality food—and lots of it—even if locations were remote and kitchens primitive. Because wages didn't vary much within an industry, meals were an important means of attracting and retaining the single men who made up a huge percentage of the work force. In fact, a good cook was probably more important than keeping bedbugs out of bunkhouses.

Food was a significant bargaining point when the Industrial Workers of the World organized early in the century, and it continued to crop up as a labor issue where men lived and ate communally. A 1940s logging boss found his Oregon camp shut down, partly because of the cook, described by the union as "an ornery SOB" who served unpalatable food and swore at his mess hall crew. Although a small logging camp might hire a logger's wife to cook, larger camps and towns recruited experienced professional cooks. A cook had high status in a smaller community, sometimes ranking second only to the camp foreman. (And his unofficial status may have been higher: he was a "monarch," declared one timber company newsletter editor.) Few cooks tolerated any complaints. As the U.S. Army discovered in 1917, when its Spruce Production Division was sending soldiers into logging camps, the camp cook "belongs to the artistic class, and has the artistic foibles, chiefly an ineluctable aversion to criticism of his art." Such criticism was likely to have "immediate and disastrous" results, an army officer reported. The government-published Spruce Production Division history provides no descriptions of such disasters, but loggers' memoirs are full of stories about camp cooks so irritated by complaints that they wrestled grouchy lumberjacks out of cookhouses or hurled meat cleavers across kitchens. The artistic nature wasn't limited to loggers, either. At a lakeside construction camp near Diablo, the cook whipped out a revolver when laborers on a Seattle City Light dam teased him about fishing out the cookhouse window.[1]

Some cooks had been trained on ocean liners and in metropolitan hotel kitchens. Others went from the woods to the hotels, recruited because of their logging camp experience, both in the culinary arts and in kitchen management. Cooks supervised as many as fifteen assistant cooks and flunkies, the men and women who served the family-style meals, made the sack lunches, and washed hundreds of plates and cups. In early years, the cookhouse staff kept huge wood stoves going for at least fourteen hours a day, raised hogs (sometimes a hundred or more), and inventoried and ordered supplies. Some cooks did their own butchering; others cut up the sides of beef and pork that arrived wrapped in burlap. As late as the 1940s, some cookhouses had no refrigeration, so cooks had to plan meals around what could be kept in screened meat sheds and root cellars.[2]

Servings in most dining halls were unlimited; laborers paid the same whether they ate two eggs or a dozen, one steak or four. Army officials setting up the Spruce Production Division in 1917 were appalled at the quantity of food offered loggers; they estimated that a logger was fed double the soldier's ration. They were also shocked at the variety of foods; to bake six different kinds of pastry for breakfast alone was unbelievably wasteful, an officer declared. One reason the army paid Spruce Production Division workers civilian wages was so the men could pay for their own meals; the mess bills were more than what regular soldiers made in salary. Not that cookhouse prices were high. In the 1930s, the cookhouses at small camps like Mowich, Oregon, offered breakfast, lunch, and dinner for fifty or sixty cents a day. In the same era, workers on Grand Coulee Dam paid fifty cents a meal. Like at logging and mining camps, servings were unlimited: as a *Seattle Post-Intelligencer* reporter said in 1939, "A man is not a man [in Mason City] unless he can eat his own weight three times a day."

The Bordeaux, Washington, dining hall of the Mason County Logging Company was typical of what timber communities provided for single workers, with long tables, backless benches, and simple white dinnerware. Food was usually served family-style from huge platters on each table. (MSCUA, University of Washington Libraries, Kinsey 213)

Menus were extensive. In Grisdale, Washington, in the 1940s, loggers were paying ninety cents a day for meals. Breakfasts included oranges, oatmeal, corn flakes, bacon and eggs, griddle cakes, potatoes, toast, muffins, doughnuts, tea, coffee, cream, and milk. The dinner menu offered two kinds of meat, fresh vegetables, fruits, freshly baked bread, biscuits, pies, cakes, and puddings. At Shevlin, Oregon, where the cookhouse accommodated a couple of hundred men, meals were less elaborate but similar in size: a lunchbox might be packed with three sandwiches, a hard-boiled egg, an apple, an orange, and oversized cookies.

Occasionally, loggers were served hot lunches in the woods; especially in the World War I era, meals were sometimes sent to the work site on a flatcar or a caboose. In later years, quality remained high, quantities vast, and prices low. Before Grisdale closed in the 1980s, loggers paid about $5 a day for steak, prime rib, shrimp, and scallops. Good camp cooks also understood the special needs of a population that was overwhelmingly young and male: in Grisdale, on the Mondays after payday, there was always tomato juice on the breakfast table for those still recovering from a weekend away.[3]

Townspeople didn't have to live in the bunkhouse to eat in the cookhouse. But however modest the prices, some couples couldn't afford the cookhouse, especially during the Depression. On holidays, though, the dining hall doors were often opened to everyone. "There will never be a meal like those the logging camp cooks used to put out for the men at Christmas," remembered Sam Churchill, who spent part of his childhood in a remote Oregon Coast Range camp. "Mother loved to have dinner at the cookhouse. She said it was better than dinner at the Weinhard Hotel in Astoria." Those who lived in Valsetz and Grisdale probably agreed; holiday meals there included Dungeness crab cocktails, oyster soup, roast turkey and chicken, asparagus, yams, Parker House rolls, pumpkin and mince pies, plum pudding with brandy sauce, fruitcake, ice cream, and cigars.[4]

Although cookhouse fare might have compared favorably with hotel cuisine, the decor wasn't as glamorous—and neither were the diners. Furniture was functional. Seats didn't have to be comfortable; few workers lingered at the table. Most finished their meals, including those extra servings of steak and pie, in minutes. A *National Geographic* writer visiting the Grisdale cookhouse in 1960 said it took seven minutes for the first man to finish his meal. After ten minutes most loggers were done, and in fifteen minutes the room was empty. Conversation was limited; in fact, it often was forbidden by early cooks. They wanted to avoid the possibility of complaints and speed up meal service so kitchen crews could start work on the next meal.[5]

There were also rules about dining hall seating. "When you reported to camp, you were assigned a stool and that's where you sat for all meals," remembered H. A. (Andy) Solberg about his 1950s summer job in Headquarters, Idaho. In less-organized dining halls, rules were implicit: a new arrival risked the ire of veterans if he inadvertently took someone's usual seat. Woman, the managers, and college students sometimes sat at their own tables, where dining was more leisurely. "Why hurry?" Solberg said. "There was never any shortage of food."[6]

Although camp bosses recognized that abundant food was important, they grumbled that meals cost more than employees paid and they kept cooks on budgets. To reduce costs, most cooks made sure dessert was on the table when men came into dinner. In the 1940s, Grisdale cooks made a hundred pies a day because the head cook believed that a logger anticipating dessert was more likely to skip an extra T-bone. Cooks irritated by accountants' close scrutiny of grocery orders sometimes quit—or threatened to. At the West Fork Logging Company's camp near Mineral, Washington, the husband-and-wife cookhouse team packed its bags when the bookkeeper refused to authorize the coconut, raisins, and walnuts needed for the seventy-five dozen cookies made several times a week. It took the intercession of the company owner to resolve the dispute. Cooks also were unlikely to scrimp on other ingredients and condiments; a 1949 story about Grisdale pointed out that there was butter, never margarine, on the table.[7]

Budgets weren't the only challenges faced by cookhouse crews, especially during World War II food rationing. Because of their importance to the war effort, some logging and mining companies were able to negotiate extra supplies of rationed goods. When rations were short, cooks expected company management to solve the problem. A western Washington cook irritated by the sugar shortage sat the full crew, including his bosses, down to chocolate pies. Every single one of them was beautifully decorated, every single one of them was made without sugar. No one had more than a bite or two of pie that night, but the point was made, and a load of sugar arrived the next day. In Holden, even a supplemental allotment from the Office of Price Administration couldn't keep the mess hall adequately supplied. After both the regular restaurant allotment and the extra sugar had been used up, a crew of drillers working for the contractor Morrison-Knudsen Company walked off the job in protest, and the resident copper miners called a brief sit-down strike in sympathy.[8]

Some companies ran farms to supply their cookhouses, and almost every early logging camp had a pig pen. Hogs ate the kitchen waste and leftovers and then eventually found themselves on the menu. At waterfront camps, workers ate fish; at Mowich, Oregon, the cook's young son caught and cleaned his daily limit of seventy-five trout after school on Thursday and another seventy-five the next day to provide for the Friday night fish fries. But most supplies were shipped in by packhorse, railroad, or steamship. Quantities were immense, especially in the larger communities. In 1941, the Holden cookhouse bought twenty-three tons of ice cream, seventy-two tons of meat, 24,000 dozen eggs, and eight tons of butter. That meant each miner was eating the equivalent of a T-bone steak and a third of a pound of bacon every day—at a time when he was paying $1.20 a day for board and room.[9]

Regardless of how little else company towns had in common, meals in the company cookhouse were huge in quantity and high in quality. Men worked hard, and they expected to eat well. The company made sure that they did, despite remote locations, limited refrigeration, stringent budgets, or wartime rationing.

5 / Education in the Company Town

When a company decided to build a family camp or a company town, a school was a necessity: children had to be educated. For the bosses, schools had an important additional effect. The social life that developed around school activities is what helped develop cohesive communities that could retain employees and stabilize work crews.

Company towns occasionally started out with company-owned districts, which allowed management to control the quality of the curriculum, the morals of the teachers—and the level of school taxes. In Potlatch, Idaho, the schools were company controlled for more than forty years, until 1948. In Ryderwood, Washington, the Long-Bell Lumber Company built an elementary and high school, and for thirty years it bought the furniture and equipment, paid the teachers, and sometimes housed them. When the company didn't own the school, it almost always influenced the selection of school board members and thus controlled school budgets and tax levies as well as teacher selection. Managers were not averse to applying pressure to school board members, especially to remove teachers believed to be union sympathizers.[1]

Whether or not the school was part of a county district, the company usually provided the building. The first schools were seldom fancy; many were nothing more than converted bunkhouses or old saw-filing sheds. In some "car camps," the schoolhouse was constructed on a rail-car chassis, just like the cookhouse and company offices, so it could be rolled into place

Children in the coal-mining community of Tono, Washington, attended class in this frame structure in the early 1900s. The schoolyard was tidily fenced, but outside the pickets were stumps and logging debris. The lettering was added when the photograph was made into a postcard. (Courtesy of Daniel Kerlee)

and ready for class in less than a day. Occasionally the company donated the land and the district put up the schoolhouse. In many communities, the employer provided both land and buildings. Sometimes these were donated or sold to the district; other times the company retained ownership. When the Gilchrist family moved itself, its timber company, and hundreds of employees to eastern Oregon in the late 1930s, it built an elementary and high school that served children from distant ranches and logging camps as well as neighboring villages and the town of Gilchrist. In Longview, Washington, the Long-Bell Lumber Company built an elementary school that it sold to the city, as planned, almost immediately. The city's first high school was a personal gift of R. A. Long, the town founder. At Port Gamble, Washington, the Puget Mill Company built the school and owned everything in it—furniture, books, even the globes. At Holden, a Washington mining community built on Forest Service land, and at Grisdale, built deep in Simpson Timber Company forests, the companies built the schoolhouses; there was no question of the districts ever owning the land.[2]

As in other rural areas in the early 1900s, most company-town schools started out as uninsulated frame structures, often just a single room with

The Kent Lumber Company built this traditional, cupola-topped school in Barneston, Washington. After children walked down the neat boardwalk from the porch and through the gate, they had to make their own path home around stumps and rocks. (Courtesy of Seattle Public Utilities, Cedar River Watershed Education Center)

a bucket for drinking water and a couple of outhouses. Some were among the best-kept buildings in camp. Photos taken in 1911 of Barneston, Washington, show a traditional cupola-topped school building, neatly sided and painted, with a planked walkway leading from the steps through a carefully leveled schoolyard. But the tidiness ended at the playground gate. Past it there was no sidewalk; in the pictures, there's not even a pathway visible between the giant stumps and swampy puddles that surrounded the schoolyard fence and the modest homes nearby. The Wilark, Oregon, lumber camp's two-room school was "wonderfully equipped for a country school," with carbide lights, a furnace, and a janitor to keep the furnace stoked, remembered Grace Brandt Martin, a teacher. Outside there were swings, a slide, and a large play shed. But despite all these amenities, it still—in 1930—had privies. A few small-town schools were almost luxurious. Before World War I, when Fairfax, Washington, had a population of 500, the coal-

More than 80 children attended school in the coal-mining town of Fairfax, Washington, in the 1920s. By then the community had a new school with a gym and a volunteer-built, heated swimming pool. (MSCUA, University of Washington Libraries, Kinsey 1961)

mining town built a new school with gym and heated swimming pool. Cedar Falls, Washington, started out with a one-room school, but by 1919, its forty-six elementary students had a two-room school with full basement, rest rooms, a play area, and a coal-burning furnace. The nearby timber town of Selleck lost its school in a fire, and so in 1930, when there were 170 students, the company built a larger structure with a kitchen, library, science labs, offices, and restrooms.[3]

Classes were often held in buildings originally designed for other uses. When Grisdale, Washington, was under construction after World War II, a carpenter took a surplus building at another logging camp, sawed it into three sections, and loaded it onto flatcars; once the pieces arrived in the new camp, they were assembled into a comfortable two-room school, complete with restrooms. In small communities, school buildings served several functions. After classes were over on Friday nights, the desks might be pushed aside so movies could be shown. On Sundays—or whenever a minister made it to camp—the building would double as a church. Sometimes it was the church that did double duty; at Roche Harbor, the sanctuary was the schoolroom until a company house was converted to a school.[4]

Like the schools scattered across farmland, the first company-town schools met for only a few months each year. By 1900, however, most Puget Sound area schools were in session for at least 120 days a year. The exceptions were those towns with only a handful of students. In Selleck, Washington, in that era, school lasted only 60 days. By 1920, children were in class for at least 150 days a year. By 1930, even in such tiny Cascade foothills schools as Nagrom, Washington, which enrolled seven, and Baldi, which had eleven, school terms were 174 to 183 days.

Most company-town schools, like schools in other early settlements, served just the first eight grades. By 1920, Washington's most populous county, King, still had forty-six one-room schools outside Seattle; they included almost all the county's company-town schools. Only three of the county's company towns then had schools with twelve grades: the logging towns of Cherry Valley and Alpine and the coal-mining community of Black Diamond. When small towns did offer high schools, they were often one-room programs, with a single teacher covering all the subjects for a handful of teenagers. In the late 1930s, when Louise Schmidt Robertson attended Klickitat (Washington) High School, the entire student body of forty was accommodated in a three-room building: a classroom, a science lab, and a typing room. In Idaho and Oregon, company-town schools weren't much different: Potlatch was one of the few company towns to offer both an elementary and a high school in the early 1900s. Some towns built both elementary and high schools but couldn't afford to operate them. Roslyn, Washington, schools had 1,000 children enrolled by 1912, but the coal-mining community had difficulty raising enough in school taxes in the 1920s and 1930s. By 1931, due to debts, the high school had to be consolidated with the school in nearby Cle Elum.[5]

In the first third of the century, it was not unusual for students to go to work after finishing the eighth grade. Depending on how far from a high school they lived, teenagers determined to continue their education could commute to high school, paying for the transportation themselves, or board in a city that had a public high school. Some paid for their room and board by working as mother's helpers or hired girls in the homes where they lived; others took part-time jobs in local stores. Those whose parents could afford the tuition enrolled in boarding schools; a few went straight to normal school, the state-run teacher training programs.[6]

When school buses were uncommon and few commercial bus lines existed, students commuted by horseback and by train. In the early 1920s, teenagers from Franklin, Washington, rode the train to Black Diamond, paying a dime a ride. Newcastle and Coal Creek teenagers either tried to get a spot in Renton's crowded high school or left home before dawn for a commute to Seattle that involved train, ferry, and streetcar rides.[7]

As the years passed, more districts offered transportation; in 1927, 64 of the 114 school districts in King County, Washington, operated buses. But routes were long, especially for high school students; some had commutes that kept them on the bus for hours. When Shevlin, the portable Oregon lumber town, was moved for the last time in 1942, high school kids rode thirty-five miles each way to Gilchrist High School. In the early 1950s, when Seattle City Light bused its employees' children to Concrete High School from Newhalem and Diablo, the Diablo students had a forty-mile ride each way through the mountains. Winter storms made the trips even longer; some nights the buses couldn't make it home, and kids stayed with classmates.[8]

In especially remote locations, commuting wasn't possible. In these communities, arranging high school educations for children meant significant disruptions in families' lives. "Wrenching," the Holden historian Nigel Adams called the decisions that had to be made after eighth-grade graduation. Parents either sent their children away or moved with them to new jobs in larger communities. In the Skagit River communities of Newhalem and Diablo, families faced this problem for almost thirty years. In these City Light dam and power plant communities more than a hundred miles from Seattle, there was no way to get kids to Concrete, the nearest town, until after World War II. Especially before Gilchrist High School was built, children from Mowich, Oregon, were occasionally sent to relatives in Portland, where parents would join them when the lumber camp closed for the winter. Occasionally, young children also were sent away: Mary Ellen Field Lacy, whose mother ran the Holden school for almost twenty years, lived with her grandparents part-time during grade school because Mrs. Field didn't want to teach her own daughter.[9]

Some parents separated to solve the education problem. Married men bunked with the bachelors weekdays and joined their families on weekends in the towns where wives kept house for schoolchildren. In Holden, while the father stayed with younger children in their home near the mine, the mother might move to a city where an older child could be educated. Some families moved only to Chelan, a boat ride down Lake Chelan. Others went to larger, more distant cities. Supporting an additional household and possibly school tuition sometimes meant another change—the mother returning to work outside the home. When Nigel Adams, who went to Holden as an infant in 1939, was ready for high school in the early 1950s, his mother moved the two of them into a small Spokane apartment, leaving her husband and young daughter behind. Two years later, Mrs. Adams moved home and the Adamses followed the example of other miners: Nigel went to board with a Chelan family until he graduated from high school. When their daughter Janet finished eighth grade, they sent her to live with an aunt in Kirkland, then a small suburb of Seattle. Other teenagers chose different options, especially in the most remote communities. Marge Haddon Stansfield spent her first year in Holden taking high school correspondence courses. Finally, she, like other children of Holden managers and professionals, finished her education at boarding school—a significant expense in an era when Holden miners earned $150 to $250 a month.[10]

The teenagers who were sent away to boarding school also felt that they missed out socially. Doran Curzon Gordon, the Holden general manager's daughter, recalled how she envied friends who attended "real" high schools with proms and ball games, not girls-only academies with curfews and uniforms. The executives' children who went from remote company towns to exclusive big-city schools sometimes also felt out of place: intimidated by the extreme wealth of day students, they occasionally suspected that they were disdained as hicks.[11]

Sending children away had other disadvantages. From Holden, the closest high school was in Chelan, a four-hour ride away on the daily boat. A high school student determined to come home could catch the *Lady of the*

Lake on Saturday morning, be home in time for a late lunch, and then leave Holden at midday on Sunday. But when children moved halfway across the state, families could count on reunions only at Thanksgiving, Christmas, and spring vacations. Returning home for a weekend was out of the question, even without considering the boat ride: getting to Chelan alone was at least a half day's drive. Via train or bus, the trip was longer and more complicated. When the Haddon sisters came home from Forest Ridge School, then in Seattle, they rode the train to Wenatchee and then took the bus to Chelan. Like almost all travelers, they stayed overnight in Chelan before leaving for the boat trip uplake or catching a flight in a small plane.

As company town populations decreased or camp locations moved, elementary schools were often combined. Children were bused, but not in the yellow school buses common today. As late as the 1930s, districts often contracted out transportation, so children might travel in wagons or trucks. The Cedar Falls, Washington, bus driver, Emmett Jackson, started out with a truck equipped with benches. When Grisdale, Washington, opened after World War II, the community's school included kids from both Grisdale, a Simpson Timber camp, and the Schafer Bros. Logging Company Olympic Camp farther into the mountains. The Olympic Camp kids traveled the three miles to and from school in a Chevrolet Carryall driven by the school principal.[12]

Whether schools were large or small, they brought company towns together, just as schools do today in most small towns. Teachers organized plays, operettas, and Christmas pageants that attracted even the bachelors from the bunkhouses. Children showed off their accomplishments in county fair exhibits and at regional spelling bees. Parents worked together on fundraisers that drew on the community's setting or local talent. In Grisdale, built deep in prime elk hunting country, mothers sold sandwiches and coffee at a temporary snack bar set up for hungry hunters. At Cedar Falls, Washington, parents paid for their playground shelter by sponsoring dances—with music by the amateur Cedar Falls Dance Orchestra—that attracted couples from several neighboring towns. Sports teams, despite the distances, competed with other schools, drawing crowds of townspeople to games. The Grisdale grade school baseball team hosted its first out-of-town opponents in 1952, when the kids from Union City trav-

Emmett Jackson drove the Cedar Falls school bus for decades. He dropped young children at the local elementary school and then continued to North Bend with high school students. Shown with Jackson in 1939 are, from left, Mary Young, Jack Young, Gilbert Brooks, Bud Brown, David Brooks, George Rauch, Theo Thompson, Jean Thompson, Helen Thompson, Marie Pomeroy, Marilyn McDonald, Kathleen Cromby, and Glenn Young. (Courtesy of Seattle Public Utilities, Cedar River Watershed Education Center)

eled the sixty-five miles into the mountains for a game. In Holden, the elementary school basketball team welcomed Chelan seventh and eighth graders, who came up on the Saturday boat, played that evening in the recreation hall, stayed the night in their opponents' homes, and then had a mine tour before returning home on Sunday. In Valsetz, Oregon, a dwindling population in the 1980s meant high school girls played on a co-ed junior varsity basketball—and then changed into cheerleading uniforms for the varsity playoffs. At Cedar Falls, high in the Cascade foothills, the determined spinsters who coached basketball in the 1920s and 1930s kept their junior high players in championship competition even if they too had to fill out the team with girls.[13]

Besides athletic events, schools sponsored other competitions. Some were peculiar to a town's industry; others resulted from the teachers' interests. In coal towns, students joined junior mine rescue teams. "We'd do a stimulated rescue. [The captain would] say, 'The arm is broken' or 'The leg is broken.' The teams were formed in school and they had mine safety men teach us," remembered Ann Steiert, whose family moved to Black Diamond in 1926. In Cedar Falls, where the longtime teacher Clara Vinup organized 4-H groups almost immediately after her arrival in the 1920s, girls sewed and cooked and canned, boys kept bees and gardened, and they all learned Robert's Rules of Order and organized a 4-H band.[14]

The classroom was sometimes the most egalitarian place in a company town or camp. Although a boss's family might live in a larger community, especially if the company town didn't offer a high school, most children of management sat in the same classrooms as children of laborers. Race, however, created different issues. When Longview, Washington, was built by southerners, they were shocked to learn from the state school superintendent that schools could not be segregated; black children were to attend the same modern schools the company had built for white children. The Long-Bell Company did not question the law, and when the first black children were enrolled in 1924, it was with the support of the company attorney, who also happened to be the school board chairman. In Vanport, Oregon, on the Columbia River, the lack of segregation in the community's five grade schools was a major complaint among residents. Henry Kaiser had recruited tens of thousands of workers from across the country for World War II jobs at his Oregon Shipbuilding Corporation, creating the first significant nonwhite urban population in all of Oregon—and also bringing in many whites who were accustomed to segregation. Like Vanport, Mason City and Coulee Dam were instant cities, put up to accommodate construction workers at Washington's Grand Coulee Dam. But because the government officials and the dam contractors who built the towns refused to rent to blacks, there were no black children in Mason City or Coulee Dam schools.[15]

By the 1920s and 1930s, Asian children were generally better accepted than black children. However, because many Asian men immigrated alone and returned home when they could afford to marry, communities had few Japanese or Chinese families. The scarcity of Asians also resulted from earlier intolerance, when Chinese and Japanese laborers had been forced out of some towns, and from the restrictions on immigration instituted after 1924. McCleary, Washington, had only one Japanese child, and Barneston, Washington, had only three or four of school age between 1911 and 1923, when the town closed. Barneston's neighboring town of Selleck, where the Pacific States Lumber Company employed many Japanese, had only about fifteen Japanese couples in the early 1920s. Although Asian and white kids in Selleck studied and played together from 9 to 3, they lived separate lives after the school door closed. They didn't live close to each other, and Japanese children often spent after-school hours in late-afternoon Japanese schools organized by their parents.[16]

Teachers were often selected by company managers, because the school board members were usually the mill or mine bosses. This was an advantage when the company supported education. When schools opened in Potlatch, Idaho, teacher salaries were set above the state average to ensure that the town could attract good faculty. Much smaller communities sometimes paid well, too: as the Depression was starting, the two teachers in Wilark, Oregon, considered themselves comfortably compensated when they each received $140 a month and free rent. About the same time, teachers in the three-room school in another timber town, Port Gamble, Washington, were being paid $130 to $165 a month. In comparison, the women who taught elementary school in Seattle in 1930 were earning an average of $220—with no housing—while the average pay for Seattle's male teachers was $240.[17]

As important to many teachers as salary were the supplies and books the company provided or made sure the district bought. Grace Brandt Martin remembered the Wilark logging superintendent who encouraged the company-dominated school board to provide an ample supply of high-quality classroom equipment and books. Many teachers of her era had less to work with; some districts made do with libraries of only 50 or 100 books. In 1920, the clay-mining town of Taylor, Washington, had 139 students but only 149 reference and storybooks. In comparison, Cedar Falls, supported by taxes from Seattle City Light, the Milwaukee Road, and Pacific States Lumber Company, had 215 books for 46 children; the Northern Pacific town of Lester had 565 books for 41 pupils.[18]

Company-town schools sometimes had resources few other communities could duplicate. One was their setting. Maude Nelson, a former Holden teacher, described her schoolyard near the copper mine as a "geological treasure chest." Another advantage was the parents. In many company towns, parents taught music and helped coach athletics, sometimes on company time. In Cedar Falls, one father whose shift ended at noon spent a couple of afternoons each week in the school basement teaching woodworking.[19]

This emphasis on academics left many company-town children well prepared when they left for high school or college. If you read the oral histories and memoirs collected from Cedar Falls natives, you'll find the longtime teacher Clara Vinup praised repeatedly. Similar stories are told by those who attended Holden School, where Florence Field was principal and a teacher for almost twenty years. At Kinzua in the 1960s, Milt Boring was teacher, principal, coach, and chauffeur to summer swim lessons. When the mill town lost its school to consolidation and the kids had to be bused out of town, Boring went on to the consolidated school with the kids, teaching, coaching, and driving the bus home late enough that everyone could participate in extracurricular activities. These small-town teachers were also credited for encouraging students to consider college, despite its significant financial commitment. In *Immigrant's Return*, Angelo Pellegrini described how his teachers, in both McCleary and nearby Elma, introduced him to the possibility of a university education. Donald Denno, who grew up in Valsetz, Oregon, during the Depression, remembered the teacher who took two Valsetz High School seniors on a tour of the University of Oregon campus and explained how it was possible for them to work their way through college.[20]

Company-town teachers often had a wide variety of responsibilities, some atypical even in rural schools. Like Milt Boring and Grisdale's Lou Messmer, many drove school buses and swabbed out toilets. An early DuPont, Washington, teacher, Wendell Laughbon, started out in 1926 teaching industrial arts, gym, and health and serving as both scoutmaster and coach. To outfit his basketball team, he collected cast-off uniforms and had them dyed in the home economics room. In communities where the school stood near bunkhouses, teachers were expected to keep children quiet during recess so that the night shift could sleep. At Holden, where the town site was set between avalanche fields, teachers and parents shepherded children between

Part of the Chelan County school system, the eight-grade Holden, Washington, school was run from 1938 to 1957 by Florence Field, shown with middle-schoolers in the mid-1950s, when enrollment peaked at 113. (Courtesy of Bill Phillips)

school and the miners' neighborhood. "We went through the slide area single file and spaced out, warned to crouch next to the snowbank if we heard an avalanche coming," recalled Sandy Wigbers Adam. Even *Life* magazine took note of this unusual problem. In 1956, when the copper-mining town was digging out from record winter snowfall of more than fifty feet, the magazine reported, "As the melt starts, the mothers will man the 'slide patrol' to rush children home from school past dangerous avalanches which herald spring." When avalanches weren't a threat, teachers had to ensure that children didn't smother in the mounds of snow that accumulated each winter. One little boy at Holden bragged that it took two teachers and three eighth graders to rescue him after he jumped from a tree stump into powdery snow. The traditional expectation that teachers would contribute to children's moral upbringing was severely tested in towns like wide-open McCleary, where bootleg liquor and moonshine were stashed everywhere—even so close to the schoolhouse that children found it while playing.[21]

A few company towns provided education for adults as well as children. Most common were the classes where recent immigrants could learn English and prepare for naturalization. Seattle and nearby districts enrolled more than 8,000 in King County's evening schools by 1928. In the Potlatch, Idaho, area, where 23 percent of the men were foreign-born as late as 1920, the community's Protestant congregation organized Americanization classes. Later the Potlatch Lumber Company sponsored the classes, which continued until the mid-1930s. The Northwestern Improvement Company, the coal-mining subsidiary of the Northern Pacific Railroad, matched community donations to the Roslyn, Washington, YMCA, where night classes in 1908 included English, mechanical drawing, and electricity. In Barneston, English classes were taught in the early 1920s by a young woman who came out from Seattle on the train, carefully chaperoned by her father. During the worst of the Depression, the Long-Bell Lumber Company encouraged the establishment of a junior college that later became part of the state community college system. In Richland, Washington, adult education classes were organized almost immediately after the government established its atomic research community; eventually these classes led to a branch campus of Washington State University. The Vanport Extension Center opened in 1946 in the Oregon war worker community grew into Portland State University.

Whether it offered kindergarten through adult education or nothing more than basic reading and arithmetic, the company-town school almost always provided both a place and a reason to come together. The building and the activities it sheltered—ball games, band concerts, pageants, even movies and church services—were key to creating the sense of community that many former company-town residents remember with such affection.

6 / Religion in the Company Town

Bosses had practical reasons for encouraging church attendance—and it wasn't usually concern for their workers' spiritual life and morals. Religion provided an alternative to carousing and helped attract the stable family men who made dependable employees. Ministers usually could be relied on to deliver conservative sermons emphasizing the work ethic and management's benevolence. Despite this, employers were still businessmen reluctant to devote valuable company land to churches. A town established with a company-built church was rare; rarer yet was a company-paid minister.[1]

The men who ran company towns seldom discouraged church services, and often it was their wives who organized Sunday schools and Bible study. But a minister usually preached in a recreation hall, the schoolhouse, or someone's home. Church buildings were unusual, especially in communities where all land was owned by the company; even more of an anomaly was the community where the boss provided churches for both Protestants and Catholics. Camps and towns without church buildings never had resident ministers, unless someone was working part-time for the company and part-time for God. Even many towns with churches were often served only on a mission basis by priests and pastors formally assigned to other parishes. Pastors to company towns sometimes spent hours on the train or boat—or on foot—to minister to their flocks.

Companies built church buildings on company land in towns like Port Gamble and Roche Harbor, Washington, and in Potlatch, Idaho. In Port Gamble, the founders of Pope & Talbot erected a white-steepled church, its design inspired by the Congregational church in the timbermen's Maine hometown. Constructed in the 1870s, it has always been owned by the company. When John S. McMillin bought a San Juan Island lime quarry and kiln, he built a tiny chapel overlooking Roche Harbor. In Potlatch, two of the earliest buildings were a Catholic church and a Union Church that the Potlatch Lumber Company intended all the town's Protestants—more than twenty denominations—to share. The federal government did much the same when it took over the Richland and Hanford, Washington, communities during World War II; it provided two chapels of standard U.S. Army design, one for the Catholics, one for the Protestants.[2]

Some town owners dictated which denomination a church would serve; others let the parishioners decide. In Port Gamble, the first services were Congregational. At Roche Harbor, John S. McMillin was a Methodist, and his chapel offered only Methodist services for decades. At Klickitat, Washington, where the J. Neils Lumber Company had moved both the owner's family and many of the employees from its Midwest mill, the services were always Missouri Synod Lutheran. In Gilchrist, Oregon, the timber company donated its original employee dining hall to the community for a church. The congregation itself chose to affiliate with the Methodist church. Some Protestant services were nondenominational by the boss's mandate. Nowhere was this lack of doctrine more formalized than in Richland. To provide "a more efficient and more effective Christianity," the government town worked through the Washington State Council of Churches to create United Protestant congregations. Each was sponsored by a nonliturgical denomination such as Presbyterian, Methodist, Friends, or Disciples of Christ that had no set order of worship. The services were general and did not necessarily use the hymnal of the sponsoring denomination. Townspeople could join a UP congregation without giving up membership in their original church or without denying that home denomination financial support; contributions were routed to churchgoers' original denominations on a prorated basis. If 20 percent of a UP congregation's members had declared themselves Methodists, 20 percent of that congregation's offer-

Built in the nineteenth century to resemble the church in the hometown of company founders, this landmark Port Gamble, Washington, church has served many different denominations. As the twenty-first century began, it housed the congregation of St. Paul's Episcopal Church. (MSCUA, University of Washington Libraries, UW 17537)

ings was sent to the Methodist church's mission board. The UP churches themselves were supported by occasional special offerings and the sponsoring denomination's mission board.[3]

Many town owners refused to finance more than one church building. Because most towns were owned or managed by Protestants, Catholics often had long trips to mass. In the early 1900s, Catholic families in Black Diamond, Washington, almost always had to walk the three miles to Franklin for services. In Gilchrist, Catholics met in workers' homes for years, with services conducted by a priest who drove the fifty miles from Bend.

In Britannia Beach, B.C., owned by the same copper-mining company that developed Holden, Washington, volunteers built a church with an entrance on each end and a wall down the middle so both Catholic and Protestant congregations could meet at the same time.[4]

Congregations sometimes affiliated with one denomination and then, a few years later, with another. If times were hard or the town population dropped, the pulpit might stand empty. When services weren't regular, parents often organized Sunday schools. For help with curriculum, they could rely on correspondence courses like Church by Mail. At Port Gamble, the early Congregational pastors were followed by a Baptist who stayed through World War I. The postwar economic slump and a dwindling congregation resulted in the church standing quiet from 1922 until the early 1930s, when an Episcopal minister began visiting from Tacoma. At Roche Harbor, when Reuben Tarte converted the lime kiln community to a resort in the 1950s, the church—still privately owned—was reconsecrated as a Catholic chapel, Our Lady of Good Voyage.[5]

Employers who did not build churches often donated building sites and provided significant financial support for the congregation. In Gilchrist, the lumber company owners donated land when the Catholics had raised the funds to construct a church. In DuPont, Washington, worship began in 1909 in an old Hudson's Bay Company building still on the town site; eventually the explosives company donated land and most of the materials for a church and provided a company house for the manse. When Lutherans in Potlatch, Idaho, preferred their own worship to the nondenominational services at Union Church, the Potlatch Lumber Company departed from its usual policy of owning all land and buildings and allowed a Lutheran church to be constructed with lumber purchased at a discount from the company. (The land, however, remained company-owned for decades.) In Brookings, Oregon, in the 1920s, the lumber company donated lots for a community Protestant church; most of the construction was financed by the wife of a company executive.[6]

Ministers were only occasionally on the company payroll. In most cases, even when the company provided the church building, congregations hired pastors and paid other bills. Henry McCleary created a church collection column on the company payroll, so his workers could contribute regularly, whether or not they attended church. The Long-Bell Lumber Company also used the payroll deduction plan in Ryderwood, Washington. The minister there received no regular salary, just whatever loggers had subscribed to donate through their paychecks. The Depression-era pastor Ted Goodwin remembered that two-thirds of his salary was paid by men who never attended church; some donated a quarter a month, some fifty cents, some a dollar. In DuPont, the King's Daughters paid the pastor and the heating bill by selling gingham aprons and rag carpets and by sponsoring cake sales, strawberry socials, bazaars, dinners, and plays. When congregations were tiny, the ingenuity of the minister might be what kept the church doors open. In National, Washington, where the logging camp had only thirty-three permanent families by the time it was sold to Weyerhaeuser in 1957, the pastor described his flock as "rich in spirit, poor in coin." So he made ends meet by driving the school bus and running the local branch of the county library. Some of Port Gamble's first resident ministers served the community both as pastor and as doctor.[7]

Ministering to remote company-town congregations meant clergy often spent days traveling. The Catholic priest who served Black Diamond,

Washington, in the early 1900s also conducted services in the nearby coal-mining towns of Fairfax, Krain, and Cumberland. The Protestant congregation in Black Diamond had a church, but it relied on visiting preachers from Seattle: one early minister arrived by train on Saturday, stayed overnight at a parishioner's home, preached in Black Diamond the next morning, and then traveled to Franklin to conduct a second service. If he was lucky, he got a ride to Franklin on a hand-pumped speeder and he returned on the train bound for Black Diamond. Otherwise he walked three miles to Franklin and, after church, the three miles back to the Black Diamond depot for the trip to Seattle.[8]

The copper-mining town of Holden, Washington, never had a church, perhaps because the village was built on Forest Service land. For a year or so, there was a fundamentalist preacher living in town, but only because he was expected to work half-time for the company. Most worship services were conducted in the gym by an Episcopal minister and a Catholic priest who made the four-hour trip up Lake Chelan every month. Because of the boat schedule and ministers' other obligations, church services were usually held on weekday evenings; after the formal services, the ministers might meet more casually with miners. Nigel Adams, who lived in the community his entire boyhood, remembered the Episcopal minister sitting in his family's basement with a group of men, drinking home-brew and talking.[9]

Communities without organized congregations, especially those with few families, were likely to have informal services on an irregular schedule—whenever an itinerant preacher came through or a nearby town's minister chose to make the trip to camp. Logging-camp mission programs were run by men (and occasional couples) called sky pilots; the name came from an early Presbyterian missionary who said he wanted to "pilot men to the skies." Several were supported by the Presbyterian Board of National Missions, which budgeted a few thousand dollars a year for ministers like L. H. Peterson and George Redden. "Parson Pete" Peterson was a logging-camp missionary who had Seattle City Light's new town of Newhalem added to his circuit-riding responsibilities in 1921; besides conducting church services, he organized social events and published a newsletter. Early in his career, George Redden evangelized in company-dominated towns like Concrete, Washington, but he spent most of his ministry based in Bend, Oregon. There

George Redden was one of the sky pilots, or logging camp missionaries, sponsored by the Presbyterian Board of National Missions. Starting in 1928, he spent more than twenty years serving dozens of logging communities such as Shevlin from his home base in Bend, Oregon. (Courtesy of Ruth Redden Cole)

the "Pastor of the Pines" ran nondenominational Protestant services in central Oregon logging communities such as Shevlin for twenty-some years starting in 1928. For much of his career, he served twenty-nine logging camps in a 22,000-square-mile area. Redden, who hitchhiked until he was given a car, visited each camp every six or eight weeks. He taught Bible school and led children's choirs that performed in church and at company picnics.[10]

Children also were easier than loggers to attract in Ryderwood, Washington, where Ted Goodwin pastored during the 1930s. Although he admitted he never could get all the Long-Bell workers to church, Goodwin's Sunday school enrolled as many as 325 in years when Ryderwood had a population of 2,000. Besides Sunday services and Thursday prayer meetings, Goodwin reached his flock with "Straight from the Heart," a human-interest column for the closest daily newspaper, and he often worked in the woods with Ryderwood loggers. A latter-day sky pilot, Jack Anderson, who traded logging for pastoring, put almost 3,000 miles a month on his car visiting southwestern Washington logging camps in the 1950s.[11]

Ministers were not always enthusiastically welcomed. The Reverend George C. F. Pringle, who served Northwest islands and inlets in the early 1900s on a mission boat, recalled that few loggers were interested in his formal sermons. "I never went hungry or lacked a place to sleep when I was back in the camps, but they seemed to have little use for a preacher," he wrote. George Redden recalled being given "the once-over" when he first announced church meetings at a Shevlin-Hixon camp. "It was my singing that brought the men out," he later said. "Many of the hard-boiled lumberjacks wouldn't take the time to hear a sermon, but they liked the songs."

When Ryderwood's Ted Goodwin first went into the woods to work, loggers demanded to know why he was there and made clear their disdain for religion in general and for sky pilots specifically. "But," he recalled, "their distrust soon changed, until I had more invitations to bring my lunch pail over to various sides than I could accept."[12]

Ethnic minorities often were served by special missionaries or ministers. At Selleck, Washington, a timber community not far from Seattle, services in Japanese were conducted once a month by a visiting white minister. By 1904, the coal town of Roslyn, Washington, supported seven churches, including a "colored Baptist" congregation. There was both a Buddhist temple and a Baptist church in the neighborhood that the married Japanese workers built for themselves in the timber town of Port Blakely, Washington.[13]

Regardless of where church services were held, it was congregations that established the first social activities in many communities. Frequently encouraged by management, church members formed Sunday schools and altar guilds, ladies' aid societies, and Epworth Leagues. They organized revival meetings, Easter cantatas, and welfare programs, even naturalization classes and local libraries. Millowner Henry McCleary's wife, Ada, helped establish both her town's church congregation in 1910 and the women's society in 1915. She and other women financed their projects—which included the community library and the children's Christmas tree—by running carnivals and rummage sales, fashion shows, silver teas, talent shows, and bake sales.

Despite the many church-oriented activities in company towns, those without church buildings and resident ministers seldom had two of the most common church services: weddings and funerals. Loggers and miners usually were married in the cities where their brides lived. There were few funerals in many company settlements because towns too small to have churches were often too small to have undertakers. Many company towns also lacked cemeteries. Sometimes this was the companies' choice. In communities built on Forest Service land, it was the federal government's.[14]

Sunday school, worship services, and congregational fund-raising projects were important in many, many company towns. They were, however, probably more important for social than religious reasons. Even when there were no church buildings and no resident ministers, church-related projects involved women, children—and men—from various levels of the town hierarchy and different ethnic groups. Like schools in small towns, church programs in the early decades of the twentieth century contributed significantly to community cohesiveness.

7 / Baseball, Bowling, Bands, and Bridge Tournaments

When the workday finally ended, the rough-and-tumble loggers and gritty miners in early Northwest camps didn't have much leisure time: they hung out their wet wool socks, read a little pulp fiction, told tall tales around the bunkhouse stove, or maybe played a hand or two of cards. Come Saturday night, if there was a town anywhere nearby, they scrubbed themselves up and headed off to the saloons and brothels. Sunday morning the men trudged back to camp, sometimes shepherded by a boss determined to keep his experienced crews, however hungover they were.

The construction of family camps and company towns didn't change this scene completely. Married men were less likely to carouse, and newer bachelor camps offered diversions like card rooms, reading rooms, and movies. But when the work was done, there were still men who headed out for beer and excitement on Saturday night. After long, exhausting days in dangerous jobs, they were not "nice nellies," as historian and politician Richard Neuberger primly noted in 1938.[1]

Company-town founders worked hard to provide more genteel amusements within walking distance of the bunkhouse. All but the smallest settlements had a mess hall that could be used for movies, dances, and shivarees; many had separate theaters, billiards and card rooms, bowling alleys, and gyms. Companies built libraries, tennis courts, and an occasional swimming pool. Bosses sponsored ball teams, brass bands, and drill teams.

They organized all-company picnics and the barbecues and dances for Fourth of July and Labor Day. The company store or the community club made sure Santa Claus came to town. As late as the 1950s, some communities had so many activities that the company hired a clerk to schedule meeting rooms. The Potlatch (Idaho) Mercantile housed the pool room, opera house, and confectionary as well as the company store, post office, and bank. For the Potlatch Amateur Athletic Club, the lumber company constructed a gym that was used until the town was sold in 1951. In DuPont, Washington, one 1920s teacher spent her summers teaching local kids how to crab and swim on the company-owned beach and play tennis on the company playground. Cedar Falls never had more than a few hundred people, but Seattle City Light still built a tennis court, a swimming pool, and a gym. Weyerhaeuser's mill town of Snoqualmie Falls, Washington, had a recreation center with dancing, roller skating, and exercise classes, a library, and a 370-seat auditorium. In Kinzua, Oregon, "the hall" had a barber shop, a confectionary, and a meeting room where the theater-style seats were mounted on two-by-fours, so it was easy to move them out of the way for the weekly dances and roller-skating sessions.[2]

The Rodgers family, first the parents and then one of their daughters, Dixie Trent, and her husband, ran the movie concession most of the years that Holden operated. (Courtesy of Gayle Rodgers Davidson)

By World War I, the most common entertainment in company-owned communities was movies. Some camps had movies before they had schools. Long before cookhouses or homes were electrified, camp bosses would hook up movie projectors to the mill generators. As a 1923 issue of the *Timberman* pointed out, little other equipment was needed: "A dining hall is suitable for the display of the pictures and an ordinary heavy piece of canvas, with several coats of white calcimine with just a trifle of blue in it, will make a very good screen." In the Long-Bell Lumber Company town of Ryderwood, Washington, movies were sometimes shown six nights a week. Through the Depression and World War II, when Americans sought escape from their

In Selleck, Washington, the Asian community was large enough in the 1920s to dominate the timber community's baseball team. (Courtesy of David Eskenazi)

worries about the economy and the war, movies grew even more important. In Richland, Washington, the government town built for atomic bomb research, theater admission was originally free. Each theater had three different features a week; one ran movies continuously from 2:30 to 11 P.M. At Holden, movie tickets cost sixty-five cents by 1948, due to the high cost of shipping first-run films up Lake Chelan. On Saturdays, though, miners could go to the movies for free and see travelogs, cartoons, and documentaries on everything from oil drilling to glassware design. Most prices were much lower. In Gilchrist, Oregon, in the company-owned theater, admission was a dime in the late 1930s.[3]

In some company towns, the Asian community was large enough to sponsor its own recreational activities. At Selleck, Washington, operated between 1908 and 1939 by the Pacific States Lumber Company, samurai movies were brought in once a month. The town had the Yamatas baseball team and the Geijutsu Club, a fine-arts organization that presented plays in the mess hall. The Japanese workers also maintained their own clubhouse for pool, cards, and other games and a communal bathhouse.[4]

By the 1930s, it was easier for workers to leave town for a weekend—or, in some cases, an evening—of entertainment. Even loggers and mine laborers were likely to own cars, and most communities could be reached by road. The reduced isolation, coupled with the financial pressure caused by the Depression, meant that few new company towns were built with recreational facilities as extensive as Potlatch's. But when new company towns were the largest communities in remote areas, they often offered more entertainment than nearby villages. In 1938, the only large town in central Oregon was Bend, fifty miles away from where the Gilchrist family had bought timberlands. So when the Gilchrist Timber Company built a town for 600 people, it provided a bowling alley with billiards and card rooms, a restaurant, a bar, and a theater for movies and plays. Families paid a dollar or two a month to belong to The Club, where adults met for formal dances once a month in the early years. For teenagers, The Club provided an after-school hang-out, complete with dancing to the latest records, ping-pong, and a stack of the latest magazines to read by the fireplace. Community sports teams used the gymnasium in the high school built by the Gilchrists. Another central Oregon community that existed from 1932 to 1950, the portable timber camp of Shevlin, also often had a population of 600. In a company-provided boxcar, the former camp clerk operated a tavern with pool tables; in a similar building, his wife ran a gift shop, complete with soda fountain, jukebox, and slot machines reserved for the women of the camp. In addition, the Shevlin-Hixon Company built a community hall for movies, school programs, church services, potlucks, and dances. A smaller company building gave Shevlin women a place to play cards, exchange recipes, and meet a couple of times a month for classes with the county extension agent.[5]

Where the company provided few amenities, camp managers often set aside land and made company equipment available for volunteer work parties. The Kosmos Timber Company boss occasionally put up a portable light plant on a company logging road so loggers could ski at night. Holden, Washington, miners used a Model A Ford engine to run a rope tow on a slope behind their homes. At Taylor, Washington, coal miners and brickmakers used materials donated by the company to construct a swimming pool over a natural spring. In DuPont, Washington, a company truck carried kids to nearby American Lake for swimming long after the town was no longer company owned. At Kinzua, Oregon, the company paid for the initial cabling so that television service was available to every home by 1955.[6]

A few towns remained extremely isolated into the middle of the twentieth century. In these, employers were most likely to subsidize extensive recreational facilities. The Howe Sound Company ran two copper-mining villages at roadless spots along the British Columbia coast for decades before opening Holden, high in the mountains above Lake Chelan, Washington. Because of the remote locations, Howe Sound ensured that each community had sports and entertainment facilities for both families and single workers. Some were company built, others designed by residents. At its Britannia, British Columbia, mine, workers had gyms and swimming pools, tennis courts and a library. At Holden, the recreation hall had a gymnasium that doubled as a theater, complete with curtains, dressing rooms, and footlights. Activities, which the company emphasized should appeal to the greatest possible number of townspeople, included mine versus mill basketball games, volleyball, concerts, and movies three times a week. Like in so many other town rec halls, there were billiards tables, card rooms, a snack bar, and a bowling alley. The Boy Scouts and Camp Fire Girls each had their own cabins, one on either side of the village.

Employers also alleviated the isolation by welcoming outsiders. Easy to reach on the company's own rail line, Potlatch, Idaho, booked its opera house several nights a week for speeches by authors and politicians, performances by touring singers, and presentations by bands or professors from the nearby state universities. At Howe Sound's Britannia and Holden mine operations, all at least a half-day's steamship trip away from the nearest town, miners were encouraged to host baseball teams from nearby communities and "big city" talent for special events. Because there was little transportation "off-project" for those working long hours on wartime atomic bomb research in Richland, Washington, the government contractor brought nationally known dance bands and entertainers to an auditorium within walking distance of employee dorms. The remote logging camp of Grisdale, far into Washington's Olympic mountain range, hosted high school bands, politicians, writers, and bankers.

Baseball, Bowling, Bands, and Bridge Tournaments

Nothing unified a company town—or any other town of the early 1900s—like baseball. Virtually every company town and many family camps had at least one team. In some company towns prowess on the baseball diamond was a guarantee of employment. "You had a job whether you knew how to work or not," one old-timer remembered. It was a good job, too: in some coal mines, baseball players were assigned to day shift, which ended at 3:30, to ensure they had time to practice after work. Some companies bought the team uniforms and built the fields and grandstands. "The company figured [that] if the people were busy and the kids were busy, they [wouldn't] get into so much trouble," said one former miner.[7]

As early as 1904, the McCleary, Washington, loggers and mill hands were vying against teams from neighboring towns. In Potlatch, Idaho, which had four local teams by 1913, management shut down the sawmill when American and National League all-stars came to town on a 1914 promotional tour. And justifiably so: the game attracted thousands from not only Potlatch but from all the surrounding towns and villages. By the early 1920s, such western Washington coal-mining towns as Roslyn, Black Diamond, Carbonado, Wilkeson, and Burnett were fielding semipro players who could hold their own against Seattle's Pacific Coast League Indians and, later, the champion Rainiers. Their Valley League also included the coal and clay miners in Taylor and the mill hands in Hobart. During the Depression and World War II, baseball remained important: Holden players, who seldom had outside competitors, divided themselves into teams by neighborhood or department. DuPont, Washington, had three teams, enough for an in-town league. At Mason City and Coulee Dam, Washington, the Inspectors competed against the West Engineers, the East Engineers, and the Laboratory; the women's softball teams included the Engineerettes and the Mamas. For some teams, weather was as much a challenge as isolation. In 1940, Valsetz was declared one of the strongest semipro teams in the Siletz Valley—but its home in Oregon's wettest community had left it "handicapped for practice by a rather rainy season," the mill superintendent told the local press. (Despite the storms and mud, the Valsetz Millers snapped back the next year to place in the state semipro tournament.)[8]

Baseball was not the only source of competition in early towns. The coal-mining towns that stretched a hundred and some miles south from the Washington–British Columbia border attracted English and Welsh immi-

84

Like many small towns, Holden, Washington, had men's basketball teams that played each other and occassionaly traveled outside for regional tournaments. (Courtesy of the family of Larry Penberthy)

grants, who brought with them games like soccer. Black Diamond's team won the Washington state soccer championship two years in a row, until some of its best players were recruited by miners in neighboring Carbonado. Basketball—played in dry, warm gyms—was popular, too. The Holden Muckers occasionally qualified for the Northwest Amateur Athletic Union tournament in Seattle. The Grand Coulee Dam site's basketball team beat the Gonzaga and Ellensburg Normal college teams and the All American Red Heads, a team of women who toured the country playing against men. Coulee Dam employees also organized a tennis club and leagues for volleyball, badminton, and fencing. Grisdale, Washington, loggers' wives formed a marching club that drilled up and down the camp lanes and then competed in local festivals and parades. Other competitions were work or community related. In 1909, the University of Washington began training mine rescue teams, which practiced first aid and rescue skills. Towns like

THOSE RED-HEADED WOMEN

MADE ONE BASKET AFTER ANOTHER

Like the Harlem Globetrotters, the All American Red Heads were a basketball team that combined sport with entertainment at benefit games from coast to coast. Organized in the mid-1930s, the Red Heads are generally regarded as the first professional women's team. They played—and usually beat—men's teams for fifty years. And that's exactly what happened at Ryderwood, Washington; the Red Heads handily trounced the loggers' team. Selected for their showmanship as well as their skill, the Red Heads were expected to dress and behave like ladies. And, yes, they were all redheads—thanks to dye or wigs if not Mother Nature. (Sources: Ted Goodwin, Stories of Western Loggers *[1977];* Women's Basketball Hall of Fame, Knoxville, Tenn., wbhof.com.)

Roslyn, Ronald, and Carbonado sent their teams to national competitions as late as 1929. Volunteer firefighters also competed: the Roslyn first aid and gas mask teams entered contests around the state and frequently came home champions. (In 1940, the Roslyn–Cle Elum first aid team even made a trip up Lake Chelan for a demonstration at the Holden Mine.)[9]

When you read the fading pages of the old company newsletters, it seems as if everyone bowled. It was the Diamond Drillers versus the Mill, the Tigers versus the Grizzlies, and in the women's leagues, the Zinc Streaks versus the Copper Queens or the Silver Stars, the Loggerettes versus the Timberettes and even the Asters versus the Snapdragons. In DuPont, Washington, where the bowling alley opened in 1911, men practiced at night while women sometimes bowled three times a day. Every year, the explosives company sponsored an interplant tournament, with bowling scores from each location telegraphed into headquarters.[10]

Besides athletic teams, nearly every turn-of-the-century town had a band. Company towns were no different, except that most were far from music stores or trained conductors. The bands played for parades, funerals, and

Starting early in the twentieth century, bowling was a popular pastime in company towns; a company-built recreation hall usually included at least a couple of lanes. By the mid-1950s, when this women's league was photographed in Holden, Washington, bowlers sometimes traveled halfway across the state for tournaments (Courtesy of Bill Phillips)

dances and, most often, on the bunting-bedecked trains carrying merry-makers to the annual company picnics. Ability and experience sometimes were as much a guarantee of a job as baseball prowess. Talent was not always necessary, however. In McCleary, Washington, several young men, none with any musical training, each contributed a dollar or two toward a set of cheap brass instruments and some how-to books. When the instruments arrived, the aspiring musicians each took one at random and stumbled through the instructions until the band could manage a tune or two. Eventually the musicians were good enough to perform, dressed up in uniforms bought used from a defunct band. Some companies provided direct subsidies for their bands. Other bosses found ingenious methods of getting employees to fund the groups: at the Shevlin-Hixon Company's first all-company picnic in 1920, the entire $350 collected in fines by the kangaroo court was donated to the recently organized musicians.[11]

Besides brass bands, communities often supported smaller groups and dance orchestras. The Shevlin (Oregon) Pine-eers, a popular trio at dances, performed on local radio station amateur hours and in Redmond and Bend theaters. In the 1930s, Kinzua mill workers formed the Wheatland Dance Band, the Melody Boys, and the Kinzuans. The Howe We Sounders provided music for dances at Howe Sound's Holden operation. Another Holden dance band was organized by Cortland Bell, the company timekeeper and sometime newspaper publisher, who recruited band members by watching for instrument cases when new employees unloaded their luggage. At Cedar Falls, Washington, the power plant superintendent, his wife, and their son made up half of the local dance orchestra. When the orchestra members were ready to dance, the community's 4-H band sometimes took over. The Powers (Oregon) Logger Band was outfitted in uniforms furnished by the company owner, Al Powers: calk boots, jeans, and blue flannel shirts. The first musical group at the Atomic Energy Commission's operations in central Washington had more unusual attire: four security guards who called themselves the Richland Singing Cops sang barber-shop melodies in their patrol uniforms.[12]

Despite the long workdays that were typical early in the twentieth century, many towns had a variety of clubs that together sponsored hundreds of functions each year. There was "an endless round of teas, luncheons and card parties," recalled a woman who went to a remote mining town as a bride in 1940.[13] Some activities were organized by church affiliates, others by local lodges of such national fraternal groups as the Eagles, Elks, Eastern Star, Rebekahs, Masons, and Moose. During World War I, communities organized chapters of the American Red Cross; after the war, they added American Legion posts. In timber communities, there was the industry-supported union, the Loyal Legion of Loggers and Lumbermen (Four L), and the Ladies Loyal Legion. The coal-mining communities had branches of Slavic, Italian, Croatian, and Lithuanian lodges. As in other small towns across America, there were study, birthday, glee, and card clubs, hospital guilds, and sewing circles. There were clubs for mothers, "bachelor girls," skiers, golfers, gardeners, and hunters. There were PTAs, Great Books groups, and the Kilowatt Kapers for couples willing to square dance with how-to phonograph records. Some purely social groups were whimsically named: the Linger Longer Club, the Thursday Night Club, and the Mistletoe Lodge. Almost every village had a community club or recreation association that organized Halloween and Christmas parties, dances, floats for parades, and special events like the Copper Queen and Atomic Frontier Days festivals. Just as in other towns, regardless of size, company-town clubs in the early 1900s presented plays and concerts and sponsored boxing smokers and progressive dinners.[14]

As improved transportation made outside entertainment more accessible or turned more laborers into commuters, many club activities lost their support. The more isolated the community, the more likely the clubs were to survive. Located in a central Washington desert far from city lights, the people of Richland organized more than 300 organizations—ranging from the Horse Heaven Howlers and the Intermountain Alpine Club to church and school groups—within a decade of their arrival at the federal government operation. There was even a long-lived Dormitory Club that sponsored picnics, barn dances, and carnivals for the single workers living in government bunkhouses. In truly remote villages like Holden, the ski club was still presenting variety shows, the Camp Fire Girls selling popcorn at the movies, and the Boy Scouts organizing fishing trips until the mine and the town closed.[15]

Potlatch's earliest clubs were organized by churchwomen. Some 300 miles away, another timber town of the same era, McCleary, relied on the Ladies' Aid to both organize and finance much of the town's social life and welfare work. During World War I, the women of the DuPont, Washington, church sponsored music programs and other entertainment for the soldiers at nearby Camp Lewis, who had no chapel of their own. After World War II, the same women's group took on a new military welfare project: sewing for the troops. For decades they met every Tuesday night to sew on patches and buttons; once a year, they drove over to what was by then Fort Lewis to make candy for the soldiers.[16]

Community groups sponsored charity projects, too. In the Grand Coulee Dam villages, thirty-five associations banded together to create the

Community Council that organized Christmas parties and holiday baskets for needy children and their families. Because of the importance of adequate medical care, company towns were among those raising funds for both nearby and distant hospitals. Grisdale's hospital guild was the only one—anywhere—in a logging camp. At Holden, the women's guild even flew in models for its 1951 "Swing into Spring" fashion show fund-raiser. (It was Eddie's Flying Service that brought in the staff of the Chelan Style Shop and its fashions, the accessories from Gurr Jewelry, and the corsages from Chelan Greenhouses.)[17]

Social standing, profession, and sometimes local geography helped determined what groups you were invited to join. The Polida Club (Potlatch, Latah County, Idaho), formed by what the historian Keith Peterson called "select" Potlatch townswomen, automatically elected women teachers to membership. In Cedar Falls, Washington, those who lived in the Milwaukee Road camp (sometimes in boxcars) or the logging camp weren't always invited to the Great Books and bridge clubs organized by the Seattle City Light managers' well-educated wives, almost all former schoolteachers. There were similar divisions in Holden, where married miners lived a half-mile or so away from managers, and in Newhalem, where the better-educated power plant staff didn't always socialize with the town site and railway operations crew. At Coulee Dam, engineers organized the Paul Bunyan Club, which announced its meetings to the public but limited its audience with program topics such as "The Smashing of an Atom." Even among the nonprofessionals, there were cliques. In mill towns, the sawmill workers might have formed one group, the logging railroad men another, and if the town had a shingle mill, its weavers a third clique.[18]

Marital status also determined what events employees were invited to. In Holden, single miners who lived in the dorms were unlikely to attend the all-company dances, especially the elaborate New Year's Eve ball, because they seldom had dates. If a miner wanted to bring a girlfriend in from Chelan or Wenatchee, there was no place for her to spend the weekend, unless a family offered to put her up. In Potlatch, Idaho, much of the social life revolved around women's groups and school activities; except for those who boarded with families, bachelors often had no interaction with married men after work hours.[19]

Clubs in company towns, like organizations everywhere, were supported with modest dues and admission fees. Many other activities were financed with community-wide recreational association or community club fees. In Carbonado, Washington, in the late 1920s, each family paid a seventy-five-cent monthly fee for admission to the nine movies. For an additional seventy-five cents a month, a family could attend biweekly dances and all of the town's other social events and athletic contests. In Holden, the mining company built and maintained the recreation hall; employees each were assessed fifty or seventy-five cents a month to pay for sports equipment, magazine subscriptions for the library, and most entertainment.[20]

Though early-day loggers may have whiled away their evenings reading secondhand books and magazines donated by big-city charities, better-stocked libraries were common in company towns and twentieth-century camps. In the early days of McCleary, Washington, several men and couples each contributed a dollar to the magazine club, which checked publications out to club members. Shortly after Potlatch, Idaho, was built, its Protestants set aside a room in their church basement as a library, primarily as a place for bachelor workers to spend leisure hours. By 1914, the Potlatch Free Public Library had been established; the company paid the librarian for more than twenty-five years and provided a monthly stipend for buying books. Communities like Holden and Snoqualmie Falls, Washington, had satellite branches of county libraries. For smaller villages and camps, state libraries shipped out trunks from their traveling libraries. Kept in the school or a spare room in the recreation hall, these collections of twenty-five or fifty books were rotated every three months. Cedar Falls, Washington, had no library, but the families of Seattle City Light power plant employees had borrowing privileges at the Seattle Public Library. When managers traveled into the city for meetings, their children sometimes went along so they could withdraw a boxful of books; others requested books by mail using a library catalog.[21]

Celebrations, whether for holidays or special events, brought communities together. In Port Gamble, Washington, the mill invited everyone in town to lunch when the grand opening of the Puget Hotel coincided with the company's fiftieth anniversary in 1903. In Potlatch, residents organized a parade and dance in 1925 to celebrate the completion of the long-awaited highway into town. For years at Grisdale, Washington, everyone in the tim-

Reading rooms were common in timber communites, even in bachelor camps. When Potlatch, Idaho, was built, the Union Church set aside a room in its basement for the Potlatch Free Public Library and its librarian, Jessie Metcalf. The Potlatch Lumber Company subsidized the library for several years. (Courtesy of the Potlach Historical Society)

ber camp turned out for the Halloween celebrations. At Mowich, Oregon, the sawmill manager opened the cookhouse for a potluck Thanksgiving meal for the seventy or eighty who stayed through the winter. At Holden, deep in Forest Service land, there were no fireworks for Independence Day, but the company organized a day of games and races with sodas and ice cream; there were cash prizes (quarters and fifty-cent pieces) for children who won the potato, sack, bicycle, and foot races. And if you won the chicken chase, you got to keep the chicken! Adults had their own contests—nail driving, log sawing, needle threading, and tug of war—with a dance to end the celebration. When the community float was ready to be barged downlake for the Wenatchee Apple Blossom Festival, Holden previewed the float with its own parade, complete with Boy Scout color guard, school patrol, and the town's new fire truck and ambulance.[22]

Sometimes the company store made sure Santa Claus had a grand entrance early in the Christmas shopping season; in other communities, he didn't appear until the holiday program, where gifts were often provided by the community club. Those who grew up at Holden remember that the presents were lavish when they were purchased with proceeds from the recreation hall pinball and slot machines. In communities like Britannia Beach and Holden, with Canadian and British influence, New Year's Eve meant a major celebration: big-city orchestras were imported, and the mine staff and management gathered for dances that were formal despite deep snow. Couples simply trudged to the recreation hall in boots; women carried their dance shoes and threw their dress hems over their arms.

Summer festivities often included a picnic. In companies with several nearby operations, the picnic might start with a special company train carrying hundreds of employees and their families through the woods. The Shevlin-Hixon Company ran elaborate parties between 1920 and 1930 for the employees in its logging camps and its Bend, Oregon, sawmills: the company band played as bunting-trimmed locomotives pulled flatcars with thousands of guests to the company picnic grounds for sausage- and pie-eating contests, egg and sack races, target shooting, and an evening of dancing. In 1930 the Potlatch Lumber Company's annual event attracted a thousand people for a day of baseball and feasting followed by an open-air dance.[23]

Chicken chases and shotgun shoots weren't the only competitions. In the autumn at Holden, miners paid a dollar each to participate in the annual total snowfall contest, guessing how much snow would fall before May 1. At Coulee Dam, winning the Engineers' Floodstakes required calculating how high the Columbia River waters would rise behind Grand Coulee Dam at the end of construction.[24]

Many communities sponsored dances, some as celebrations, some as fund-raisers. When the new Mason City gym was finished in 1938, a thousand employees of the Grand Coulee Dam construction contractor danced

About 1910, when the local brass band led this parade through Ravensdale, Washington, the coal mining community had 1,000 residents. The business district is on the left, the mining operations on the right. (Courtesy of the Museum of History and Industry)

to music provided by an eleven-piece "all-star" band brought halfway across the state from Washington State College. When Kinzua, Oregon, was almost ready to start up its sawmill in 1928, the couple who ran the Kinzua Mercantile held their own festivities in the new store building. At Cedar Falls, Washington, the community financed construction of a schoolyard play shelter by sponsoring a season of dances.[25]

Card parties were also an important part of community social life. They

too were sometimes fund-raisers. At Cedar Falls, bridge became an obses-
sion after the power plant superintendent's sister came to visit. Because she'd
just finished contract bridge lessons, she taught everyone in the little settlement how to play. And they played "morning, afternoon and evening
for years afterward," recalled one longtime resident, Grace Sherman
Brooks. At Potlatch, women remember playing bridge—and hosting bridge
parties—despite disliking the game. It was what everyone did, explained
one woman.[26]

Marriages were another excuse for parties. The old-fashioned shivaree
was a favorite way to fete a bride and groom, especially because few weddings took place in logging camps or in the company towns that lacked
churches and ministers. The newlyweds returning to camp after their marriage sometimes found coworkers waiting on the honeymoon cottage
steps to be entertained with food and drink. At Holden's Honeymoon
Heights, the first dozen families included ten newlywed couples; the frequent shivarees suggested the neighborhood's name. (They also led to the
construction of a life-size plywood stork, which could be rotated to point
at the next home expected to announce a pregnancy.)

Even when roads were limited and cars uncommon, some company-
town residents managed an occasional day away. In towns like Taylor, Washington, that had regular rail service, clay miners and brickmakers could
catch an early Sunday train and spend most of the day in Seattle. When
Holdenites didn't have the time for a half-day boat trip to Chelan, some
rode the company bus down to the lakeshore and then were picked up by
the Moore's Inn boat for a short cross-lake trip to the popular resort. By
the 1930s many loggers had cars and could take off after work, despite the
Depression. Just before hard times closed the Valsetz, Oregon, mill in 1931,
summertime movies were discontinued because too few people attended.
"The roads are in good shape now," reported the Polk County paper in its
"Valsetz News Items" column, "and many drive to town for the weekends."[27]

When they didn't have gas money or ration stamps or the weather was
bad or the city was simply too far away, those who lived in company towns
had other means of entertaining themselves and socializing. For easy cama-
raderie, little could compare with the daily wait for the mail. Laborers and
managers alike gathered to gossip while they stood at the depot or the bus
stop or the dock. In Holden, even when the snow was several feet deep,

mothers pulled preschoolers on sleds to the store for a bit of shopping while they waited to see what—and who—had come uplake that day. In Valsetz, Oregon, the mail came in on the late afternoon train for decades, so until the early 1950s mill hands and loggers could finish work in time to walk together to meet the mail. Sometimes household tasks drew audiences, especially in power plant towns like Cedar Falls, where employees acquired electric appliances as soon as new models were available. "The first automatic washer in camp belonged to the Crombys and everyone flocked to their basement to watch the clothes in the Bendix," recalled Mary Jo Brown Adkins. In camps without power to homes, neighbors played cards and gathered around gigantic battery-powered radios, especially for special events like championship prizefights. (In a logging community, reception would be improved when a "high-climber" carried an antenna to the top of the tallest tree in the neighborhood.) Even in communities with electricity, workers got together to listen to sportscasts. At Ryderwood, Washington, when few homes had radios, loggers clustered outside the train station to hear a broadcast of the 1926 Dempsey-Tunney heavyweight prizefight.[28]

Families hiked, fished, and hunted; some mills even closed for a few days for fishing and again during hunting season. On the hottest summer days, the brave swam in the glacier-fed streams and the determined went berrying. Armed with leftover lard buckets, mothers and children avoided both bears and brambles as they picked flavorful tiny blackberries. In the timber town of Selleck, Washington, the company made a celebration of berry-picking; once a year it ran a flatcar full of families deep into logged-off territory where the bushes were thick with berries. For their forts and playhouses, children sometimes had abandoned cabins and shanties; others appropriated the packing cases in which new furniture and appliances had arrived. Kids who didn't have cats and dogs might adopt wildlife: at Cedar Falls, an orphaned fawn and raccoons went from house to house, begging for stale bread and other scraps. Some animals could even be lured into the house with the right bribe.[29]

The berry-picking and secluded forts, the snowballing across rooftops and the animals that scampered along the path to school are only part of what people remember about their childhoods in company towns. These adventures compensated for what kids couldn't have because of the towns' settings: few company towns had paved sidewalks, so many children didn't

So many company-town employees hunted and fished that local meat markets weren't always well patronized. In Valsetz, fishermen didn't even have to leave town to catch their limit. Bill Beyers, right, a mill electrician during the Cobbs & Mitchell era, often invited John C. Heffley, left, and his son John A. to fish in the mill pond. Photo taken about 1940 on the boardwalk leading to the Beyers home. (Courtesy of John A. Heffley)

learn to roller skate, and in those towns without electricity, no one, regardless of how indulgent the parents, could have an electric train.

Company-town settings also led to other simple pleasures. At Holden, high in the North Cascades, winter brought a quiet beauty. When nights were clear, movie-goers sometimes walked home under starry skies and then bundled up to go back outdoors and sled on the deserted road. During the day, children slid to school on toboggans built from corrugated tin scraps they had scavenged from mine buildings. Teenagers skied all the way down to the town site from Honeymoon Heights and then sent their skis back up the mountain in a company truck (and if the boss wasn't watching, the skier maybe got a ride, too). At Cedar Falls, one power plant employee's autumn bonfire of leaves was a much-anticipated event for the children who roasted potatoes in the fire.[30]

Especially after electricity simplified housekeeping and weekends were extended to two days, townspeople took up crafts and hobbies. Men built toys, furniture, skis, and even boats and campers. In Holden, almost every-one in town eventually stopped by Chuck Dolfay's basement to check the progress of a runabout construction project—and to question how Dolfay would get the finished boat out of the house and down to Lake Chelan. In the mid-1950s, Newhalem workers equipped a community craft workshop with a lapidary shop, potter's wheel, and woodworking tools. Women sewed, crocheted, embroidered, and dressed dolls for the local bazaars that bene-fited local charities and distant hospitals. And, said one Coulee Dam wife, "We hobby like mad. Photography, and music and square dancing and Book-of-the-Month and hunting and gardening and again gardening."[31]

There were other kinds of recreation, too. In Potlatch, Idaho, although pros-titution was officially forbidden and waitresses and maids who "departed from the path of virtue" were forced out of their jobs and out of town, a carful of "ladies" from Spokane still made an occasional visit in the early 1900s. In Holden, built on government land, the Forest Service prohibited brothels, but old-time miners recall hiking or rowing uplake from Lucerne to a "hotel" called Edgemont (and, perhaps more aptly, Pecker Point). In southwestern Washington, where the last whorehouses didn't close until the early 1960s, prostitutes weren't quite so secluded. When a trio of McCleary sixteen-year-olds set up a local newspaper in 1925, they discov-ered that the tenants on the second floor of their office building included "Big Betty, the toast of the moonshine set." But Big Betty and her cowork-ers were generous about subscribing to the paper and bought a discreet $2 ad each week to promote "Liberty rooms, soft drinks, candy and cigarettes." The early editor, Roy Craft, later recalled, "This was perfectly normal in McCleary as we also had wide-open gambling and bootlegging joints."[32]

Although many company towns were officially dry, making beer and wine often drew little criticism. (Some company store managers, however, monitored how much yeast and sugar were charged by unemployed loggers and suggested that credit was for necessities, not beer.) In western Washington coal towns, home-brew was a typical refreshment at baseball games. A worker's status usually determined how much tippling was tolerated. Because of their importance in maintaining workers' morale, logging-camp cooks sometimes could order unlimited quantities of alcohol-based flavorings. One Shevlin-Hixon cook is even known to have operated a little still on the back burner of the cookhouse range.[33]

In the woods outside McCleary, Washington, it was easy to stumble over stills. "When the nation went dry, McCleary went wet," wrote one longtime employee, Ernest Teagle. The town even had a label for its own moonshine. The town owner, Henry McCleary, was known for bailing out employees caught by the law, and the law itself often had a hand in the moonshine and bootleg operations. In 1927, the local sheriff, several of his deputies, and lawmen from neighboring cities were among a couple of dozen men indicted in a "rum conspiracy." To get a load of liquor into the remote copper-mining village of Trinity, Washington, bootleggers once disguised themselves as a nun and a priest. In other communities, inaccessibility worked to the bootleggers' advantage. In Wilkeson, Washington, where everyone came in on the train or down the one street, coal miners could easily watch for unfamiliar cars that might carry federal liquor inspectors. To reach the more isolated Lester, liquor inspectors could only drive as far as Kanasket; once they got on the train there, someone from the railroad depot would call up to the station at Lester. Before the inspectors ever arrived in the Northern Pacific community, the home-brewers would have thrown out their mash. "The town just reeked with liquor," recalled Gertrude Murphy, a longtime resident, but because nothing was ever found in a house, no one was ever arrested.[34]

Along with closing their eyes to home-brew and bootlegging, company managers weren't always too concerned about when and where workers hunted and fished. Especially during the worst of the Depression, when many men got only a few days of work a month, there was greater tolerance for poaching. Even in camps without electricity, where out-of-season kills were obvious because fresh game was hung out on the porch, the bosses said little. Neither did the law: at Ryderwood, Long-Bell's southwestern

Washington logging community, nobody worried too much about whether the hunting or fishing season was open, recalled the long-ago minister, and the game warden stayed away at least part of the time.[35]

Because poker could lead to fights, some early logging camps outlawed card games. Later, however, card rooms were put to almost constant use. In villages like Holden, where miners worked on shifts, a high-stakes poker game never seemed to end; when one man left, another took his place.

Few company-authorized histories mention the gambling or the beer halls or the brothels. Corporate publicists focus on the wholesome entertainment— and, indeed, it's hard to find a company town that didn't offer an astounding schedule of games, meetings, celebrations, and fund-raisers. This social life was typical of other small towns of the era, but it was easier to sustain because of the facilities the company built, the subsidies it provided to cover operating costs, and the community-wide dues assessments. The isolation of many of the company towns increased the importance of local entertainment and encouraged the participation of even new arrivals.

8 / The Importance of the Company Store

Whether it was a couple of shelves of chewing tobacco, work clothes, and liniment or a three-story building stocked with everything from ice cream to automobiles, the company store has been called the most typical feature of a company town. Maligned for uncompetitive prices, poor selection, and oppressive credit policies, company stores often have been blamed for ensuring that employees stayed indentured. As the 1950s entertainer Tennessee Ernie Ford sang about Appalachian coal miners, "I owe my soul to the company store." Despite the negative image company stores may have today, they—like general stores and groceries in small towns all over America—were community gathering places. Workers stopped at the store to collect their mail and maybe their paychecks; it might have been where they had their hair cut, their shoes repaired, and their cars filled with Mobilgas. In some towns, the company store was the one institution that endured long after the houses had been sold, the schools consolidated, and the post office closed.[1]

There were a few Pacific Northwest employers that paid only in scrip, the company's own currency. But unlike in some other company towns in the U.S., no Northwest employers refused to redeem the scrip for cash. In fact, some Northwest employers didn't issue scrip, refused to set up company-owned stores, and discouraged employees from buying on credit. Some undoubtedly were determined to avoid the appearance of extortion. Others wanted no part of the work—and the risk—of running stores, banks, hotels, restaurants, and barbershops. These employers leased space to private retailers and occasionally monitored the prices these stores charged. They encouraged townspeople to shop by mail and telephone and provided display space for traveling salespeople. Where company stores did exist, some were operated as corporate profit centers, their managers expected to provide quality, selection, and prices that would attract the widest possible customer base. Especially during the Depression and strikes, a few company-store operators took a paternalistic approach to ensure that workers' families could eat: they relaxed credit policies and occasionally reduced prices.

The Potlatch (Idaho) Mercantile is probably the best example of a company-owned store with a mandate to serve an entire region. Started with clothes, groceries, and patent medicines when the Potlatch Lumber Company town was under construction, the Merc by 1907 had three floors of merchandise including groceries, ice, furniture, millinery, shoes, jewelry, drugs, toys, and hardware. Later it would add farm implements and cars. Its sales and holiday festivities attracted not only townspeople but distant farmers and businesspeople who had to travel hours by horse and buggy. It was a million-dollar store, and deservedly so, in a rural region where the nearest city was almost a hundred miles away. Similar selection was available starting in 1905 at the Lumbermen's Mercantile, which boasted that it offered "Everything from a needle to a locomotive." The L & M was not strictly a company store: it was founded by executives of two companies, Simpson Timber and the Mason County Logging Company, and headquartered near Simpson's Shelton, Washington, offices. But it served all of Simpson's employees, whether they worked in town or in an isolated camp. The main store did indeed offer everything from sewing notions to logging equipment, although the smaller outlets had more limited stock. The Grisdale camp store was equipped with a soda fountain, and it sold work clothes next to the groceries and the ever-present snuff. After Simpson bought out the Henry McCleary Timber Company in the early 1940s, Lumbermen's opened a McCleary branch store. The grand opening photos show suit-clad salesmen displaying racks of tailored clothing.

Both the Merc and the L & M, like metropolitan department stores of the era, tailored services to their customers. In Potlatch, the Merc had a

In Valsetz, Oregon, Cobbs & Mitchell built an elaborately detailed structure to house the company store, post office, and general offices. It burned in 1939, in a fire that threatened the entire community. (MSCUA, University of Washington Libraries, Kinsey 647)

cobbler, a hairdresser, and a sewing studio complete with machines where women could make their own clothes. Its out-of-town customers could stable their horses at no charge in the Merc's barn. Its meat was fresh from the Potlatch Lumber Company's own farm, where chickens, cattle, and hogs were butchered daily for more than thirty years. The company farm also provided sausage and dairy products. Both stores had special promotions. On Merc Sales Days in the early 1900s, the giveaways were sometimes free lunches, free movies, or free stud service from the company farm's prize bulls and stallions. Lumbermen's sponsored fashion shows on its upper floors and pig shows down in the feed department. By 1935, it employed fifty during peak season, making it one of Shelton's larger employers. It is "the finest small town store of its kind," enthused the *Mason County Journal.* Some other company-town stores attracted similar praise. No record exists of its size, but the first store at the Weyerhaeuser Timber Company camp at Vail, Washington, had many satisfied customers. "The company's store did a good business before the holidays. . . . Residents of Vail, who live in the nice, new cottages, and the men from the bunkhouses find the store a great convenience," reported *Camp & Mill News* in 1929. In Kinzua, Oregon, mill workers could buy—or special order—almost anything from a candy bar to a car at the company store. They could charge everything and finance most purchases, without interest, at $25 a month. The Roche Harbor Store run by the lime and cement company had a monopoly in its harbor, but it solicited business from all over San Juan Island; by the 1940s it was advertising its specials—whether asparagus, outboard motors, or Sherwin-Williams paint, Bisquik, boats, or batteries—in the island-wide *Friday Harbor Journal.*[2]

This selection and service was not universal. Some stores didn't claim to offer anything other than emergency supplies. In Mowich, Oregon, the fourteen-by-sixteen-foot store shared space with the post office and carried only such basics as kerosene, coffee, beans, canned goods, and soap.

Storekeepers in company towns did expect to have captive markets. This was especially true when the company ran its own store and permitted no competition. Those who grew up in some western Washington coal towns in the early 1900s remembered having to hide purchases made in other communities. In some towns, peddlers, even farmers with local produce, had to sneak in after dark. Starting in the 1930s, the contractors at Grand Coulee Dam didn't outlaw peddlers in Mason City, but any stranger coming to town—especially a salesperson—had to have a permit. Some bosses didn't own the businesses in their towns, but they owned the land and determined who could run what kind of shop and who could trade there.[3]

Even when workers weren't required to shop in town, bosses often made doing so more convenient by locating the paymaster's office in the company store. "Consequently, very little of the money received ever left the

Although the Henry McCleary Timber Company paid in cash, employees could charge scrip against the next paycheck at a 10 percent premium. It was accepted at face value by McCleary merchants, but redeemed by the Bank of McCleary (run by the McCleary brothers) at a 10 percent discount. (Courtesy of Steve Willis)

building," recalled Torger Birkeland, who visited Port Gamble, Washington, in 1910. Forty years later, the grocery at Holden benefited from a similar policy: paychecks weren't issued from the store, but that's where town residents got their "tin," the mining community's scrip.[4]

A surprising number of Northwest employers deliberately stayed out of retailing. Even when the company chose to own all the property, storekeepers could lease building lots or retail space. Henry McCleary owned almost none of the businesses in his town. His mill workers lived in someone else's hotel, ate in someone else's dining room, and bought their clothes and tobacco and beer in other people's stores and saloons. (But they cashed in their scrip at his bank.) Frank W. Gilchrist followed the same example when he built his mill town in eastern Oregon in 1938. He designed a block-long structure with space for a grocery, liquor store, drugstore, hairdresser, barbershop, and dry cleaners, but he didn't own any of the businesses. Unlike in McCleary, however, Gilchrist businesses had no local competition. At Shevlin, the portable Oregon logging camp of the same era, one woman got into retailing by providing sewing notions for other women. Each time the camp moved, her store in a converted rail car got a little larger; by the time the Shevlin-Hixon Company was sold in 1950, Florence's Gift Shoppe offered work clothes, sporting goods, toys and greeting cards, small gifts, and such services as a soda fountain and hairdresser. Meanwhile, Shevlin residents could buy their groceries in the sixteen-by-forty-foot rail car converted to a camp store. Florence Olson's husband ran it for a while, and then, during the Depression, a Bend grocer used the space for a branch store. Holden operated for about ten years with nothing other than a tiny commissary; in the late 1940s, the first floor of one bunkhouse was converted to a grocery store that was run as a concession by the Price Cash Store, which also owned stores in Chelan and Manson. (Its customer services included delivery, often made by sled in the winter.) After a management change at the Price Cash Store, the concession was let to a small supermarket chain called Peter Rabbit. But neither grocery had a monopoly; some Holden families continued to place orders by mail with Safeway and other distant supermarkets.[5]

Obtaining merchandise for company-town stores, especially those in the most remote villages, meant careful planning for the store managers, who sometimes saw wholesalers' sales representatives only once a year. Getting supplies delivered required meticulous scheduling and back-up plans. In Holden, most supplies had to be delivered to the dock in Chelan once or twice a week and then barged up Lake Chelan. When the road to Grisdale, Washington, was closed by snow or mud, milkmen and wholesale grocers sent supplies into camp via the Simpson Timber Company railway speeder.[6]

Especially in the company-town stores that continued to operate into the mid-1900s, retailers had to offer reasonable selection, quality, and prices because they had competition. Townspeople may not have been able to go to shops next door, but often they rode the train or car-pooled into larger towns. Like other small-town residents, they shopped by mail, both from such catalog retailers as Sears, Roebuck and Montgomery Ward and from metropolitan department stores. Some company stores, determined to

The Importance of the Company Store

HOW DID GROCERY PRICES COMPARE?

Richland Villager grocery ads for late 1949 and early 1950 show Campbell's tomato soup was on special, three cans for twenty-nine cents, while Kellogg's Pep cereal cost fifteen cents, Rice Krispies nineteen cents, and Spry shortening eighty-nine cents. About the same time, Holden's Price Cash Store was advertising Campbell's tomato soup for two cans for a quarter, a box of Post Toasties for eighteen cents, and Swiftning shortening for eighty-nine cents. In comparison, in Seattle suburbs like Bellevue, Heinz soup was three cans for thirty-two cents, a box of Rice Krispies was fourteen cents on special, and Crisco and Spry were each eighty-five cents.

expand their market area, kept their prices comparable to—or lower than—prices in general stores in neighboring villages. At other company-town stores, prices were high, but with some justification: shipping costs to their remote sites were higher and many stores offered credit, which increased operating costs. Many company stores in the Northwest charged no interest on charge accounts, even for major purchases. Few stores were large, which meant selection was limited; those that chose to carry only the best-quality merchandise had correspondingly higher prices. As the Depression-era Ryderwood, Washington, pastor Ted Goodwin later noted about his logging camp's company store, "We bought on credit and we squawked about the high prices. But the facts are something else. Those prices were not so high, after all. The stuff was of good quality. . . . And the credit was awfully handy." Sometimes prices just seemed higher: in Holden's branch of the Price Cash Store, regular prices were no different than those charged in the closest city, but the miners complained that they missed out on the loss leaders typical in city supermarkets.[7]

Some stores deserved criticism. Housewives struggled with local grocers who carried nothing fresh: no fresh fruit or vegetables and only cold cuts in the meat case. Others complained about the quality of the food. When grocers insisted on selling last week's delivery before they put out new stock, lettuce might be wilted, bread stale, and meat moldy. Prices, of course, were not discounted. Some local grocers and butchers had other jobs like running the company cookhouse and could only open their shop doors for a couple of hours a day.

In some of the most remote communities, there were no stores. The only option was finding a grocer who delivered—even from forty or fifty miles away. There was no grocery at the Seattle City Light community of Cedar Falls, so meat and vegetables came up from nearby North Bend. When it was time to place orders, the city power plant telephone operator would call each home in turn, first for one grocer, then for the other. The Mowich, Oregon, logging camp opened before the town of Gilchrist was built, so the closest large grocery stores were sixty-some miles away in Bend. Because Mowich had a telephone only in the lumber company office, the Bend grocer would arrive each Tuesday during the summer to take orders and return on Friday to make deliveries and take orders for the next week. Until World War II, the Mowich "milkman" was the Southern Pacific, which carried deliveries from a Klamath Falls, Oregon, dairy. There was a company store at Valsetz, Oregon, during most of the town's existence, but during the worst of the Depression, when logging and sawmill operations were shut down, the single-car Yellow Jacket brought supplies the forty miles from an Independence grocer by rail. Later, as the economy improved, a Dallas, Oregon, grocer started up a route to Valsetz. Even with oversized tires on his truck, weather and the rutted road frequently made the thirty-mile trip so harrowing that the driver's success was deemed newsworthy: in February, 1935, the Dallas paper reported that the grocer had "braved the snow and mud to resume his weekly route." When the Holden mine opened in the late 1930s in a remote mountainous spot accessible only by boat, each family sent its grocery order down to Chelan on the steamship with a check for the estimated cost. A day or two later, the groceries came the forty miles uplake, with an envelope of change in each family's order. When they were hoisted onto the dock, the boxes of groceries were set out in the order that they'd be delivered, for the convenience of the mining company worker who drove the groceries up to each miner's home.[8]

Long-distance shopping could be both frustrating and amusing, especially when orders were misunderstood or goods were hard to come by. In

Cedar Falls, where the telephone service was poor, housewives might get lamb when they wanted ham, or tomatoes when they had tried to order potatoes. For the brides who set up housekeeping at Holden's most isolated neighborhood, groceries were carried in by the aerial tramway, or the skip. Occasionally the skip tipped its load out all over the mountainside; other times the delivery included surprises. "If they didn't have what we wanted, they'd substitute," recalled Ruth Bley, who went to Holden in 1938. The North Bend grocers took similar care of their customers during World War II rationing: the delivery might include cigarettes, which were so scarce they wouldn't even have been on the grocery order.[9]

Company-town residents relied on mail orders, peddlers, and traveling salesmen for ethnic and specialty goods and seasonal fruit. Some of the Japanese communities in Puget Sound area company towns ordered their favorite foods by mail; others depended on Seattle's Asian merchants who sent salesmen out monthly to take orders. In the 1930s, the Japanese workers were also served by a man who sold food and Asian sundries from a pickup-size truck with doors that opened up to display inventory in the truck-bed space. Peddlers and farmers sold fruit and vegetables, especially during canning season. Traveling salespeople also sold clothing. In the early days at Kinzua, Oregon, the local newspaper announced when "ladies' wearing apparel" was being shown at the local hotel by a Portland shopkeeper. A representative for made-to-measure tailored clothing visited such small communities as Holden a couple of times a year to display samples in the recreation hall and write up orders.[10]

Big-city storekeepers solicited business from distant communities, where people might not go out for months at a time as late as the 1950s. The pages of publications like *Camp & Mill News* are full of small ads promising prompt service on mail orders. In the especially remote village of Holden, the post office handled an unusually high volume of money orders and parcel post because of the mail-order business. Furniture, fabric, and everyday clothes were purchased from catalogs like Sears, Roebuck; other merchandise came from Chelan and Wenatchee stores. "Immediate delivery," promised Valley Hardware in its *Holden Miner* ads for major purchases like Coleman floor furnaces and oil-burning water heaters and seasonal gifts like skis, ice skates, and Westinghouse electric sheets. Building materials and heating oil also were shipped uplake on the mining company's barge. Special purchases like the formal gowns for New Year's Eve dances were sent in from such Seattle carriage-trade department stores as Frederick & Nelson. Dancing shoes came in from Seattle, too: women uncertain of their sizes traced their feet on paper and mailed the sketches to stores, which shipped shoes out on approval. The many women who sewed had to order patterns by mail; sometimes a seamstress could convince a pattern company or a department store's fabric department to send a catalog that would be on display at the library.[11]

Not everything came from a store. Gardens were common, especially during the Depression and during World War II. Where the growing season was short, the rain relentless, or the soil rocky, families still managed to grow peas and carrots, beets and radishes, potatoes, onions, and lettuce. They picked berries and ordered crates of fruit from nearby orchards for canning. When Potlatch, Idaho, was built in the early 1900s, the company built a communal barn where employees could rent space for their cows. At Mowich, which like many other early logging camps lacked any formal town site planning, some backyards had pigsties as well as rabbit pens and chicken coops. Especially in remote areas, fish and game were often on the table. At Roche Harbor, Washington, lime-company employees ate clams from San Juan Island's beaches; as the pioneer maxim went, the banquet table was set when the tide went out. Just like in farm homes without electricity, many company-town families canned beef and venison. When the weather was very cold, some Mowich loggers kept the deer they'd shot hanging on porches, covered with heavy cloth.

Some company towns, like other small communities, had a greater variety of stores in the early years when poor transportation encouraged townspeople to shop at home. High in the Cascade Mountains, far from any city, the coal town of Roslyn, Washington, supported many privately owned businesses. By 1904, the retail district included eighteen saloons. In the 1930s, the Ryderwood, Washington, logging "camp" had a population of 2,000, but only a fifth of the loggers had cars. The community had a barber, hairdresser, "valetorium," butcher, drugstore, and cafe, as well as the company's general merchandise store, which sold furniture, large and small appliances, clothes, and groceries. For laborers working on Grand Coulee Dam in desolate central Washington during the same years, the contrac-

The Ryderwood Cafe was one of many businesses serving hundreds of Long-Bell loggers by the mid-1920s. Note the boardwalk, a typical substitute for paved sidewalks in timber towns. (Courtesy of the Longview Public Library)

tor's camp department sold clothing, groceries, hardware, and jewelry and operated both a beauty parlor and soda fountain in what it called "a complete shopping center under one roof." About the time Henry McCleary sold out, his town included a bowling alley, theater, cafe, insurance agency, cigar store, pharmacy, beauty shop, florist, Golden Rule grocery, and at least a couple of taverns.[12]

In other communities, it was the later years that reduced the dependence on mail orders. In Holden, the postwar era brought not only a grocery, but variety and dress shops. The variety store operated by a blinded

Some companies minted lightweight coins for use in their towns and neighboring communites. The Howe Sound Company redesigned its scrip in the early 1950s, adding the heart-shaped center hole to its fifty-cent pieces. (Courtesy of Linda Powell Jensen)

miner, Fred Wigbers, and his wife sold fishing and hunting licenses, fishing tackle, shotguns and ammunition, appliances, army surplus gear, and Christmas toys. If none of the stores carried what a miner needed, both the grocer and Wigbers handled special orders. At the post office, the postmaster, Al Holzhauer, also sold magazine subscriptions. Holzhauer's wife, Ruth, ran a gift shop in their home, selling the finer quality china and vases that the Wigberses didn't carry. Some home businesses eventually moved to the town site. Helene Bell started her dress shop in an extra room in her house but later took over the old company commissary space next to Wigbers and Holzhauer.[13]

Some company towns had banks; some were branches of banks in neighboring towns, others founded by company owners. In Roslyn, the Northwestern Improvement Company invited the Cle Elum State Bank to open a branch in 1907, mostly for the convenience of the coal-company payroll staff. The McCleary brothers ran the Bank of McCleary for more than twenty years until shortly after Henry McCleary sold his company in the early 1940s; then the brothers paid off their depositors and liquidated. The Potlatch State Bank was supported by the Potlatch Lumber Company, even through financial crises, until a larger operation bought it out in 1940. Many timber communities were served by "outside contact men" from institutions like the Seattle Dime and Dollar Savings and Loan Association, which (according to *Camp & Mill News*) "spread the gospel of thrift and savings." At Barneston, Washington, the many Japanese workers sent their bank deposits to Seattle with the sales representatives from Asian merchants.

Holden, like the Oregon communities of Gilchrist, Valsetz, and Shevlin, never had a bank; miners could mail deposits to their checking accounts with Chelan or Wenatchee banks and charge "tin," the mine's metal version of scrip, against their paychecks. Little metal disks, each worth fifty cents, could be used to pay for almost anything in Holden, even for boat fare out and for goods in a few Chelan stores. (To play the slot machines in the recreation hall, however, miners had to have cash.)[14]

Most company towns and some camps had basic services like barbershops, although in a camp the barber might have been a logger moonlighting in his corner of the bunkhouse. At Cedar Falls, the Seattle power plant village, the single retail business for most of the community's life was a combination post office and barbershop, where the Cedar Falls postmistress and her barber husband sold stamps, haircuts, candy bars, and cigars.

The hotel in a community of a couple of hundred people often was a mess hall with tiny rooms on the upper floors; in a larger community, the hotel may have boasted elegant dining rooms and guest rooms fit for presidents—of the country as well as the company. In McCleary, where the McCleary Hotel is today a historic landmark, the timber company owner's wife, Ada, selected the silverware and china; she and her husband, Henry, in formal evening dress, crossed the unpaved street between their home and the hotel for dinner each weekend. In Washington's San Juan Islands, the waterfront Hotel de Haro at John McMillin's

Potlatch Lumber Company Potlatch, Idaho, scrip. (Courtesy of David Ownbey)

Roche Harbor Lime & Cement Company hosted such dignitaries as President Teddy Roosevelt.

Regardless of the size or sophistication of a town's retail district, it was an important part of community life. Even a tiny commissary gave people a gathering place, an excuse to visit with the storekeeper and their neighbors.

9 / Forty Miles from Nowhere

Today many company-town sites are suburbs, but most started out as remote little villages. A look at old county maps and fading time-tables provides a sense of the isolation that was common to most of the Northwest's company towns. Many were truly twenty or thirty or forty miles from nowhere, reached only by trail or railroad or a once-daily boat. People went "in" and stayed there for months, sometimes years, especially when rains turned the rutted paths to mud or winter storms brought down avalanches and rock slides. "Going out" was an event worthy of notice in the local newspapers as late as the 1950s. Returning home meant being greeted at the depot or the dock by neighbors eager to hear about the trip outside.

Most people got to and from camp with employer-built transportation. As late as the middle of the twentieth century, some companies were still laying track for their own railroads and running steamships and barges. In the early days, almost everyone arrived by train or boat: laborers and company executives, visiting dentists and pastors, new babies coming home from the hospital, salespeople bringing samples—even the Internal Revenue Service and the liquor inspectors. The train or boat brought everything a worker or the company needed: the mail and the weekly payroll, groceries, milk and medicine, furniture, fuel oil and building supplies, Christmas toys, coffins and cars.

The Northwest's very earliest company towns—waterfront communities like Port Gamble, Port Ludlow, Seabeck, Port Blakely, and Roche Harbor—

relied on boats to bring in employees and take out the lumber, logs, and lime. In the beginning these vessels were sailing ships. Many were company owned. The Port Blakely Mill Company owned as many as nine ships; the Roche Harbor Lime & Cement Company ran a brigantine between San Juan Island and San Francisco. Later, steamships cruised the Pacific coast, Puget Sound, the Strait of Juan de Fuca, and the Columbia River. They ran to lumber camps at Pysht and Neah Bay and to roadless riverfront cannery towns. Some came north from San Francisco and the Eel River—or south from Portland and Astoria—to isolated Oregon coastal settlements. Smaller boats cruised the inside passages, the rivers, and the large lakes like Chelan and Coeur d'Alene. For most of these villages, boat transportation was vital; without it the towns would have died. In Brookings, Oregon, there was a logging railroad but no coastal highway until the mid-1920s; in Brookfield, Washington, where Joseph Megler built a Columbia River cannery in 1873, there was no road out until 1951. No one could drive to the Howe Sound copper-mining operations in British Columbia until well after World War II; the site of the company's Holden, Washington, mine still relies on daily boat service up Lake Chelan.

Despite the importance of boat travel, towns often lacked wharves. Without them, equipment and supplies—even locomotives and sawmill generators—had to be hoisted onto barges for the trip to the beach. When construction began in 1912 at Brookings, the lumber company crew swung its machinery ashore from a cable connected to ships at anchor. Passengers, including the founder John Brookings himself, arrived via what Brookings called the same "wild ride." Timber camps were even less likely to have docks; people from tiny straitside communities on the Olympic Peninsula would come out in skiffs to meet steamers cruising westward from Seattle. Mailbags would be exchanged and visitors would clamber between the boats whether the seas were calm or rough.

Long after highways had made most company towns accessible by car, there were communities in Oregon and Washington mountain ranges that remained dependent on boats or trains. Nowhere was this more common than in Washington's North Cascades. These mountains are not America's highest, but they may be its steepest, making transportation of both people and goods a challenge even when weather is fair.

Perhaps most isolated was the copper-mining town of Holden, east of

Holden, Washington, has always been reached only by boat. During the mining era, visitors and residents rode up Lake Chelan on the Lady of the Lake *or on smaller boats like this* Speedway. *A Howe Sound manager, Wellington Phillips, and his wife, Elsa, standing center, were among those aboard in this mid-1950s photo. (Courtesy of Bill Phillips)*

the crest of the North Cascades. An occasional adventurer backpacked through the peaks to Holden, but nearly everyone came via boat, on the *Lady of the Lake* or the smaller *Speedway*. In the mining days, the boat took four hours to chug the forty-some miles of Lake Chelan between Chelan and Lucerne, where the mine owner, Howe Sound, maintained a dock twelve miles from the Holden town site. The boat made only one trip daily, and it carried only passengers, mail, milk, and small freight; larger shipments had to wait for a barge.

The Howe Sound Company shipped its employees' cars up and down Lake Chelan on the company barge at no charge, so the cars traveled atop the copper ore canisters to save space. (Courtesy of Vivien Weaver)

In twenty years of operation, the Holden tug and barge never missed a trip—regardless of weather. When visibility was poor, the tug operator used reflectors along the lakeshore to determine his location or timed the boat run so that he knew when to turn into the mining company dock. On each trip downlake, the barge carried 250 tons of copper ore concentrate. On its return trips uplake, the same barge carried in groceries and the shipments from Sears, Roebuck. Employees' cars went on a barge every time a family made one of its unusual trips outside, but because the company shipped cars at no charge, they were hoisted atop the five-ton ore canisters to save space.[1]

After the snow started to fall in October, Holden, like such other North Cascades towns as Newhalem and Diablo, sometimes found itself cut off from the world by avalanches. In the worst of winter, it wasn't unusual to get more than a hundred inches of snow a month. Men worked around the clock to keep the road clear for trucks carrying concentrate to the dock. Then they went home and shoveled their house roofs, to prevent cave-ins and broken windows from the weight of the snow. Because snowdrifts filled every usual parking spot and because even a single snowfall could be heavy enough to demolish them, cars were stored for the winter on the lakeshore or barged down to Chelan to rented garages. The executives visiting from Howe Sound headquarters and others who traveled to camp sometimes found their stays unexpectedly extended by avalanches. Even those who came up the dozen miles from Lucerne could find it impossible to get home because of snow slides. In March 1950, the crowd that traveled up one Friday night for movies in the Holden recreation hall ended up sleeping over when the road was closed. When the road was blocked only in one place, people occasionally walked over the slide; they'd get a ride up from the lakefront to the avalanche site, climb over the snow, and then be met by someone who had driven down from Holden. More than once, a miner on the Holden side rescued the mailbag from the midday bus stuck on the other side of an avalanche.[2]

Between the first of May and the end of September, Holden residents could be fairly certain they wouldn't have snow, but travel outside was still cumbersome. Single miners sometimes reported that they hadn't been downlake for three or four months; for those with small children, trips were usually less frequent. One mother recalled four years without a respite. Getting downlake was a long trip—and made longer by the bus schedule. To catch the bus to the dock, miners walked to the townsite; in the early years, for those families living near the mine portal, the first leg of the trip was a steep, dusty trail three-quarters of a mile long. Because the bus was run for the convenience of those arriving at Holden, it arrived at the dock when the boat was traveling uplake to Stehekin. Those traveling downlake could board the boat then, ride another hour uplake and then ride down-lake the entire fifty-mile length of Lake Chelan. Miners who wanted a less expensive and shorter boat trip preferred to wait at the Lucerne dock for a couple of hours until the boat stopped on its way downlake. For those who had young children dressed up for the trip to town, this long wait meant an exhausting challenge, keeping kids clean and off the beach. Going far-ther than the town of Chelan presented its own travel challenges because

The same businesses that rented cabins on Lake Chelan often operated the midday bus that brought mail and visitors up from Lucerne to the mining village of Holden, Washington. The post office still stands at the north end of the hotel. (Courtesy of the family of Larry Penberthy)

of the difficulty in coordinating boat, bus, and train schedules. The boat didn't arrive in Chelan until 6 P.M., so almost everyone overnighted in Chelan before continuing their trips.[3]

To provide for the miners who seldom went out, state and federal agencies sometimes shipped in representatives. So that residents could renew driver's licenses and buy car licenses, a couple of Washington State Patrol employees worked a few days a year at a makeshift desk in the recreation hall. To ensure that income tax returns were completed correctly, deputy collectors from the Internal Revenue Service's Tacoma office traveled across the state and spent three days—probably at that same recreation hall desk—working with Holden residents.[4]

Forty or fifty miles west of Holden as the crow flies, the Seattle City Light towns of Newhalem and Diablo were roadless for decades. Those who worked in Newhalem relied on the city's railway or a pack trail for both passenger and freight service for more than twenty-five years. For the people in Diablo, seven miles farther east into the mountains, the little electric train was the only way in or out until 1954. The route west of Newhalem was begun in the 1930s by the Civilian Conservation Corps as a one-car-wide Forest Service road. Even in 1949, traveling on it was "abnormal" and "unnecessarily dangerous," the state highway department was told when a thousand people from Newhalem and neighboring Marblemount petitioned for improvements. When the road from Newhalem was extended east into Diablo, most of it was surfaced—but some parts remained just a single lane wide.[5]

Because an avalanche could destroy railroad tracks and eliminate all traffic into the communities, Newhalem and Diablo people might go weeks without mail, medicine, or groceries. One longtime resident remembered being overjoyed when someone hiked in with eggs and yeast after she'd been "slid-in" for a month. In January 1925, the towns were cut off for three weeks; in the winter of 1945–46, slides covered the railroad tracks that extended from Newhalem east to Diablo. A few years later, in early 1949, winter snows again isolated Diablo. To get food in and people out, a powerhouse had to be shut down and a power tunnel drained so that people could hike through it into the community. Sometimes the City Light workers were marooned on the train: one Saturday night in early 1937, the train heading home from Rockport found itself stopped by a wall of snow to the east. When the engineer began to back up, to try to return to Rockport, he discovered a new slide blocked his way west. It took hours for crews from Newhalem and the CCC camp to clear the way, and it was three days before regular train traffic resumed. Rock slides were also common. In 1959, when all eight grades of the Diablo school were bused west to Newhalem for a play performance, the kids reported that the rock slide en route was an "added attraction" of the trip. Rocks were an especial danger during the construction of the North Cascades Highway, when vibrations caused by heavy equipment brought tons of rocks down. In 1962, after two construction workers were buried by rocks, officials were fearful that the weight of the school bus might cause another serious slide. So the Diablo children heading to school in Concrete each day were required to put on hard hats and walk a stretch of the old road, while their driver eased the empty bus along. Despite decades of effort, there was no road of any kind across this range until the North Cascades Highway was completed in 1972, and it remains only a seasonal route: east of Seattle City Light's Skagit towns the pass still closes in winter. Even today, those who live in Newhalem and Diablo must prepare for slides that can close the road leading to their communities.[6]

Other mountainous communities were harder to reach. At Trinity, Washington, where construction of a copper and silver mine started after World War I, trains came no closer than Leavenworth, twenty miles away. Miners and their families traveled via a road that was closed six months of the year. A trip out in the winter was almost an expedition; getting a pregnant woman to Leavenworth one January took three days by sled despite fair weather.

Like in Newhalem and Diablo, it was the railroad that provided the lifeline to dozens of company-owned towns well into the middle of the twentieth century. By 1900, hundreds of timber companies were building their own railroads; between the end of World War I and the beginning of the Depression, there were an estimated 1,500 company-owned railways in Washington, Oregon, and Idaho. Some ran a mile or two, others a couple of hundred. Simpson Timber Company's railroad was the longest regional line in miles—and the longest lived. Eventually it had hundreds of miles of its own track, and it was still operating as the twenty-first century began. Most companies built logging railways, but some lines were organized as common carriers, authorized to carry passengers and other companies' freight. In Idaho, thousands of passengers rode the Washington, Idaho & Montana Railway built by the Potlatch Lumber Company. Many of the WI&M's competitors, however, were common carriers in nothing more than name: they never sold a passenger ticket or carried freight other than logs and lumber. Their owners sought common-carrier status for the privileges that came with being a public works: common carriers could condemn rights-of-way, while logging railways could not; common carriers could block the construction of saloons within five miles of the railway right-of-way; and common carriers were eligible for lower tax rates and more favorable freight rates on other railroads. Many of the railroads didn't live up to their names, either. Despite its founders' ambitions, the WI&M never reached Montana; only three of its sixty-seven miles of track ran into Washington. The Bordeaux brothers' Mason County Logging Railroad wandered for eighty-five miles all over the Black Hills of southwest Washington, never once crossing into Mason County. In Oregon, the Kinzua Corporation's Condon, Kinzua and Southern Railroad ran only the thirty-some miles from the Union Pacific tracks at Condon to Camp 5 at Wetmore.[7]

Very common were the short, temporary spurs that logging companies built into forests; as the closest trees were taken down, the spurs were extended farther into the woods. When all the marketable timber had been cut, the rails were taken up to be reused again and again. When logging companies were liquidated during the Depression or when they traded their trains for logging trucks, many of the rails were scrapped and sold to Japan.

Timber communities weren't the only ones dependent on railroads. Many coal- and clay-mining villages never had roads; those who didn't ride the train traveled by foot. When the only paths were steep, narrow trails intended for packhorses, people walked the rails, even when that meant taking children across the open trestles that spanned deep ravines. Moving to or from one of these landlocked towns meant packing everything—including the family cow—into a railway boxcar.[8]

Even when roads did exist, railroads were sometimes the only comfortable means of travel. When distances were great or winter weather severe, trains remained important for decades, especially for those who didn't drive or were reluctant to venture far on narrow roads with old cars. The seven or eight miles of road between North Bend and Cedar Falls, Washington, was "just a ledge on the mountain, curving round about between the stumps of trees," an early teacher recalled. The minister who served Ryderwood, Washington, was more critical about the route into the Long-Bell Lumber Company community: "Every car that goes to Ryderwood takes a beating coming and going," he wrote in the 1930s. "You hold your breath as you edge around each yawning crater." In Valsetz, a timber village in western Oregon's Coast Range, the Valley & Siletz Railroad wasn't the only way out, but for years it was the best; the unpaved road to camp was a rough series of 130 switchbacks that could be impassable with snow or mud. In 1941, the road's condition was infamous enough to warrant being the topic for a chamber of commerce meeting in the county seat.[9]

Until the early 1920s, passenger trains were so important that lines like

Forty Miles from Nowhere

The sharp angles and porthole windows of the McKeen Motor Car distinguished this self-propelled train, built from 1905 to 1917 by William McKeen, a Union Pacific executive. To serve Polk County, Oregon, logging communities, the Salem, Falls City, & Western Railway used a gas-powered McKeen nicknamed the Skunk because of its exhaust. (Courtesy of Daniel Kerlee)

the Pacific Coast Railroad ran extra Sunday trains named the Picnic Line and Fisherman's Line. From towns like Taylor and Hobart and Coal Creek, just like in thousands of other small towns across America, brickmakers, mill hands, and miners rode the train to the big city for entertainment, shopping, and necessities like a trip to the dentist. They caught the National Park Branch of the Milwaukee Road into Tacoma from Harding, Kapowsin, Clay City, Eatonville, or all the way out in National, the logging town near Mount Rainier National Park. In Cedar Falls, Washington, in the Cascade foothills, housewives could finish the breakfast dishes, catch the morning train westbound for a day of shopping in Seattle, and be home again in time for dinner. Those married to railroad employees traveled free on a pass; for Seattle City Light families, a ticket was seventy-five or eighty cents.[10]

Some of the trains were pulled by steam locomotives; others were self-

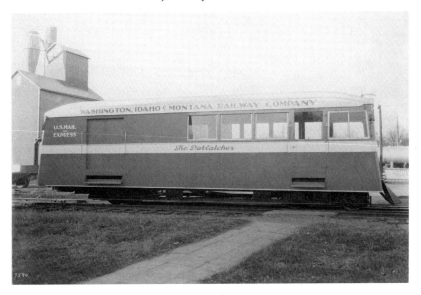

Self-propelled passenger trains could be operated economically because they required only a single crewman. When the Depression forced cost-cutting, the Bug and its successor, the Potlatcher, replaced steam locomotives and passenger cars on the Washington, Idaho & Montana Railway. Photographed in Princeton, Idaho, about 1950, "The Potlatcher" ran from 1937 until 1955. (Courtesy of Potlatch Corp./forestphoto.com)

propelled, gas-powered vehicles. Many were a single car, with separate compartments for the engine, freight, and passengers. In Kinzua, Oregon, one of the lumber company's first purchases was a "gasoline railroad coach," bought in Portland and delivered by flatcar. The Goose, which resembled a trolley car with a cowcatcher, carried twenty passengers and mail on its daily run from nearby Condon. On the WI&M, when the Depression forced cost-cutting, the steam locomotive and two passenger cars were replaced with the Bug, a Studebaker that company mechanics modified for rail use. It ran until the end of 1937, when a trolley-style vehicle, the Potlatcher, took over, getting passengers and mail into Potlatch until 1955.[11]

Common carriers like the Northern Pacific and the WI&M had passenger cars complete with cushioned seats and windows. So did a few logging railroads: as late as the 1960s, the Weyerhaeuser Timber Company ran a Sunday night loggers' special with comfortable coaches to carry crews back to its logging camps. But even when the seats were cushioned, the ride might

Forty Miles from Nowhere

JITNEYS, GALLOPING GEESE, AND DOODLEBUGS

The little trains that chugged in and out of company towns with a few passengers and the daily mail are affectionately remembered as the Galloping Goose, the Skunk, or the Doodlebug. Designed to replace costly, cumbersome steam locomotives on branch and interurban lines, these were self-propelled cars with gas-electric or diesel-electric engines that could be operated with a single crewman. Some were glorified speeders, vehicles modified for gasoline engines in a logging company or railroad's shop. Others were manufactured by General Electric, the J. G. Brill Company, Mack, or the Union Pacific's McKeen Motor Car Company. The McKeen train, built between 1905 and World War I, had a streamlined design with porthole windows and a cowcatcher attached to the prow-like front. A submarine on wheels, one reporter called it. Other doodlebugs (so nicknamed because they "doodled along," making frequent stops) had more traditional train shapes. The engineer sat in front, separated from the passenger section by a freight compartment. Some of these little trains seated sixty or seventy. Another vehicle common on short runs was a rail bus, a truck cab attached to a truck-box or a bus-style passenger section. Some say the Galloping Goose name came from the way they wobbled over the tracks and from their unusual horns. But a rail bus wasn't the only vehicle to be called a Galloping Goose: little trains of other designs, like the one running into Ryderwood, Washington, were also nicknamed the Goose. (Sources: Milwaukee Road Collection, Milwaukee [Wisc.] Public Library; Maury Klein, Union Pacific: The Rebirth, 1894–1969 [New York: Doubleday & Co., 1989]; and "Colorado Railroad Museum," coloradomuseums.com (2002).

Incline railways, among the most dangerous of railroads, were common where log-gers, miners, and dam builders needed transportation up extremely steep slopes. This 3,400-foot railway, built with a 57 percent grade, moved logs and supplies between Manley-Moore, Washington, and its logging camp three miles away. Even steeper inclines were built at Holden and Diablo, where the railways went almost straight up. (MSCUA, University of Washington Libraries, Kinsey 1991)

have been rough because the track had been laid for logging trains. Most logging railways didn't have coaches, so passengers rode on wood benches in the caboose, which also contributed to the bumpy trip: a caboose's box-car-type springs didn't absorb much, and the slack between dozens of cars loaded with logs meant that the caboose often swayed crazily. "You had to hold on tight to stay on your seat," recalled Pete Replinger, who worked for decades on the Simpson Timber Company railroad.[12]

Travel could be a little faster—but not necessarily more comfortable—in a speeder, a gas-powered railroad engine that was originally nothing more

Gas-powered speeders, often built in a timber company's own shop, moved passengers, supplies, and mail more economically than locomotives. This Weyerhaeuser speeder ran between Vail, Washington, and nearby logging camps. Weyerhaeuser Archives identify the man standing in the middle as Ed Hendrickson, then the cook at Cherry Valley Lumber Company, a Weyerhaeuser affiliate near present-day Duvall. (MSCUA, University of Washington Libraries, Kinsey 5014)

than a motorized handcar. Some were Model T Fords equipped with flange wheels so they could run on rails. Timber companies used roomier speeders that could deliver supplies and haul a logging crew. Some speeders had only an enclosed cab; waist-high walls were all that protected the loggers. Some had roofs and benches, but no sides. Others, like Simpson's, were always enclosed; the speeder called Kalakala that served Grisdale was a plywood-sided box, about twenty-two feet long, with wooden benches. The only light came from small windows on one side and the cupola created to give the driver better visibility. Speeders were an important means of getting passengers and freight into landlocked camps and towns or where roads were poor. As late as 1946, when Simpson built Grisdale, speeders were used to travel the forty-seven miles to Shelton until the last several miles of road near camp could be graded and surfaced. Even after the road was improved, it was often closed by the heavy snows of winter and early spring rainstorms. The children who lived in Grisdale remembered with fondness the orange-painted speeder with its squeaky whistle. Adults were less enthusiastic. Ann Messmer, whose husband ran the camp school from 1947 to 1950, had to return home from Aberdeen, Washington, via speeder with her newborn baby: wedged in between supplies for the company store and the cookhouse, she sat on milk crates with the infant on her lap and a side of beef swinging in front of her. Even Simpson management acknowledged that speeder rides weren't the most comfortable. In 1949, when winter storms brought six feet of snow to some timbered areas and closed logging around Grisdale, the company magazine reported, "Family men in Grisdale are riding the speeder 'Kalakala' nearly 40 miles to Dayton each day they log. It is a long, cold and bumpy ride, but it keeps men working."[13]

Loggers usually traveled to camp or to the day's work site on vehicles that, regardless of design or origin, were called "crummies." Some were converted handcars or surplus cars from interurban lines; some were single cars with benches that were pulled by locomotives. At Ryderwood, loggers went out in boxcars equipped with benches, fifty men to a car. The most unusual transportation was probably the used passenger coaches, complete with upholstered seats and steam heat, that the Washington lumberman L. T. Murray bought to carry loggers into West Fork's Mineral-area work sites in the 1930s. Other bosses loaded men on flatcars: loggers who worked at the Kosmos Timber Company in the 1930s and 1940s huddled together as they were hauled miles through rain and snow. Worse off were the loggers who had to ride skeleton cars; there were no benches and no handrails, so the crews had nothing to grab except the planks they sat on. A man who lost his balance could easily fall to his death.[14]

More dangerous yet were the incline railways and aerial tramways. Incline, or vertical, railways used stationary engines to pull cars up grades as steep as 70 percent. Riding an incline railway was so risky that some bosses made employees sign waivers absolving the company of any responsibility for accidents. Used where timber and mining companies wanted to avoid carving switchbacks out of steep hillsides, incline railways also carried equipment, supplies, and passengers at dam sites where the only other option

"A highlight for visitors," said Seattle City Light about the Diablo incline railway ride offered tourists on the Skagit. Built for the construction of a dam, this railway is one of the United States' steepest, rising 313 feet in its 560-foot length for a 68 percent grade. (Courtesy of the Museum of History and Industry)

was blasting roads out of cliffs. At the Seattle City Light village of Newhalem, the incline railroad built to haul rail cars up for dam and power plant construction and maintenance was soon commandeered for tourists. Promotional brochures called the trip up a 68 percent grade in an open freight car a highlight for visitors. At Howe Sound's Britannia, British Columbia, mine, getting down the mountain from the Townsite community to the neighboring Britannia Beach for social events or to catch the boat to Vancouver required a fifteen-minute ride in the incline railway's open flatcar, standing between oil barrels. When the company began development of its Holden Mine, a vertical tramway was intended to transport supplies and ore between the Lake Chelan shore and the mine more than 2,000 feet above, but it was abandoned as soon as a road was built. With grades ranging from 52 to 75 percent and heavy loads, engines wore out quickly.[15]

Both Howe Sound mines had aerial tramways, or skips, that carried supplies and household goods up the mountain. At Holden, the skip was nothing more than an open steel box, about seven feet long and three feet wide. Operated by the miners and their wives themselves, the "bucket" would jump off its cable as it descended if run too fast. Both the Britannia and Holden communities relied on skips for years; at Holden, when recent college graduates and their brides turned the original mine village into Honeymoon Heights, groceries, heating oil, building supplies, furniture, and appliances all came up in the tram car. When they moved in or ordered something special, women watched apprehensively as their belongings dangled from a cable. Skips also had to be used when tragedy struck; at Townsite, during the deadly 1918 flu epidemic, the aerial tramway carried down a dozen miners' bodies at a time for shipment to Vancouver mortuaries.[16]

The train was an important part of both business and community life in almost every inland company town for decades. In many communities, people met at the depot on Sunday evenings to hear about their neighbors' trips to town; on weekdays, they gossiped and drank coffee as they waited for the train carrying the mail and papers. As young Dorothy Anne Hobson wrote in the *Valsetz Star* in 1940, "Every night when the mail comes in we stand in the postoffice lobby and cackle and laugh something fierce." Even when the train didn't stop, children ran along the tracks to wave to the engineer and watch the train crew grab outgoing mail from a hook and fling arriving mail from the baggage car. During World War II, kids and adults alike stood at the depot and waved to soldiers passing through on troop trains. In Ryderwood, Washington, the depot was where the loggers without radios gathered to hear broadcasts of prizefights; in Valsetz, it was the polling place on Election Day.[17]

When the Depression forced logging companies to reduce costs, many replaced trains with trucks. In 1930, trucks carried only a few of the logs headed for sawmills; ten years later, more logs were being shipped by truck than by rail. Without the geographic constraints of railroads, timber companies had more freedom in where they logged. As loggers became commuters, many of their little camps and towns closed. Because these new powerful trucks made other extractive operations possible, however, company towns continued to be established. In Holden's mountainous setting, building a railroad was prohibitively expensive because of the grade between the mine portal and the lakeshore. Only when a truck had the power to haul tons of copper concentrate down miles of switchbacks could the mine operate economically. At Trinity, another hard-rock mine built in the Washington Cascades, the closest railroad was miles away: the silver and copper ore was milled year-round and shipped out by truck starting in the spring, when the mountain road reopened.

When roads were built to company towns, few were paved, regardless of whether they were taxpayer or company owned. In mill towns, where only flawless boards were sent to customers, lumber was often used to cover both streets and sidewalks. In Potlatch, built in 1906, the main streets were originally planked to reduce dust and mud. In the Booth-Kelly Lumber Company town of Wendling, Oregon, the first roads were covered with sawdust; later they were planked, and wood-slat sidewalks were built. As late as the 1920s, some roads were still puncheon or corduroy: some boards or logs were laid crosswise; others were built "fore-and-aft," with two strips of planks laid end to end to support vehicle wheels (but no provision made for two vehicles side-by-side.)

As roads improved, buses became important. In the earliest days, these often were nothing more than touring cars that had been lengthened to accommodate fifteen passengers. By 1910, some towns were served both by rail and by motor stage. As early as 1917, the Carbonado-Wilkeson-Tacoma line ran three buses a day to the western Washington coal-mining towns. Bus fare was a dollar or two, depending on destination. As the Depression started, it cost $.75 for the round trip on one of the four daily stages between DuPont and Tacoma and $1.85 between Black Diamond and Seattle. When Grace Brandt Martin was earning $140 a month as a Wilark teacher, she was paying $1.75 to travel the couple of hours into Portland to visit friends. Howe Sound operated its own commuter bus between the Lake Chelan shore, where about fifty workers lived, and the Holden mine. For the midday bus used by travelers, the fare was fifty cents, perhaps because the mine issued "tin," or metal scrip, in fifty-cent units.

A few company towns existed long enough to be served by air. At Grisdale, Washington, injured loggers could be evacuated and firefighters flown in starting in 1949, after the men in camp volunteered to clear an emergency landing field. At Holden, after World War II, Eddie's Flying Service started with a three-passenger floatplane that flew up to the lakefront dock and into local fishing spots. Harriet Wilbour, whose husband was the office manager at the mine, brought her newborn son home from the Chelan hospital in the plane in 1951. A few years later, when the Wilbours, with a toddler and two other young children, couldn't all backpack from Holden to Domke Lake for a weekend, they drove down to Lake Chelan so Mrs. Wilbour and their youngest could fly to the fishing resort. Other couples used Eddie's or Ernie Gibson's competing Chelan Airways to fly home after honeymoons, and the managers' teenagers occasionally caught the plane when heading back from boarding school or college. Air service also meant that the seriously injured or ill could be sent down to the shore by Holden ambulance and then flown to city hospitals.[18]

Despite the isolation, families chose to stay in these remote locations. At Cedar Falls, Washington, some Seattle City Light employees passed up chances to transfer to jobs in the city. The tiny village in the mountain foothills was a peaceful, rural setting; especially during the Depression, workers valued the decent pay, guaranteed vacations, free rent, and unlimited electricity. At Simpson Timber Company's Grisdale camp, thirty-some miles into the south Olympics from the closest town, a few employees stayed most of the four decades of the camp's existence. They were accepting of the fact that it would take them at least an hour to get anywhere; even in 1982, the last sixteen-mile stretch of rutted dirt road leading to Grisdale was described as "the road to destruction."[19]

Women who did not work suffered the most from the isolation, especially during the winter when they were cramped inside dreary homes with small children. At Holden some homes received no direct sunlight for months during the winter; even management houses received little light because of the high mountains and accumulated snow that blocked windows. Although evenings were busy with potluck suppers, sports leagues, and club meetings, days often were very long. The only link to the outside was the mail; few remote communities had telephone service. Long-ago residents remember people who succumbed to the strain, those who fell victim to alcoholism and depression.

These old-timers also remember the ingenious solutions to the isolation. A new Roslyn, Washington, doctor, arrived in December 1918 after a taxi ride over dirt roads from the Cle Elum train depot. Because Snoqualmie Pass, the cross-state highway, wasn't kept open during the winter then, the doctor shipped his car to Roslyn on a freight train. In Concrete, Washington, merchants watched out for Seattle City Light workers who needed to make connections at Rockport for their train ride home to Newhalem and Diablo. The local theater was famous for posting an employee outside the building to listen for the train whistle when movies ran extra-long; as the train drew near, the theater owner, C. B. Stickley, stalked down the aisle with the warning, "All out for the Rockport train."[20]

Other extremely isolated communities had their own versions of Mr. Stickley. Those who had to travel outside alone as teenagers have fond memories of the men and women who encouraged and protected them. In Cedar Falls, where ice and the occasional flooding at Rattlesnake Lake could make the trip down a steep, winding road treacherous, the longtime school bus driver Emmett Jackson is remembered both for his careful driving and his devotion to the Cedar Falls kids. Childless himself, he drove the young children to the Cedar Falls school and then took their older brothers and sisters on to high school in North Bend. At his own expense, he drove them to the state 4-H fair, on their school picnics, and to weekend sports events, where he sat in the bleachers and rooted for "his" kids. At Holden, the company bus driver is recalled just as fondly by some 1940s residents. "I never came home for a weekend or a vacation that I didn't see the bus waiting at the dock and Les Garrett out waving to everyone," wrote Betty Bickford Christianson, who boarded in Wenatchee to attend high school after her parents went to Holden during World War II. "You knew you were coming home to friends and family." Others remember the mine's downlake agent, who sometimes provided a lift from the train station for Holden teenagers en route home from boarding schools, and the maternal innkeeper at Campbell's, then a quiet lodge on Lake Chelan, who looked out for the girls uncomfortable about overnighting alone in town before their journey uplake.[21]

In the end, the transportation systems that allowed company towns to survive contributed to the towns' demise. The roads that made it easy to leave for a day led to the consolidation of schools, declining participation in the local clubs, and rebellion against the company store. With decent roads and cars, people could commute from homes they could own in communities where they had chosen to live. Eventually, the roads made it easier for companies to consolidate operations and haul raw materials to larger and newer mills and factories, to close down the mills and mines and factories that once had made the company town necessary.

10 / Getting the News in Company Towns

The news came slowly to company towns. Especially for those people who lived in remote settlements high in the mountains, newspapers were at least a day old, and radio and television reception was undependable. Few homes had telephones; mail service, despite the mail carrier's pledge, was frequently interrupted by snow, slides, and floods.

To alleviate the sense of isolation, companies with many locations often circulated company-wide newsletters with gossipy comments about promotions, retirements, bowling scores, and hunting trips. For truly local news, an employee sometimes initiated a village newspaper that could be produced after-hours on the company mimeograph. Other employees created low-wattage broadcast stations or strung wires to improve radio and television reception. If the postal service wouldn't take responsibility for delivering the mail to the camp, the boss usually did, hauling the mailbags into the company store or office.

Most little towns had newspapers of their own in the late 1800s and early 1900s. Company towns were no different, although towns with no privately owned businesses did not have independent papers. Even where management encouraged publishers, papers often struggled. In McCleary, Washington, the town owner, Henry McCleary, was so anxious to see a paper succeed that he donated a building lot as the prize when the *McCleary Stimulator* held a subscription drive in 1925. Produced by three high school students who eventually sold the paper in order to pay for college, the *Stimulator* survived a few years. It was followed by a mimeographed sheet, the *McCleary Observor,* the community's only newspaper through the Depression.[1]

Company-town papers often were produced by volunteers or part-timers who used manual typewriters to cut mimeograph stencils and who hand drew the ads and illustrations. The *Holden Miner, Valsetz Star, Skagit Static,* and *Mason City Columbian* were filled with chatty articles about school operettas and town band concerts, baseball games and club variety shows, births and weddings, visiting relatives and two-for-one specials at the company store. "The kind of weekly newspaper every publisher dreams about," the *Wenatchee Daily World* called the *Holden Miner* in 1954. Cortland Bell was publisher, editor, writer, and cartoonist—but only autumn through winter. When spring arrived, Bell quit publishing and went fishing. However, because he made only $300 or $400 a year on the newspaper, Bell worked full-time for the Howe Sound Company as timekeeper and served the community as constable.[2]

More professional were publications like the *Richland Villager,* which even in its first issues had a paid staff, commercial typesetting, and photographs. Issued by a nonprofit organization, the *Villager* started out in 1945 as a twelve-page weekly. Over its five-year life, it grew fat with community news, sports reports, a locally drawn cartoon, and the same syndicated features found in Spokane and Seattle papers. Delivered free to every home long before that was typical for community newspapers, the *Villager* declared that its mission was "to contribute to the welfare, recreation, comfort and entertainment and education" of Richland residents. When the paper was launched, the editor promised that it would be "full of news about you and your friends and neighbors," but that it wouldn't "tell you what happened yesterday in London, or in Washington, or even in Seattle." Some people claimed it didn't even tell what happened in Richland. Carefully controlled by the federal Atomic Energy Commission, the *Villager* got only the news that the AEC wanted released. Especially in the early years, months might go by without an issue that mentioned the AEC. Instead, the newspaper's front page headlined the government's ban on trailers and carts in driveways, the upcoming Easter egg hunt, and the openings of the library and the preschool. When a reporter from Seattle's morning daily, the *Post-Intelligencer,* and the *Villager* editor tried to interview Richland's top federal official, they were rebuffed. And "rightly so," wrote the *Villager* editor

Launched in 1945 by a nonprofit group controlled by the Atomic Energy Commission, the Richland (Wash.) Villager *was an attractive, but carefully censored, weekly. Readers got movie schedules and the dog pound inventory, but little breaking news—local or national. (Courtesy of the Richland Public Library)*

the next week. They had asked the "wrong questions" about "the plant," he said, apologizing. "We should have known better." Ironically, the next issue of the *Villager* carried a front-page editorial comment about how the newspaper had "zealously guarded its constitutional liberties"—presumably the right to a free press—"while living up to the rigid censorship controls so necessary because of the fearful secret we all kept."³

Another *Villager* had similar goals. "Share it!" exclaimed the first issue of the DuPont, Washington, paper in 1966. The editor didn't want gossip or rumors, but news of former residents, new grandchildren, sons in the military—"even a legitimate gripe can be newsworthy." In her introductory edition, the grandmotherly editor, May Munyan, said the paper would publish twice monthly unless there was enough news to justify a weekly. And if there wasn't enough news, well, then it would come out monthly.

Like its sponsor, the DuPont Garden Club, the *Villager* didn't want controversy. Instead, Munyan and her staff filled the four typewritten pages of each issue with "Sparks from the Fire House" (by Fire Chief John Sparks), "The Pastor Ponders," wedding, engagement, and birth announcements, obituaries, PTA reports, corrections and additions to the village telephone directory, lawn watering restrictions, and, of course, Garden Club news. Edited on a card table, the *Villager* was delivered to every DuPont household free by the Girl Scouts. Like the *Holden Miner,* the *Villager* too took a summer hiatus; its break coincided with the vacation of the community church minister, who ran the mimeograph machine. The schedule and content satisfied the readers: when Munyan was ready to retire in 1974 and announced that the paper would cease publication, the neighborhood kids gathered 107 signatures on a petition asking her to reconsider. She did, and the paper continued until just before the DuPont powder works closed up in the mid-1970s.[4]

The most famous company-town newspaper was probably the *Valsetz Star,* begun in 1937 by the nine-year-old daughter of the cookhouse manager in Cobbs & Mitchell's Oregon Coast Range timber community. Dorothy Anne Hobson's monthly single sheet was also written on a card table, and then mimeographed in Cobbs & Mitchell's Portland headquarters. Thanks to Cobbs & Mitchell, it was distributed both in Valsetz and across the United States. It was read by sawmill employees and loggers, lumber dealers, trade journal editors, and a wide variety of celebrities, including the First Lady Eleanor Roosevelt, the former president Herbert Hoover, the presidential candidate Wendell Willkie, and the child film star Shirley Temple.

In 1939, the *Christian Science Monitor* talked about how Dorothy Anne's paper had attracted so much attention that postal employees "have beat a path to her town, if not her door." Her comments were so insightful, said the *Monitor,* that they "might have come from the typewriter of a real columnist rather than the pencil of a grade-school girl." When four years of *Star* issues were collected in a book and published in 1942, the Cobbs & Mitchell executive Herbert Templeton wrote, "Dorothy Anne has become a national figure, with subscribers and friends in nearly every state of the union, as well as South America, Hawaii, and the Philippines." Marshall Dana, who was then the managing editor of the *Oregon Journal,* one of Portland's daily papers, added that Dorothy Anne had been "touched by

It was over lunch in the Valsetz cookhouse that Dorothy Anne Hobson, shown (front center) with her parents Henry and Ruby (front left) and their dining hall crew, told Herbert Templeton, a company executive, that the town needed its own newspaper. Starting at age 9, she wrote the monthly Valsetz Star. *Circulated by the Valsetz owner, Cobbs & Mitchell, the paper received national recognition. When she went away to school and closed down the paper in late 1941, the farewell party was broadcast to CBS stations from the Pacific Ocean to the Mississippi River. (*MSCUA, *University of Washington Libraries, Kinsey 680)*

the spark of genius." Her reporting was sometimes rather casual (with sports reports like "The Valsetz high school football team lost to Perrydale forty or fifty to nothing" and weather predictions like "Too Hot for Words"), but the editor's note that opened each issue provided perspective on everyday life as the Depression ended and World War II threatened. Some comments were pithy, others poignant. In 1938, when the sawmill (and the generators that powered it and the entire camp) shut down because Valsetz loggers were on strike, she wrote, "There is lots of trouble in the world but we can't hear any of it because none of our radios say anything on account of the men wanting ten cents more so our camp is dark and down and we have no electricity, only coal-oil lamp." In September 1941, as the turmoil in Europe and Asia continued and she began eighth grade, Dorothy Anne told her readers, "We have been saying our prayers for a long time, and always we have prayed for peace, but now it doesn't seem to do any good."[5]

As companies grew, many also had organization-wide publications, issued monthly or quarterly, that sandwiched news from remote operations between announcements from headquarters. A few, like the *Kinzua Graphic* and its successor, *The Forest Log*, were slim enough to be inserted in pay envelopes; others were magazines. Written by personnel or public relations departments, house organs like the *Simpson Lookout,* the Brooks-Scanlon Deschutes *Pine Echoes,* the Shevlin Hixon *Equalizer,* and the DuPont Powder Company *Better Living* kept employees informed about former colleagues who had transferred to other locations and fostered intracompany competition for War Bond sales, safety records, and productivity gains. Cute names were common: begun in 1919, the *Deschutes Pine Echoes* published news from its camps and railroad in a column entitled "Chips, Barks and Bent Rails"; the box factory, sawmill, and shipping yard news was headlined "Edgings and Trimmings," and the editorials, "Sawdustrials." Simpson ran baby pictures of employees' children in "Second Growth."[6]

Company towns also got mentioned in larger cities' papers. The 1930s Ryderwood minister, Ted Goodwin, wrote regular columns for the *Longview (Washington) Daily News,* and he even joined the press corps when President Franklin D. Roosevelt toured the Northwest in 1937. The *Palouse (Washington) Republic* routinely carried news of Potlatch, Idaho; the Dallas, Oregon, *Polk County Itemizer-Observer* published an occasional "Valsetz News" col-

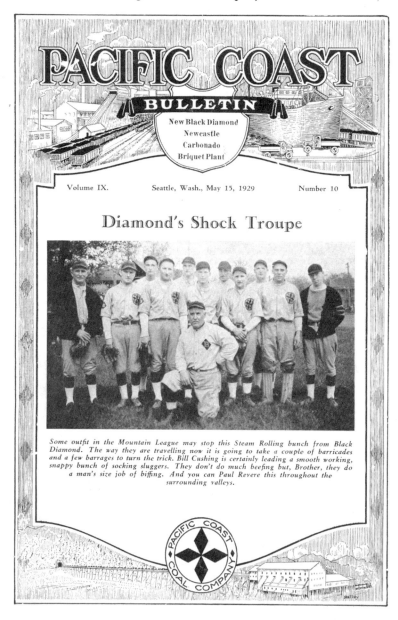

PACIFIC COAST BULLETIN

New Black Diamond
Newcastle
Carbonado
Briquet Plant

Volume IX.   Seattle, Wash., May 15, 1929   Number 10

Diamond's Shock Troupe

Some outfit in the Mountain League may stop this Steam Rolling bunch from Black Diamond. The way they are travelling now it is going to take a couple of barricades and a few barrages to turn the trick. Bill Cushing is certainly leading a smooth working, snappy bunch of socking sluggers. They don't do much beefing but, Brother, they do a man's size job of biffing. And you can Paul Revere this throughout the surrounding valleys.

Each community operated by the Pacific Coast Coal Company had its own page of news in the company magazine in 1929. Events of interest throughout the company, such as the Black Diamond baseball team's winning streak, got extra coverage and even photographs. *(Courtesy of David Eskenazi)* umn, just as the *Fossil (Oregon) Journal* ran Kinzua news. DuPont parties, Red Cross projects, and church programs were described in the *Tacoma Sunday Ledger* as early as World War I because of Roy Hull, the powder company's purchasing agent, who freelanced for several papers after hours.

Telephone service came to many Pacific Northwest communities in the 1880s, often through the organization of mutual or stock companies that each served only a single neighborhood or town. Similar independent systems served company towns like Potlatch and Kinzua. But logging camps, even large ones, often had no telephones. At Mowich, Oregon, opened in 1934, an emergency meant running to the telegraph at the Southern Pacific railroad siding; it was two years until a telephone was installed—and then there was just one, in the Deschutes Lumber Company office. When Grisdale, Washington, was built in 1946, the only public telephone was at the store; when the camp closed in 1985, there was still only one phone for residential use. Long after most towns had dial telephones and long-distance service, some remote communities had nothing but operators and local telephone service. When operators went to lunch in towns like McCleary, no calls could come in or go out. At Holden, where the copper mine operated until 1957, all outside messages, including those to corporate headquarters in New York City, had to be relayed via the Washington Water Power Company's telephone line. Only one person could call out of the village at a time.[7]

A few towns had their own broadcast systems. In the early 1940s, a Valsetz mill worker built a low-powered radio station and produced broadcasts each evening for his neighbors, playing records, reporting local gossip, and announcing shift changes at the mill. When he was tired, the station went off the air for the night. In Kinzua, a couple of hundred miles away, the pine mill financed the first work on a cable television system, and volunteers finished up the project so that every home in town could be wired by 1955. Things weren't quite as sophisticated at Holden, where a geologist frustrated with poor television reception from the distant Spokane stations created what he called cable television, wiring the management houses and bunkhouses to an antenna erected high atop a pine tree.[8]

Almost every settlement, however small, had mail service. For decades, most towns got their mail via rail. In communities where the train didn't stop,

In the 1950s, the Headquarters, Idaho, post office served hundreds of Potlatch Lumber Company employees and their families. It was combined with the only local gas pump and a small store that sold snacks, sundries, work clothes, and snuff—but no liquor. (Courtesy of Potlatch Corp./forestphoto.com)

the incoming mail was simply heaved from the baggage car as the train chugged past; the outgoing mail was hung in a leather pouch by the tracks and grabbed by rail workers. To reach villages and camps served only by boat, the postal service sent the mail out on steamers. Although most logging camps received their mail via the company train, a few had their own postmasters.

Shevlin, Oregon, moved its post office building, its staff, and its official name whenever the community of 600 relocated to a new site. The postal service assigned the name Shevlin to a Shevlin-Hixon Company logging camp, never expecting that the site of the post office would change several times before Shevlin-Hixon sold out in 1950. Although postal officials had to approve each move, regional inspectors didn't always keep up with the location changes. One, unaware that Shevlin had moved, drove to the site near La Pine to find shade trees, the outlines of lawns, and the remnants of outhouses—but no people, no houses, and no post office. It was two days later before the postal inspector arrived at the new camp site, twenty miles away.[9]

Getting mail in Grisdale, Washington, the last logging camp in the continental United States, was more of a problem. Although the post office provided daily service when Grisdale was built in 1946, officials soon cut deliveries to three times a week between April and December and offered no service at all in the worst of winter. The post office initially claimed that the road to Grisdale was so poor that deliveries couldn't be made daily, but ten years later, after both the county and Simpson Timber had improved the route, loggers were still getting limited mail service. When the postal service wouldn't deliver, the 500 people at Grisdale had to rely on the company bringing in the mail via logging truck or train.[10]

Just as a storekeeper might double as postmaster in an ordinary small town, the post office in the company town was usually located in the company store or the superintendent's office. Some towns offered private boxes; in others, employees and their families used general delivery, where mail was held until someone stopped in to claim it.

The postcards and penciled notes sent from company towns are among the few remnants of daily life in Tono and Port Gamble and Black Diamond. The pictures of the schools and the stores and the snowstorms taken by itinerant photographers show us what the towns looked like in 1900 or 1920 or 1940. The letters mailed to friends in Seattle and Spokane and Portland, along with the tattered copies of long-ago newsletters, help us visualize the school operettas and the basketball tournaments, the bowling leagues and baby showers, the church choirs and charity bazaars. It is these fragments from company towns that create an understanding of company-town life.

11 / When the "Dead Whistle" Blew

D eath, dismemberment, disease, and fire. Threats that couldn't be ignored in industries that had the highest mortality rates of their era or in remote sites that were far from medical help; in villages where trees grew dangerously dry each summer and where steam locomotives sent sparks flying on either side of the tracks. There were other dangers, too: methane gas explosions, abandoned mine shafts, runaway trains, avalanches, lightning storms, fast-running rivers, and wandering bears and cougars. And, as in every other community before penicillin and immunizations and decent sanitation, people worried about gangrene and blood poisoning, polio and typhoid.

Lumbering killed more men in the Pacific Northwest than anything else: five times as many as any other turn-of-the-century industry. Most died in the woods, crushed by a log, scalded in a steam locomotive's derailment, or blown into pieces when dynamite misfired. The sawmills weren't much safer: men were maimed and killed when they were dragged into saws or struck by errant logs. Missing fingers were commonplace; missing arms and legs were not unusual. The U.S. Army officers studying sawmills in 1917 for the Spruce Production Division were shocked to find tick marks on sawmill walls representing the number of limbs lost; fingers were severed so frequently that nobody counted them. Five years later, the industry was still averaging several accidents a day in Washington state alone; in one twelve-month period, 825 men were killed or permanently disabled. Even into the

1930s, accidents were regarded as routine. One Cedar Falls man remembered Washington State restrictions on local logging companies; they each could only kill or injure four people a month before being shut down, he said, "and they usually ran clear up to their quota." The pages of the small-town newspapers are full of accident reports. One week it was a logger killed in Valsetz or someone maimed in Black Rock, the next week a crew scalded in a derailment or a fireman smothered with sawdust when he was feeding the kiln. At Port Blakely alone, there were 142 injuries in 1904—almost three a week. "It is hard to estimate," one logging community historian wrote, "how many human sacrifices there have been to the great god Timber through death and maiming of loggers."[1]

Each logging camp had its own train whistle to signal an accident so serious that work had to stop. The "dead whistle," it was called by kids in Sam Churchill's Oregon logging camp. Whenever it sounded, women would gather on the railroad tracks in front of their homes. "If the great machines remained silent you knew the worst had happened—somebody's husband or father wouldn't be on the crew train when it rolled into camp at the end of the day. He wouldn't be on it ever again," Churchill wrote. Decades later, the families at Grisdale, Washington, would share his emotions. "We would gather at the car shop, waiting for word, each hoping our man wasn't the victim, praying no one had been killed. That was the hardest thing about logging camp life. We were never quite free of that fear any day our men went to work," remembered the wife of a cat driver.[2]

Until the 1940s, an injured man usually came out of the woods on a logging railroad flatcar or speeder after being carried from the accident site. Sometimes it took two or three men to hack a path for the four or six who were carrying the stretcher. When the trees or the terrain didn't allow for a stretcher, the injured man might be packed out on a strong coworker's back. In Simpson Timber's early years, a flatcar would carry a logger to isolated Shelton, Washington, which had no paved roads out of town until the 1920s. The company owner's wife might have sat with him while they waited for the sternwheeler that could get the man to Olympia and a hospital. In McCleary, Washington, injured employees were hauled out on a railroad handcar to the nearest depot and then sent the hour or two by train into Tacoma. When Allan Teagle was hurt, he made the trip accompanied by none other than the company owner Henry McCleary himself.[3]

When there were no roads and the train wasn't running, the sick or injured got little more than first aid and prayers. In 1927, an Oregon logger paralyzed in a forest fire accident near Black Rock couldn't get out because the same fire had damaged the logging train trestle. As late as 1948, it took almost eighteen hours to get help for those injured near Newhalem when an avalanche destroyed part of a Seattle City Light camp. Besides directly causing injuries, the slide knocked in cabin walls, which toppled stoves and started fires. The slide also cut off electrical power to the camp. Then snowslides blocked both the railroad and the road between camp and the hospital.[4]

When accidents were fatal, the dead men came out on the logging train, but sometimes not until the end of the workday. If a man working deep in the woods was killed instantly, the body might be carried out to the landing and set aside until the rest of the crew had finished its shift. His family wouldn't know of the death until dinnertime, when the boss brought the news.[5]

Many timbermen died not in the woods but on the logging railroads. "Staying alive around the logging railroad was looked upon as a sort of game," according to the logging historian Kramer A. Adams. It was a game with an appalling number of losers. Even a derailment, so commonplace as to be uneventful, could kill or seriously burn men when steam spewed out of overturned locomotives. Trestles, built only of wood for decades, were not always well constructed or well maintained; some collapsed under the weight of a locomotive or cars heavy with giant logs. Others burned along with trees when fire swept through the woods. Most dangerous were the runaway trains that could speed down the mountain at eighty miles an hour, out of control because of bad brakes, too heavy a load, icy rails, or steep terrain. These runaways could destroy everything in their path. Some derailed before their crews and passengers could jump to safety. A few trains picked up enough momentum to race all the way back into camp, crashing into buildings or tearing apart the mill. Some runaways rolled themselves to a stop. Others damaged little more than the crew members' egos. No one was injured when an out-of-control train roared back into a World War I–era camp in the Oregon Coast Range, but the engineer earned himself an unflattering nickname from the loggers who had to dig out the rail cars that had landed in the camp latrine pit.[6]

Volunteers ran the fire departments in company towns, usually with equipment donated by the company. In Potlatch, Idaho, the first fire engine was a retired logging truck. (Courtesy of Potlatch Corp./forestphoto.com)

Mining camps and towns had their own tragedies. In the coal mines, methane gas and dust explosions, cave-ins, and accidents often were fatal. Too often the mines injured or killed an entire family or neighborhood. If there was a chance of survivors underground, the mine rescue team would be summoned. Much like volunteer fire departments, these teams had been trained through a University of Washington program and equipped with protective clothing and huge, fish bowl–style helmets.[7]

At the Holden copper mine, there was almost always a doctor on hand; even when he went on vacation, a relief physician was brought in. But the mining town's four-bed hospital wasn't equipped for specialized surgery or life-threatening illnesses. A seriously injured laborer had to be loaded into an ambulance and driven over twelve miles of rough, winding road to the Lake Chelan shore. Then—if he was still alive—he faced a four-hour boat trip and another ambulance ride to the closest hospital. Sometimes the miner had to wait for the arrival of the regular passenger boat; other times the Forest Service boat would make an emergency run to get him downlake. Once or twice, an injured miner was taken out by the company crane operator. The boat trips were slow and often cold and frightening, especially after dark and when winds whipped the lake into swells. After World War II the ill or injured could be flown out, but only in good weather and only after the drive to the lakeshore; there was never airplane service from the Holden town site.[8]

Everyone who worked in the Holden office was drilled on how to report accidents. When an emergency call came from the mine, someone called the doctor, hoping he wasn't already busy with a patient. Once the doctor was on his way to the mine portal, or entrance, an office worker arranged for his railway ride underground to the accident site. Finally, the mine super-intendent and mine foreman were alerted so they could accompany the doctor underground. It was up to the bosses to determine how to notify the miner's family. With almost no telephones in private homes, a Holden family's first news of an accident came when the "meat wagon," as the kids called it, drove into the miners' neighborhood to pick up the injured man's wife for the trip outside.[9]

Fire—in the mine, the mill, the factory, or power plant, in the woods, in the town site—was an ever-present danger. Wherever steam-powered logging trains ran, sparks from their fireboxes could ignite grass and dry timber. Logging camps and mill towns like Potlatch, Idaho, usually had round-the-clock surveillance, especially of mills. Smoking was forbidden on the job and in the bunkhouses. Even so, "Fires" was a regular column in the *Timberman* industry magazine. Lightning storms brought another threat of fire. Marian Thompson Arlin, who as a girl in the 1920s and 1930s lived next to the Cedar Falls power plant, said she was terrified when light-ning struck the high-voltage tower. Many towns had fire hydrants and fire engines. Virtually every community had volunteer firefighters, sometimes both men and women, equipped by the company. Some volunteers drilled regularly and attended specialized training classes, but those without expe-rience were also expected to help. At Holden, the miners practiced extin-guishing house fires, and they were called out when forest fires spread along Lake Chelan. In 1951, when fire broke out four miles from Grisdale, 300 loggers worked day and night to stop the blaze on Forest Service land. Some communities even trained children to fight fires: at DuPont, Washington, in the 1920s, boys between eight and twelve made up a junior fire patrol

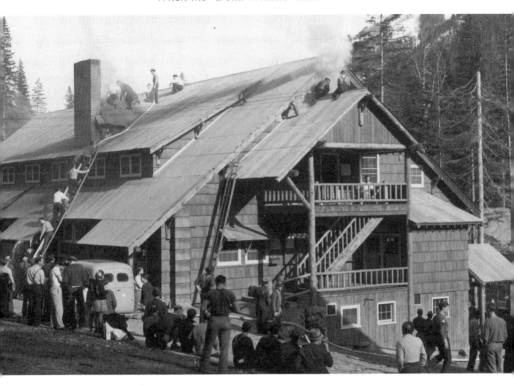

Most Holden, Washington, miners doubled as volunteer firemen. Several got experi-
ence with hoses and ladders in April 1940, when a chimney fire damaged the structure
that housed the dining hall and hotel. (Courtesy of the family of Larry Penberthy)

that took responsibility for getting hose carts to the fire, freeing up adults
to pump water. Forty years later, as the DuPont volunteer crew dwindled,
the fire chief pleaded with his neighbors to show up for drills; when a trans-
former dripped hot oil in 1969 and set a garage afire, it was two women
who got the fire truck out when the alarm rang. (They were the two smallest members of the crew, and one of them was pregnant, reported the local
newspaper editor, chiding the other volunteers.)[10]

A fire threatened everything in town: jobs, homes, lives. Villages and
camps set deep in the forest were especially vulnerable when a fire started,
because they could be surrounded by flames. The only way out was by rail,
and if the train itself was trapped by fire, women and children had to flee
down the tracks and over the trestles, hoping to outrun the blaze. When

Whites, Washington, caught fire in 1902 during the Yacolt Burn that devastated western Washington and Oregon, some families saved themselves and their belongings by loading up a Northern Pacific flatcar and coasting it the five miles to Elma. In the 1912 fire that struck western Washington's Skagit County, loggers and their families—without a train car of any kind—hurried along the rails, abandoning a just-finished English Lumber Company camp. Everything left behind burned, including the hogs being fattened behind the cookhouse. Rather than run, some hid: at Cedar Falls, Washington, a group of women once sheltered their children inside a hollow chamber of the Seattle City Light dam. At nearby Taylor, townspeople put their valuables in the clay mines while they fought a 1910 forest fire that threatened the village.[11]

Some fires were fought without conventional equipment. At Potlatch, Idaho, the first fire engine was a converted logging truck. In Roslyn, Washington, the volunteer fire department organized in 1925 had only hose carts for more than twenty years. Not until 1947 did the firefighters get a truck—and then it was another city's discarded 1914 model LaFrance. In those few communities with running water, women stood guard on their own house roofs with garden hoses while their husbands joined fire brigades. Some communities also turned to unusual preventative programs: at DuPont as late as 1959, the explosives company reduced the risk of grass fires on its undeveloped land by maintaining herds of deer and cattle that grazed on the vegetation in open fields.[12]

The mountain settings that writers called picturesque and enchanting had their own dangers. Avalanches remain a winter hazard at the Seattle City Light's Skagit River power plants, where the seven miles between Newhalem and Diablo are threatened by several avalanche zones; even today, slides sometimes isolate the communities. Holden too was built among avalanche fields, and the few who still live there are occasionally "slid in" for days at a time. In mining days, the snow damaged homes and threatened lives. Thanks to vigilance, only one slide resulted in tragedy in all the years the mine operated: a miner in a hurry to get home bypassed the bulldozed path where he would have been safe and was swept to his death. His body, buried under six feet of snow, was found later by his dog. Ever mindful of this danger, teachers and mothers guided their children across the avalanche field that separated school and home; the staff in the mine office, perched several hundred feet above the homes, kept binoculars within reach so they could look across the Railroad Creek valley and see if moving specks on the snow meant children had climbed too far into slide areas. One winter the office manager had to climb part way up the slope to guide five children down slowly enough that an avalanche wouldn't be triggered.[13]

Drowning was another occupational hazard, especially for the lumberjacks who ran logs downriver each spring. Mill ponds were less of a threat, except to children who tried to sneak a dip. But the fast-running rivers were risky for both adults and children. At the Grand Coulee Dam construction site, few workers survived a plunge into the Columbia. In Holden, Railroad Creek was one of the few places children couldn't wander. Fearful of the glacier-fed river's torrents, parents never forgot the danger of drowning.[14]

In communities where mining and construction required blasting, bosses took additional precautions. At Holden, the Honeymoon Heights neighborhood near the mine portal was evacuated every time dynamiting was scheduled. In Cedar Falls, Washington, the power plant operator could telephone every home simultaneously to warn mothers to bring their children indoors before a blast. Telephones at Cedar Falls were also wired for emergency signals; when five short rings sounded, everyone picked up the phone and helped a mother locate a missing child. Parents in many communities used whistles—sometimes a different pitch for each family—to summon their children.[15]

Bears were a nuisance and a danger in remote camps. Attracted by the smell of food, they wandered in from the woods. In both Grisdale and Holden, bears came close enough to be shot from bunkhouse windows and porches. In Holden's early days, when some miners were still living in old cabins, one family returned from a short summer vacation to find a hole in its roof where a bear had fallen through; he ripped apart most of the kitchen before he was able to scramble out. Years later, a bear wandered the main road so frequently one spring that parents worried about their children's half-mile walk to school. At Cedar Falls, deer destroyed gardens and raccoons sometimes ripped the screens off the coolers used before refrigerators were common. But both deer and raccoons were better tolerated than the bears who raided the vegetable patches. At the City of Seattle's

Company towns often had resident physicians or at least nurses or medics. Many employers also built small hospitals. This facility was built in Tono, a Washington coal-mining community, before World War I. (MSCUA, University of Washington Libraries, 22144)

other projects, high in the North Cascades, bears even crawled onto the raft that supported a floating camp built for construction workers; when the cook was away, bears broke into the food supply hut.[16]

Critics of company towns and company-paid physicians have complained about doctors who were unable—or unwilling—to diagnose problems, especially those resulting from industrial hazards and polluted water. But some early company towns had better medical care than communities of similar size or remoteness, because companies often ensured that a doctor or at least a nurse was available. In McCleary, Washington, the doctor and nurse who arrived in 1913 when a new hospital was built were still on the job in 1926; the next doctor stayed until 1942. In Port Blakely, Washington, the same doctor served the mill town for forty years. At Snoqualmie Falls, Washington, the timber company hospital had forty beds and two doctors on staff in 1929. In Valsetz, Oregon, "Doc" Spry wasn't really an M.D., but he provided first aid and hurried the most seriously ill or injured out on the railroad or in his makeshift ambulance. Up on the Skagit River,

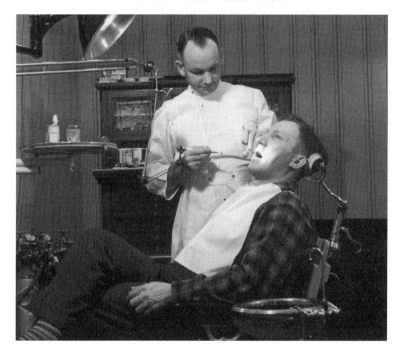

Doug Dewar, a Chelan dentist, made monthly trips to Holden, Washington, where the Howe Sound Company had installed a dental chair in the mining community's small hospital. (Courtesy of the family of Larry Penberthy)

Seattle City Light brought in a doctor for emergencies—but that could be a lengthy, demanding trip. In 1937, when a worker ripped his face open, the doctor was rushed to Diablo, the end of the railway, and then he walked—six miles in eighteen-inch-deep snow—to reach the patient.[17]

Although some companies initially provided health care only for employees, other doctors served entire families from the time the town was established. Employees often paid for their care through monthly payroll deductions; a dollar a month was typical as late as the 1940s. In many cases, however, the fee covered only injuries and illnesses, not routine physicals and obstetrics. Some doctors and nurses provided prenatal care but wouldn't deliver babies. Especially in the most remote company towns and camps, women "went out"—often several days before their due dates—for childbirth. They stayed with family or friends or at motels until labor pains began. Early in the century, a pregnant woman might have checked into a hospital a week or two before her due date. By the Depression era, few could afford that; loggers' wives from Mowich, a central Oregon camp, remember racing the sixty miles of narrow, winding Highway 97 to Bend, sometimes reaching the hospital only minutes before their babies arrived.[18]

Even with medical care, people suffered from gangrene and blood poisoning. Children developed polio and had to be shipped out to big-city hospitals. Middle-aged men, their heart disease gone undetected, dropped dead. When doctors were able to identify appendicitis, they had the challenge of getting patients to an operating room before ruptures threatened death. Up on the Skagit River projects, some early appendicitis victims were evacuated by sled. In 1947, a moment of carelessness on the icy path outside the Holden Fountain Lunch put the village's resident doctor on a boat to Chelan for treatment for his own broken leg.

During the influenza epidemic that killed millions of Americans just as World War I was ending, schools in company towns, just like classes everywhere, closed down, clubs canceled meetings, churches sometimes met only for open-air worship, and soccer leagues delayed their seasons in an effort to check the spread of a disease that was claiming entire families. There were less serious problems, too. In the 1920s, after two Cedar Falls children came down with scarlet fever, the top executive at the City Light plant, along with another manager, had to move into the bachelor bunkhouses for five weeks because their houses were quarantined.

Death and disease and illness brought out the community in company towns. At Holden, when heart disease forced Maude Nelson to leave her teaching job, her students' mothers helped her pack and company executives themselves crated her television and radio for the trip outside. At Grisdale, Washington, when the young son of the school principal, Lou Messmer, and his wife, Ann, faced surgery, the loggers donated enough money to cover the medical bills. In villages where losing the breadwinner often meant losing your hometown, neighbors and bosses did more than carry in casseroles to the bereaved. At Holden, miners had a voluntary payroll deduction program for making donations to a grieving family. Companies sometimes paid for funerals, even for children who had drowned after sneaking into company reservoirs. When employers didn't help financially, unions and lodges often organized benefit plans. By 1908, the coal miners union in Roslyn, Washington, ensured that each working man donated a dollar to the family of anyone killed while working, so a new widow might receive $1,200 to $1,400. Other help was more personal: when a new widow at Holden had a truck barged uplake so she could move her family out, she found a group of miners on her doorstep, ready to take over all the loading. Some were neighbors who had known her for years; others were bachelors from the dorms who had worked with the dead man.[19]

Employers also authorized the use of company equipment when tragedy struck. In Newhalem, when a three-year-old fell into the river and was swept downstream, City Light power plant officials reduced the water passing through the power plant turbines to drop the river water level so volunteers could search both banks of the Skagit. Howe Sound managers used a company bulldozer to divert the flow of Railroad Creek when a Holden child's body had to be recovered after a drowning.[20]

Despite the close-knit communities, funerals often were quiet services far from home and the comfort of friends. There was no church and no minister at Holden, so the dead were shipped downlake in one of the coffins kept in the company warehouse. Funerals were conducted in Chelan, the closest town, or wherever extended family lived. Holden neighbors seldom attended the services, because the mine ran around the clock; leaving for a funeral would require a miner to miss at least two days of work. In such remote towns, a death meant a lengthy, involved trip out for both the dead and the survivors, regardless of the family's stature in the community or financial resources. In landlocked Washington coal towns, where no roads existed and the only transportation was by train, a death meant summoning the undertaker and a coffin on the next day's train. In the early 1900s, when someone died in the Northern Pacific coal town of Melmont, neighbors carried the coffin from the station to the home. The next day they carried it back, so the mortician could accompany the body to the town where the funeral would be held. Family members traveled to the funeral by train—if they could afford the fare—or by hand-pumped rail speeder.[21]

Some companies, like the Grand Coulee Dam contractors and the operators of the Holden mine, provided compensation for the widowed and disabled. As early as 1919, some timber companies paid the bereaved as much as $2,000 in life insurance. A few offered opportunities to work: at Holden, a miner blinded at work was asked to open a variety store; a laborer who lost his leg was retrained as a mess hall cook. A longtime Port Blakely, Washington, shopkeeper was offered his first job by the Port Blakely Mill Company at age thirteen; the fifty cents a day he earned was important to a family left fatherless by a mill accident. Other employers ignored the widows and orphans. In Wilkeson, Washington, where the first mine opened in 1878, there were no serious accidents until just before Christmas 1917, when six men were entombed after a tunnel collapsed. Each of the dead miners was a father; one left seven children, all younger than twelve. That new widow was "stooped" and "sobbing" about the loss of her "good provider," the Tacoma reporter Frances Stone wrote, but "life will be resumed in each household, for the children must be brought up."[22]

How the Wilkeson widows could afford to bring up their children wasn't a question that Frances Stone asked. Death and disability were common problems in the first half of the twentieth century, regardless of where people lived. As one company magazine reported about a 1948 fatality, "The accident appeared to be one of those things which will happen now and then." People in company towns may have been at more risk because of the type of work they did and the isolated communities in which they lived, but they often had the advantage of a local doctor and hospital. They also had a built-in support system that sometimes extended past neighbors to coworkers, bosses, and even company executives.[23]

12 / Depression and World Wars

Perhaps more than any other part of America, company towns were insulated from the effects of war and economic recession. Wartime demand for timber, coal, copper, power, pipe, and explosives kept mines and mills running around the clock. When the peacetime of the 1920s brought production lulls and eventually the Depression of the 1930s, the structure of a company town protected its people: there were no property taxes to pay, no businesses to go bankrupt, and no banks to fail. Many companies watched out for their workers: the bachelors usually were laid off, but most married men got at least a few days of work each month. When war came again during the 1940s, workers were often exempted from the draft but frozen in their jobs at bureaucrat-decreed wages.

When World War I began in the Balkans, American bosses felt it first in their employment offices. Just as demand soared for products like lumber, immigration was cut off, eliminating an important supply of low-cost labor. Many American men went into the military before the United States entered the war in April 1917. Turnover in logging and sawmills, always high, was estimated to be at least 600 percent in 1917—and probably closer to 1,000 percent. The American government was slow to defer loggers and mill workers from military service despite the desperate need for lumber for barracks, truck bodies, munitions boxes, and especially for spruce to build airplanes. By October 1917, the industry was short 7,000 loggers. With orders skyrocketing and their work force depleted, timber companies put both boys and women to work. At the Henry McCleary Timber Company, which then claimed to be the world's largest door manufacturing factory, women put on special-order overalls and assembled fir doors, working eight hours to a shift instead of the ten hours then standard for men. Three hundred miles away, the Potlatch, Idaho, box factory replaced men with young boys, but when still more workers were needed, the company turned to women.[1]

Timber companies worked extra shifts to produce lumber for everything from barracks to ships, but the most significant demand was for boards for the wooden airplanes for the new U.S. army air force. Companies like the Potlatch Lumber Company cut high-quality, extra-long western white pine for wing beams. Even more important for aircraft frames was Sitka spruce, a splinter-resistant wood found almost exclusively in western Oregon and Washington. Determined to almost triple the production of spruce, the War Department in August 1917 organized the Spruce Production Division. Men experienced in logging and sawmills were recruited to work under military officers but in private industry and paid civilian wages. Eventually some 30,000 men worked in 234 Pacific Northwest camps, cutting and milling lumber and building roads, railroads, and mills.[2]

World War I also put coal miners back to work. Oil had stolen the market from coal in the first years of the twentieth century, but soldiers and sailors got most of the petroleum supply once the war started. With Americans again forced to use coal, production reached a record in Washington state in 1918.

Hundreds of company-town residents went to war—in one kind of uniform or another. A DuPont, Washington, woman was among those who joined the Red Cross and entertained troops in Paris; a pair of Roche Harbor, Washington, brothers went to Europe with the Marine Corps and, when wounded, were honored in the waterfront Hotel de Haro by the local Red Cross and the Roche Harbor Lime & Cement Company president, John McMillin himself. The McCleary minister, the first clergyman in southwestern Washington called up, served in the medical corps.[3]

The war brought a fervent patriotism. Bosses erected flagpoles, where workers and their families often met for a flag salute each morning before work. Every possible group and institution—postmasters, school classes, factory departments, and stores—ran war savings campaigns. In DuPont, the women sold more Thrift Stamps than any other chapter of the Minute

WORLD WAR I IMPROVED LOGGERS'
WORKING CONDITIONS

The Spruce Production Division, organized in World War I to help loggers provide lumber for aircraft, was directly responsible for improved working and living conditions for loggers. Before the United States Army would release soldiers to work in a timber community, the camp had to pass a military inspection: decent food, decent bedding, clean sheets once a week, and reasonable fees for room and board. Bryce P. Disque, who headed the Spruce Production Division, also campaigned for the eight-hour day; with the six-day week that would remain standard for years, Disque's efforts reduced loggers' work weeks to forty-eight hours. (Source: Ellis Lucia, The Big Woods: Logging and Lumbering—from Bull Teams to Helicopters—in the Pacific Northwest *[1975], pp. 77–78.)*

Women of Pierce County. The powder-company town never had more than 600 people, including men, women, and children, but in one Liberty Loan drive, 199 people bought war bonds, for a total contribution of $28,500. That was more than $140 per person, in an era when T-bone steak sold for twenty-two cents a pound and houses rented for $15 or $30 a month. The fervor wasn't always positive. In some towns and camps, it led to attacks on neighbors; those who refused to buy war bonds were sometimes forced out of their jobs. People with German names, even if they weren't recent immigrants, also were at risk. Especially in timber communities, patriotism flared into hysteria about a union called the Industrial Workers of the World. Denounced as socialists, the Wobblies were accused of sabotaging the war effort; they were believed to be starting forest fires, driving spikes in logs to wreck sawmill equipment, and organizing work slowdowns.[4]

World War I also brought a flurry of new social activities. Women organized Red Cross chapters to roll bandages and knit for soldiers; in little Washington communities like McKenna, Harding, National, and Fairfax, the community halls and schoolrooms were commandeered by groups that sometimes sewed every day of the week. Men sponsored fund-raisers like boxing smokers to pay for the boxes of tobacco, candy, and toiletries sent to hometown boys. The little gifts and well-wishing weren't limited to local soldiers; in Alpine, built along the Great Northern tracks, women put on their Red Cross uniforms and passed out candy and cigars as troop trains passed through the timber town. Sometimes it was an executive's wife who spearheaded the activities: in southwest Washington, Ada McCleary organized Red Cross chapters and wrote personal letters to hometown boys sent overseas. DuPont women provided lodging for the wives and mothers of soldiers stationed at neighboring Camp Lewis. Their Red Cross group, started with fourteen members in April 1917, numbered 400 a year and a half later. Members made thousands of surgical dressings and sewed masks, ambulance pillows, and almost 500 "helpless case garments." In logging camps where Spruce Production Division troops were supplementing civilian crews, the army organized social activities through its Bureau of Morale, which sent singers, musicians, speakers, and chaplains "to educate, to instruct and to inspire" (as the military phrased it). In other communities, local matrons sponsored dances for the troops, complete with carloads of closely chaperoned young women. Company towns near military bases worked hard to provide wholesome recreation for soldiers, too. Camp Lewis, within walking distance of DuPont, had no chapel of its own, so the DuPont church pews overflowed with doughboys for the Sunday services and the frequent social programs. One musical program attracted 450—including 100 for whom there were no seats. "The program . . . , and especially the forty-eight homemade cakes and the fifty young women, made a great hit," the Tacoma paper reported.[5]

After the armistice a postwar slump hit many company towns. The overnight end of military orders forced executives to look for new markets and means of reducing expenses. In 1921, coal-mine executives announced a pay cut of almost 25 percent. The laborers, already frustrated over dangerous working conditions, frequent layoffs, and poor living conditions, shut the mines down. Some unions didn't settle for more than two years— and by that time, the industry was facing death again. Wilkeson was one of many western Washington coal towns where when the miners did finally go back to work, it was at lower wages and with their livelihood threatened by competition from oil and the better-quality coal mined elsewhere. Some miners never got their jobs back: in Taylor, Washington, the mines filled with water during the strike and could not be successfully reopened. As the industry died, the coal towns did, too. By 1924, in all of Pierce County, Washington, fewer than 800 men worked in coal mining. A few miles north, at Coal Creek and Newcastle, the mines reopened—but not for long. By 1929 the Pacific Coast Coal Company had closed its doors and was selling workers' houses for $25 each.

Some communities boomed during the 1920s, only to see their industries collapse as the effects of the 1929 stock market crash reverberated all the way west. Burdened by debt, many companies struggled, eliminating extra shifts and consolidating operations. Some closed factories down completely for years. Manley-Moore, which owned a western Washington timber village, was one of the first to go under; deep in debt when the crash came in 1929, the company sold out to the Eatonville Lumber Company, which ran the mill only until the early 1930s. At the Potlatch Lumber Company, the mill shut down in the fall of 1931, not to reopen until 1934. In Wendling, Oregon, a Booth-Kelly Lumber Company town, the mill closed but many laid-off employees chose to stay, supporting themselves by cutting and selling firewood and by hunting. In Valsetz, Oregon, the mill, the camps, the store, the bunkhouses, the mess hall—and the power plant—all closed in mid-1931. It would be 1936 before operations returned to their previous level. A few men were kept on as watchmen or got seasonal work as firewardens. Some left their families in Valsetz and took whatever short-term jobs were available in other timber communities. The families who stayed weren't completely isolated: the Cobbs & Mitchell Yellow Jacket brought in mail, groceries, and visitors six days a week. School enrollment dropped, but classes continued.[6]

Hard times in the mills, mines, and plants also meant hard times for town site maintenance. The best-kept towns grew a little shabby; those that were already rundown became obviously dilapidated. People who couldn't afford token rent set up shanty towns at the edges of communities. Even where operations were adding employees, townspeople often did without. The municipal towns of Newhalem and Diablo had to increase power plant staff to meet the growing demand for electricity from Seattle City Light customers, but taxpayers opposed the rate increases that would have provided more housing or better town services for the employees.

Many employers made a commitment to protect their workers from the economic crisis. The bosses cut wages, let houses go unrepaired, closed bunkhouses, and eliminated subsidies for libraries and recreation programs; they also reduced rental rates and allowed unpaid rent to go uncollected. They kept the schools and the banks open, relaxed company store policies on credit, and sometimes even cut store prices. They let townspeople raise rabbits, chickens, and other livestock in their backyards. Especially in remote camps, bosses were apt to ignore the poachers who kept meat on the table and the moonshiners who earned a little cash income. Most important, managers worked hard to provide for their best employees. Unsold inventory often stacked up because the company kept operations going as long as possible. By shortening work weeks, bosses guaranteed that each worker got at least a small paycheck. In much of western Washington and Oregon, many mill workers got three six-hour workdays a week in 1933; the lowest paid earned twenty or thirty cents an hour, or about $21 a month. Married men were usually the last laid off, and even after a mill or mine closed, bosses sometimes kept fathers working on clean-up and mill maintenance. At Roche Harbor, employees were kept busy on make-work construction projects that included the owners' mausoleum.[7]

What Sam Churchill said about the post–World War I recession was also true during the 1930s:

> If there was going to be a depression, the Western Cooperage camp was about as comfortable a place to sit one out as you can imagine. The company provided worker houses, so there was no rent or taxes. We depended on kerosene lamps for light and the only telephone was in the company office. And during the summer, spring and fall we were virtually surrounded by foods that nature provided.[8]

Towns like Cedar Falls, stabilized by regular paychecks from Seattle City Light, the Milwaukee Road, and the Pacific States Lumber Company, were even more sheltered from the economic crisis. "There was no Depression here," said Jack Young, remembering the free rent, electricity, heat, and water in Cedar Falls. But, as another Cedar Falls native noted, no one was naive: "People hung onto their jobs," said Marian Thompson Arlin. Even in a relatively affluent community, people made do or did without: Arlin's clothes were all home-sewn and she learned to ski using how-to books from the library and skis built in her father's basement shop. A woman who grew up in the Cedar Falls Milwaukee Road camp, where toilets were communal, remembered that toilet tissue was carried to and from the bathroom: it was too expensive to share. Kinzua, Oregon, didn't go untouched by the economy, but it had only one Depression-era shutdown—and that lasted all of a week. The Kinzua postmaster, a relative of the town founder, took a pay cut to $1,300 a year, however, thanks to newly elected President Franklin D. Roosevelt's wage reductions for federal employees. Some schoolteachers in the county saw their paychecks slashed by $300 a year to as little as $750. At Klickitat, Washington, the sawmill ran all through the Depression, but everyone in town cut corners—even the boss's family. A few communities were busier than they had been: in Taylor, the clay-mining and brick-factory town not far from Cedar Falls, one longtime employee recalled many, many twelve-hour days making water and sewer pipes, in demand probably because of government-funded sanitation projects intended to eliminate typhoid.[9]

Like Cedar Falls in its relative isolation from the Depression was Coulee Dam, the community built by the Bureau of Reclamation for professional and management staff at the Grand Coulee Dam construction site. Secure in their federal jobs, the officials were astounded by the number of people who journeyed to windswept central Washington on just the hope of work. As the historian Paul Pitzer wrote, the Depression left one-third of the nation's labor force with nothing to do. Desperate and afraid, thousands came to the dam site from everywhere, to live in cars and caves and cardboard shanties, waiting for the chance at a job. And with good reason: in 1933, even unskilled laborers at the dam site earned at least $.60 an hour and paid only $1.50 a day for meals and lodging.

In the towns where free rent and a garden weren't enough, some employers created their own welfare programs. The Long-Bell Lumber Company appointed a company welfare administrator to assess the needs of unemployed workers. Almost two dozen local organizations were asked to contribute at least $10 a year to the Longview Welfare Bureau, which ran a thrift shop and food bank; as the Depression deepened, those still employed at Long-Bell were also asked to donate $1 a month to the Bureau.[10]

Workers also took care of each other: Ryderwood's Depression-era minister recalled the old chewing tobacco tin where people covertly dropped in a coin or two whenever they could, to help out the most impoverished families. Neighboring farmers left their surplus vegetables nearby for soup and stew. In McCleary, Washington, any family without a wage earner was helped by the community relief fund, which took no funds from county, state, or federal governments. In Coulee Dam and Mason City, the Grand Coulee Dam site towns, social and charitable organizations sponsored Christmas parties and food baskets. At work parties in the community, women made toys and sewed children's clothes; firemen repaired donated toys. At a benefit theater matinee, admission was free for anyone who brought canned goods or a glass of jelly for the food baskets. A benefit bridge party was so successful that in 1939 the community funded the holiday charities with a single large card party.[11]

The companies that had limped through the early 1930s were not guaranteed survival as the Depression eased. Timber companies were especially vulnerable. Conflict in Japan and China had eliminated an important market: lumber exports to Japan and China had decreased by more than 80 percent between 1934 and 1938. Some timbermen were out of trees and tired: Henry McCleary sold out to the Simpson Timber Company and his town survived, but the Bordeaux brothers closed down their Mason County Logging Company, shuttered its town of Bordeaux, and sold most of its land to the state. In 1939 the Pacific States Lumber Company, exhausted by years of labor unrest and depressed markets, called it quits and closed down both its business and its town of Selleck. At Taylor, the coal and clay mines were closed by the end of the 1930s; the City of Seattle, determined to protect its watershed from pollution, continued its drive to shut down Taylor's remaining brick and tile plant.[12]

Within a few years, however, the advent of war in Europe meant a sharp increase in production and a population surge for other companies and their communities. No place was there greater potential for a bonanza than in the woods of western Washington and Oregon, which then provided more than a quarter of all American lumber. Forest products were called America's most important World War II industry and justifiably so: it was an era when wood and wood derivatives were used in everything from airplanes, truck bodies, ships, and wharves to PT boats and pontoon bridges, explosives, gunstock, and barracks, a time when it took three trees to equip and maintain a single American soldier. Even before Americans were climbing onto troop ships, the crisis in Europe brought what the historian Stewart Holbrook called "a demand for lumber the like of which had never been seen. . . . Pearl Harbor set loose a new and greater demand which continued unabated through the war years and after."[13]

Labor shortages meant that even those lumber companies with a guaranteed supply of logs had difficulty meeting sales demand. Never the best-paying industry, forest products lost well over a fifth of its peacetime workers to the draft and the much higher-paying jobs in shipyards and aircraft factories. By mid-1942, Washington state shipyard wages were on the average almost 50 percent higher than the pay in timber operations. Sawmills had difficulty running at capacity because they lacked skilled workers. In Gilchrist, Oregon, the mill sometimes had only enough labor for one shift. Most serious was the situation in the woods, where few experienced loggers were left. By September 1943, when crews across America were short more than 100,000 loggers, some Northwest companies were operating with only two-thirds of the workers they needed. At camps like Kosmos, Washington, it was even worse: the company could fill only 200 of its 450 positions. Shevlin-Hixon shut down its Bend, Oregon, mills for weeks so that loggers at camps like Shevlin could catch up with the demand. As loggers left the woods for defense jobs, it was harder to get trees cut. With too few logs coming out of the woods, prices shot up. Large lumber mills, guaranteed that the government would buy their output, outbid smaller operations and shingle mills for the few logs available. With no raw materials, many mills shut down, and their towns died.[14]

Fire, always a danger in logging camps, became a more serious issue with the skeleton crews of the war years. Loggers fought their own companies' fires as well as joining Forest Service crews to combat fires on government land, so every day of fire—wherever it was—meant a delay in getting logs out of the woods. Steam locomotives, which threw off sparks that ignited brush along railroad tracks, were only one of the fire hazards. People on the West Coast were convinced that their forests were the targets for Japanese incendiary balloon bombs drifting across the Pacific Ocean on high wind currents, especially after a Japanese pilot tried to firebomb the woods near Brookings, Oregon, in late 1942.

Labor shortages also created a serious problem in nonferrous mines.

Some miners were drafted and then, just as the demand for copper sky-rocketed, others enlisted or left for defense-industry jobs. Because of copper's importance to the war, the United States Army furloughed soldiers to work in copper mines starting in the winter of 1942–43, but most of the men sent to the mines were inexperienced. Those who did have mining experience had worked in coal mines, not hard-rock operations. Many were unaccustomed to the hard labor of mining and quickly drifted on to other jobs. A "fiasco," the media called the furlough program, and accused military commanders of using it as a means to eliminate "misfits and problem soldiers." The government quit drafting experienced copper miners and tried to freeze them in their jobs, but by late 1944, the number of men working underground had plummeted. Between the beginning and end of 1944, the copper-mining labor force decreased by 38 percent. At mines like Holden, the managers tried to replace miners with conscientious objectors and even transients imported from the streets of Spokane.[15]

Like loggers and miners, teachers eventually were able to get draft deferments, especially in fast-growing communities. As Americans migrated across the country to take defense-industry jobs, regions like the West grew rapidly; schools couldn't keep pace with the need. In Richland, Washington, where the federal government's atomic bomb research project almost overnight transformed a village of 247 into a city of thousands, the schools ran double shifts. Some smaller communities had almost no teachers. In August 1942, the school superintendent in Wheeler County, Oregon, had only one teacher for Kinzua and two other towns—instead of the three or four she needed in each school—and none at all for the new school at the Kinzua Pine Mills' Camp 5. (In fact, school would not start at Camp 5 until January, when a teacher was found.)

With these shortages, married women who had been forced out of the classroom had an opportunity to return to teaching. Those who had already retired were entreated to register for wartime assignments. But many women chose the better-paying industry over education. For good reason: a woman with no factory experience could earn $2,400 to $3,000 a year working swing shift in Seattle's Boeing plant or the shipyards; even in a sawmill, a woman might make more than the $1,600 paid many teachers. Employers desperate for help successfully used patriotism as a means to get women back to work. In Wheeler County, Oregon, where 40 percent

When World War II broke out and men went to war, timber companies recruited women to help satisfy the increasing demand for wood products. The Lumberettes, as management called them, worked at the Snoqualmie Falls (Washington) Lumber Company. (Courtesy of the Weyerhaeuser Company Archives)

of the men went to war, women—whether or not they had children—took over. Kinzua, the county's largest town, had more than a hundred children in school and many still at home, so the community organized a day nursery that would free more mothers for work in the sawmill. Even in mining communities like Holden, women replaced men; no women worked underground for Howe Sound, but some took traditionally male jobs like timekeeper and sampler.[16]

In timber towns like Potlatch, Idaho, where all the women mill workers had been laid off after World War I, the lumber company began to recruit them again. The Snoqualmie Falls Lumber Company, a Weyerhaeuser subsidiary in Washington's Cascade foothills, used "Lumberettes" in physically exhausting operations like the green chain, pulling newly cut lumber off a moving chain conveyor for additional processing. Women replaced men both in the Gilchrist Timber Company office and in the mill; some were just teenagers who took the good-paying jobs as soon as they were eligible for work permits. In a few operations, women worked in the woods, ran logs on the rivers, and fought fires. At Kosmos, a former teacher spent a winter working out in the snow as a log scaler. At Kinzua, when an over-heated motor set the sawmill afire in August 1942, men and women worked four hours to save the precious equipment. Using gas masks hurried to the mill by the county defense coordinator, they struggled through smoke and heat to quench the blaze and salvage the saws. "All the courage of an army under battle stress was shown by these men and women," declared the mill's general manager in the company newsletter.[17]

Labor wasn't the only wartime shortage that affected company towns. The scarcity of tires and gas had a serious impact on employer-owned com-munities, especially the remote settlements where trucks and cars had begun to replace trains. Before World War II, virtually all of the rubber used in the United States was imported from the Far East. By early 1942 Americans had no source of rubber. Because almost half of the rubber imports were used in automobile tires, they were the first product of any kind to be rationed. Logging companies had only limited leverage with the ration boards: army trucks needed the same kind of tires that loggers used. In January 1942, when the first tire rations were announced, Wheeler County, Oregon—home of the Kinzua Pine Mills and several smaller lum-ber mills—was granted only a dozen truck and bus tires and ten tubes. Gas rationing, begun in May 1942, aggravated the labor shortage. Many employ-ers had shuttered their bunkhouses during the Depression and supple-mented the resident crews of family men with commuters. Now the bunkhouses and cookhouses had to be reopened, and logging superin-tendents struggled to find men who would live in the woods. They also strug-gled to keep their longtime employees; in small camps like Mowich, Oregon, loggers quit their jobs and left because they couldn't drive the sixty miles to Bend on a gas ration of three gallons a week. Grocers, denied extra gas rations for delivery service, couldn't always manage to serve distant cus-tomers. Nor could company-town and camp residents rely on the main line railroads for transportation: busy with war freight, trains no longer stopped in little settlements.

Just as they had in World War I, most company-town residents supported the World War II effort, both on and off the job. Even tiny towns like Kinzua collected thousands of pounds of rubber in scrap drives. Women solicited donations of old white sheets, pillowcases, and shirts that could be cut and rolled into bandages. Their clubs knit for sailors, made quilt tops for the Red Cross, and donated books for military libraries. To support the USO and Red Cross, townspeople planned dances, turkey shoots, and carnivals where war stamps were the only currency accepted. Some civic groups packed gift boxes of candy, cigarettes, and paperback books to hand each local draftee as he departed for the induction center. In Potlatch, Idaho, and Holden, Washington, women and girls organized letter writing clubs to ensure that local boys received regular mail from home. Holden residents also invited flyers from the nearby air force bases uplake for baseball games, dances, and overnight visits in miners' homes. At Cedar Falls, Washington, when troop trains were scheduled to pass by, both adults and children would often gather at the depot to wave to the soldiers en route to the Pacific theater. Men too old for the military organized themselves into Home Guards; both men and women joined civil reserve units. In Oregon's Polk County, just a few miles from the Pacific Ocean, loggers and sawmill workers fearful of Japanese invasions formed what they called guerrilla bands in Valsetz and several nearby logging camps. A "sharpshooter band, organized in platoons under experienced woodsmen," was necessary, the local paper reported, because of the isolated communities' "strategic" locations.[18]

Children had their wartime projects, too. Near Cedar Falls, where logging companies had once run railroad spurs hither and yon, kids were dismissed from school to help on scrap drives; small children pulled out the loosened spikes, and the biggest boys pulled up entire sections of old railroad track. At Holden both boys and girls learned to knit scarves, leg warmers, and afghan squares. Holden teenagers attending high school in downlake communities found themselves picking fruit one harvest season, when the schools closed so that kids could help during a farm-worker shortage. In the *Valsetz Star*, the young editor Dorothy Anne Hobson reported that she and her friends hadn't been able to get much scrap for the national aluminum drive: just a few old pie tins, an egg poacher and her father's brandnew cocktail shaker.[19]

Companies supported both their military personnel and the people on the home front. Many employers sent their company newsletters to former employees now in uniform; the Snoqualmie Falls Lumber Company went a step further and mailed newsletters to everyone from the Snoqualmie Valley who was serving in the military. Just as Boy Scout troops and school classes competed on sales of War Bond stamps, company departments vied against each other or nearby towns to sell more War Bonds. Right after Pearl Harbor, the Kinzua Pine Mills set a quota of $5,000 a month for war bond sales. In Valsetz, when the sawmill superintendent took over as chairman of the Red Cross drive, the town donated the equivalent of $4 for every man, woman, and child, raising more than $2,000 of the $9,000 contributed in the entire county. Valsetz residents gave more than money: "Valsetz Saves Day at March Blood Bank Here," exclaimed a headline in the local paper, which pointed out that it was the thirty-eight pints of blood from Valsetz that put Polk County over its quota in one blood drive.

Both laborers and their families prepared for bombings and medical emergencies. Homes were fitted with blackout curtains, and the outdoor lights were dimmed in every community within 150 miles of the Pacific Ocean; the military feared that street lamps, car lights, and even traffic signals might silhouette the ships at sea and make them easy targets for enemy submarines. In Cedar Falls, where elegant street lamps had brightened the night and no one ever turned off their lights because electricity was free, the little Seattle City Light town was finally dark. People with basements stockpiled blankets, canned goods, and first aid kits; emergency supplies were stored in community air raid shelters in recreation halls and gymnasiums. Men, women, and even children took first aid or home nursing courses: eight million copies of the Red Cross first aid manual went to American homes in 1942, making it the best-selling book of early wartime.[20]

With many foods rationed, almost everyone gardened; 40 percent of the vegetables produced during World War II was grown in Victory gardens. Employers set aside land for communal gardens and allowed tenants to dig up their yards for smaller vegetable patches. In Cedar Falls, the gardens were carefully fenced—although not with much success. The raccoons were almost impossible to keep out of gardens, and bears weren't even always deterred by electric fences. In Potlatch, where Victory gardens became so popular that the company ran a lottery for plots, the town site department plowed up vacant lots and converted the old lumber storage area to a garden. In Holden, late snowfalls and early frosts kept the growing season short; in 1945, almost two feet of snow was recorded in April, and eleven inches

Groceries were rationed during World War II, so a shopping trip meant taking along ration coupons. In communities like Holden, where there was no store, miners sent their ration books to Chelan by boat along with their weekly grocery orders. (Courtesy of Gayle Rodgers Davidson)

fell in October. But despite the weather and the rocky soil, miners grew raspberries, radishes, peas, carrots, beets, potatoes, onions, and lettuce. When the crops were harvested, company-town families, like others across America, canned. For those unfamiliar with the process, extension agents taught Food for Victory classes. Because sugar was rationed, making jam sometimes took cooperation; in Holden, families with leftover sugar traded it for the fruit preserves other women made. Besides fruit and vegetables, people put up venison; few homes had freezers, and with ration stamps limiting how much meat people could buy, hunting remained as important as it had been during the Depression.[21]

With wartime shortages and government-dictated six-day work weeks keeping people close to home, many company towns revived the sense of community common in earlier years. They organized Halloween parties and Christmas caroling and met for monthly potluck suppers in church halls. Clubs like Kinzua's Rip It and Stitch It held handkerchief showers, and Holden's Winston neighborhood hosted informal cribbage tournaments, playing in one miner's house one night and another's the next. Neighbors even socialized over routine jobs like laundry; housewives sometimes washed together to conserve the rationed gas that powered their washing machines.[22]

Crises had contradictory effects on company towns. Some towns were better isolated from the day-to-day problems caused by Depression and war. Others fell victim to major economic changes caused by these events. Still others wouldn't have existed without the crises. In some towns, it was demand, not Depression, that killed off the communities. Because shingle mills in towns like Kerriston couldn't compete for logs when raw material prices soared during World War II, the mills closed and the towns faded away. Other towns wouldn't have boomed without crisis: Depression-era government work-relief programs created Coulee Dam and kept clay kilns in towns like Taylor manufacturing sewer and water pipe. World War I's Spruce Production Division built railroads and lumber mills that became postwar headquarters for western Washington and Oregon timber operations. Twenty-five years later, the weapons and warships for World War II led to the establishment of Richland and Vanport.

13 / Fame—Even If Fleeting

E ven before George Pullman's model town drew trainloads of gawk-
    ers, company towns attracted attention. The result of someone's
    experiment or dreams, Northwest towns were often the best or the
biggest or the last of their kind. Thanks to natural resources, they produced
the most copper, the best clay, the longest timbers, the most power. Their
locations gave them notoriety, too: the longest winters, the most rainfall,
the hardest to reach. One drew national attention as the only spot in the
continental United States ever bombed during wartime. Occasionally and
unfortunately, a town found itself scrutinized because it was the worst: the
dirtiest or the most dangerous. Besides the *Life, Fortune, National Geographic,*
and *Saturday Evening Post* photographers and the newsreel film crews who
documented the record snowfalls, the biggest trees, and the newest dams,
company towns attracted movie makers who used the secluded settings and
spectacular scenery as backdrops for both documentaries and feature
films. And, like other small towns across America, the Northwest's company towns spawned at least minor celebrities: from Edward R. Murrow
to a Munchkin to Marilyn Monroe's press agent, from the inventor of flying
cars to a nine-year-old newspaper editor.

Opened just after the turn of the century, the mine at Britannia, British
Columbia, grew famous for out-producing every other copper mine in the
British Commonwealth; its sister mine at Holden produced almost all of
Washington state's copper in the 1940s and 1950s and much of the copper

Snow at Holden, Washington, always accumulated quickly. But during the winter of 1955–56, when Holden received more than double its usual snowfall, the main road was narrowed to the width of an alley, and homes were reached by open-topped tunnels. The record 615 inches resulted in a three-page feature in Life. *(Courtesy of Harriet Wilbour)*

used by the United States in World War II. But these Howe Sound Company communities drew as much attention for their carefully platted towns, roadless locations, and mountainous settings. "The most romantic and poetically entrancing region of the Cascades," gushed a local reporter about Holden. At the 1939 World's Fair in New York, photos of this just-completed model village were included as part of the fair's theme of Building the World of Tomorrow. In later years, publications like *Life* would chronicle the village's record snowfalls, and national radio quiz shows like "Answer Man" would document its remoteness. In a three-page feature in 1956, *Life* reported that a wall of snow and ice blocked the light from the village school's seventh-grade classrooms: "But Holden grouches little about snow."[1]

Even after Holden closed, *National Geographic* and *Sunset* continued to send crews up the lake. "Here lay Valhalla," rhapsodized one writer. Enthused another: "The most inviting living space in all the Cascades Range. . . . The trail beyond Holden gives you a pocket edition of the best of Cascade scenery." Reality was sometimes acknowledged. Although a 1968 *National Geographic* feature on the North Cascade mountains emphasized the "labyrinth of high, ragged peaks amid deep valleys," the writer also admitted, "A broad yellow scar, waste from a processing plant, persists after 10 years. No grass, not even a blueberry bush, covers the poisoned tailings."[2]

Grisdale, Washington, a logging camp that operated from 1946 until 1985, was a fascinating anachronism. The last American family logging camp outside Alaska, it was new when other camps were being razed. As Dave James, a longtime Simpson Timber Company public relations executive, wrote, the more the other camps disappeared, the greater the interest in Grisdale. Early visitors came from as close as Canada and Mexico and from as far away as Europe and Australia. People who couldn't visit wrote: Simpson received letters from all over America from children who had read about Grisdale in *National Geographic* or their social studies textbooks. Early in its history, Grisdale had gotten an incongruous taste of fame: it hosted the southern California winner of the radio program "Queen for a Day." The contest queen, who spent a rainy November day in the woods, got a tenderloin steak for lunch, a tree-topping demonstration, and a tea party with Grisdale women. Convinced that logging camps were all wretched shantytowns, the media—whether journalists, cookbook writers, historians, or photographers—couldn't stop praising this well-planned little timber village. Typical of the hyperbole was the logging historian Stewart Holbrook's description in 1952: "It is technically a logging camp, yet few loggers have seen its likes. It has beauty and an air of permanence that set it apart. The men who built it obviously had an eye for comfort. . . . It is a logger's dream camp come true." *National Geographic* writers called it "a company town that has a heart" and "a glimpse of a vanished past." Grisdale also attracted attention because of its weather: it could expect as much rain in a month as Seattle received in a year, with annual rainfall once exceeding 190 inches. Valsetz, a logging and mill town due south of Grisdale, was repeatedly recognized as Oregon's wettest spot: 5 inches a day wasn't unusual in the winter, and the annual total was often 160. In 1950, when 72 inches of rain fell in the first three months of the year, Valsetz was even profiled by an Associated Press feature writer, who claimed people had to be six feet tall to live in the town or else they'd drown.[3]

Two other "last towns" that drew media attention were Gilchrist, Oregon's last company-owned town, and Port Gamble, the last timber town in Washington. Built almost ten years before Grisdale, Gilchrist stayed a company town until the early 1990s, all of those years owned by the same family-controlled firm. Port Gamble, probably the longest-lived company town in the entire country, was historic before communities like Grisdale and Gilchrist were even started; its pristine nineteenth-century church and Victorian houses, many reminiscent of the town founders' Maine home-town, are tourbook favorites, and the entire town has landmark status.

Even after they closed, company towns continued to attract attention, either for their mystique as modern-day ghost towns or for the communities' success in finding new directions. When the Pacific Coast Coal Company shut down its operations in Carbonado, Washington, the *Seattle Times* headlined its story, "The Birth of a Ghost Town." Visiting Holden a few years after it closed, a *National Geographic* crew wrote, "Today it is a ghost town. Television antennas still sprout from the battered roofs of its silent cottages. Stop signs punctuate its empty streets." About the same time, another *National Geographic* writer chronicled the Long-Bell Lumber Company camp's transformation into a senior citizen community:

> Ryderwood, a logging town that ran out of logs, seemed destined for ghost-township—until an enterprising real estate developer made it a haven for retired folk. They have come from all over the country, to hunt, fish in their own lake, work on houses and gardens, and kick up their heels at Saturday night dances.[4]

Another company town found itself revived—at least in fiction—more than sixty years after it was razed. Alpine was built deep in Washington's North Cascades in 1910 and demolished in 1929, after its mill closed, but it was reintroduced to the world in 1992 when a Seattle writer, Mary Daheim, wrote her first novel about an Alpine newspaper editor turned sleuth. Today Daheim, whose mother grew up in Alpine and graduated from the town's tiny high school, has turned out more than a dozen mysteries set in the

2. Strong her men and great her beauty
   Swift and sure to do her duty,
   First her country's call to heed
   With men and money every need.

3. Let us offer up a prayer
   That before another year
   Every man now over there
   May be with us over here.

"In the mountains of the West, In a Valley near the crest lies a Gem of fair renown,"
wrote Mrs. C. L. Clemans, wife of the Alpine Lumber Company co-owner, in "Alpine
Song," published in the program for the company's eight annual banquet, in 1918.
(Courtesy of Mary Daheim)

community. (Her first, *The Alpine Advocate*, chronicles the heroine's financial struggles as publisher of the local paper, which did once exist—but as
The Blabber.)[5]

The massive effort it took to construct Grand Coulee Dam—and the
almost unbelievable quantities of power this new dam generated—attracted
prestigious visitors and, predictably, national publicity. Presidents and
princes were among those who wound around the switchbacks leading down
the coulee; Franklin D. Roosevelt and Harry Truman came, along with Norway's Prince Olav, Ethiopia's Hailie Selassie, and dozens of members of
Congress. Some came to marvel, others to complain about pork barrel politics. "Coulee detractors ask where in blazes the boosters think they are going
to sell 900,000 kilowatts," noted *Fortune* in 1937. *Fortune* editors themselves
commemorated the project by publishing eight pages of Margaret Bourke-
White's photographs of the dam in addition to commissioning a painting
of the dam site that the magazine spread across two pages. *Harper's* called
the dam the "biggest thing on earth"; the *Saturday Evening Post*, the "eighth
wonder of the world." National radio shows broadcast from Grand Coulee
by celebrities like a young Chet Huntley helped attract a third of a million
visitors in 1938 and hundreds of thousands more in 1939. Some of the media
attention spilled over to Mason City and Coulee Dam, the central Washington towns built for those constructing the dam. Mason City, where dam
contractors lived, drew notice because of its large-scale use of electricity.
"A unique experiment in domestic heating," reported *Pacific Builder &
Engineer* in 1935, which enthused, "The employee moved into a cozy, all-
electric home that gave him a happy outlook on life, and aids, indirectly,
in building the Grand Coulee Dam." A few years later, the "chimney-less"
community was still enough of a novelty to attract the attention of *National
Geographic.*[6]

Earlier Washington state dam projects received their share of national
publicity, probably due to the continuing public relations efforts of J. D.
Ross, a longtime Seattle City Light superintendent who saw tourism as an
important second industry for the Skagit River power projects. As early as
1925, *Scientific American* gave the projects a two-page spread full of photos. Later articles focused on Ross as much (or more) as on the dams. In
1936, *Collier's,* a national weekly magazine, titled its story, "It Can't Be Done,
Can't It?" and emphasized Ross's indefatigability: "Ross has been doing the

impossible all his life." A few years later, *Harper's* eulogized Ross with an extensive story that claimed Skagit tours were a public service operated at no profit. (To employees who grumbled about his spending on tourism, however, Ross had insisted that it was tourists who "paid the way" at Newhalem and Diablo.) Even after Ross was gone, the publicity continued; in 1953, a media tour brought reporters from as close as the Seattle daily papers and as far away as the *Wall Street Journal* and *Sunset* magazine.[7]

War also put company towns in the spotlight. Almost twenty years after its mill closed and the town had shrunk to a beachside hamlet, Brookings, Oregon, found itself in the news when a Japanese seaplane tried to firebomb the surrounding forest early in World War II. The only community in the Lower 48 ever attacked, Brookings made headlines again decades later when it invited the Japanese pilot back for a visit. Another waterfront Oregon community, Vanport, got a half-page in *Business Week* in mid-1943, thanks to being the country's largest wartime housing project. "The nation's newest, most unusual city," said the magazine. In a story headlined "Kaiser's Kids," *Newsweek* described how the shipbuilder Henry Kaiser had created Oregon's second-largest school system. Vanport's unusual demise—the entire community floated down the Columbia River when a dike broke during a 1948 storm—brought it pages of additional national publicity. Richland, developed by the government at the same time as Vanport, found itself profiled on the front page of the *Wall Street Journal* when Congress was trying to get out of the company-town business: "Most everyone agrees that seven years of Government ownership and controls have created a snafu that won't easily be untangled. The whole thing is shaping up as a $100 million headache for U.S. planners and taxpayers." A few years later, the publicity was more positive when *Look* magazine named Richland one of its All-American Cities.[8]

Company-town operations were occasionally described in extensive detail, complete with blueprints and site plans, for professional journals like *Reclamation Era* and *Mining World*. Other writers recounted their experiences for lay readers. In 1929, the *Atlantic Monthly* devoted pages to "Sitting on Dynamite," a young man's tale of two weeks' work at the DuPont Powder Company. The logging historian Stewart Holbrook wrote sometimes glamorized tales of life in the woods that ran in popular magazines like *American Mercury, Reader's Digest,* and the *New York Times Magazine*.[9]

When Elizabeth Taylor visited Holden to film Courage of Lassie, *released in 1946, she posed near the Howe Sound Company dock on Lake Chelan with several Boy Scouts. From left are the Rodgers twins, Robert and Raymond, and their brother Dean, Jerry Webb, Lee Carey, and Joe Smith. (Courtesy of Bill Phillips)*

Seeking the highest mountains, the deepest ravines, and the tallest trees, both movie stars and bit players brought Hollywood excitement to company towns. DuPont matrons flocked to the set when the silent movie heartthrob Richard Barthelmess filmed *The Patent Leather Kid* near the Washington explosives town in 1927. His usual co-stars like the Gish sisters and Mary Astor weren't in the cast, but Barthelmess's performance got him nominated for an Oscar in the first Academy Awards competition. During World War II, Holden children found the young Elizabeth Taylor buying sweets in the Fountain Lunch and playing in their sandbox between takes on *Courage of Lassie*, released in 1946. School kids remember getting a break from classes to watch Lassie being filmed in Railroad Creek. Both adults and children also were invited to a performance by the dog and his handlers in the recreation hall. A few families were close enough to the movie sets to chuckle about how even the alpine scenery had to be enhanced; one man watched the movie crew paint and rehang the apples that Taylor ate in the film.[10]

Far more dramatic were the scenes that sent old locomotives and loads of logs off trestles and over cliffs. In 1926, Buster Keaton filmed *The General* near Black Rock, Oregon, and the Willamette Valley Lumber Company logging camps. A vintage Oregon & Southeastern locomotive met disaster—just as scripted—on a 110-foot-high temporary trestle. For *God's Country and the Woman*, produced near Longview, Washington, in 1936, forty loggers worked as extras in a Warner Brothers film that sent several carloads of logs tumbling over a cliff and down into the Toutle River. For *Ring of Fire*, filmed near Grisdale in 1960, the producer got state permission to destroy an old locomotive on the abandoned trestle over the Wynooche River. When one of the Hollywood cameras didn't catch the engine's 300-foot fall into the ravine, Metro-Goldwyn-Mayer bought fifteen feet of footage that a Grisdale bulldozer operator had shot with his home movie camera. Several other employees had bit parts or worked behind the camera with the movie crew. More conventional scenes for the same film were shot in Vernonia, Oregon, a timber town near the site of Clark & Wilson's long-ago Wilark. Thirty years later, portions of the Patrick Swayze film *Point Break* were photographed in Wheeler, another Oregon coast community founded as a company town.[11]

Washington and Oregon company-town sites attracted film crews as different as Disney and the federal government. Grisdale was still operating when it was the setting for a United States Information Agency documentary featuring the veteran Simpson Timber high rigger Frank Brehmeyer. Most of the central Oregon logging camps were gone, however, by the time the pine forests were attracting stars like Richard Boone in *Have Gun, Will Travel*, John Wayne and Katharine Hepburn in *Rooster Cogburn*, and a couple of dogs and a sassy cat in *Homeward Bound: The Incredible Journey*. Brookings, once an isolated southern Oregon coast village, was the setting for *Timber*, released in 1977. A decade later, *The Year in Lincoln Plains* was filmed not far from Kinzua, Oregon, by then a tree farm. Astoria, Oregon, which was the market center for dozens of little logging camps, including the Olney camp where Sam Churchill grew up, is today a popular location for such movies as Steven Spielberg's *Goonies* and Arnold Schwarzenegger's *Kindergarten Cop*. Even the Teenage Mutant Ninja Turtles and Madonna have been to Astoria.[12]

Cedar Falls, Washington, substituted for the Rocky Mountains when parts of the 1981 John Belushi movie *Continental Divide* were filmed at the local train depot. Locals were proud of the Seattle City Light employee Cecil Geelhart, who had a tiny role. Neighboring North Bend was the setting for the *Twin Peaks* television series about the same time. Dick Van Dyke filmed *The Runner Stumbles* in Roslyn, Washington, in the 1970s, but the old coal-mining town was really introduced to the world in 1990 when it was turned into fictitious Cecily, Alaska, for the quirky *Northern Exposure* television series. A frequent backdrop in the show was the faded Northwestern Improvement Company sign still visible on the long-ago company store. Another mountain town, Seattle City Light's Newhalem, was one of the settings for Matthew Broderick's *War Games* in 1982; nearby Diablo Dam has shown up in several thrillers. In 1992, Robert De Niro and Leonardo DiCaprio were on location just a few miles away in Concrete for *This Boy's Life*, about the author Tobias Wolff's boyhood home in Skagit County.

Some of the people who grew up in company towns would become media darlings; others would work to create celebrities. Roy Craft, who as a teenager ran one of the first newspapers in McCleary, Washington, went on to Twentieth Century Fox and a job as Marilyn Monroe's press agent; he claimed credit for the famous photo of the actress with her skirt billowing up over a heat grate. Another McClearyite, Clarence "Major Mite" Howerton, worked on-screen with Judy Garland; reportedly only twenty-eight inches tall, he played a Munchkin in *The Wizard of Oz*, took bit parts in other movies, and appeared for two decades with the Ringling Brothers, Barnum & Bailey circus. (In between gigs, the adult Howerton would dress in children's clothes and wander the streets of McCleary, mischievously shocking passersby with his cigars and obscenities.) The community's third entertainment-world celebrity was the musician Cecil "Primo" Boling, who grew to be almost eight feet tall.[13]

McCleary's man of letters was the award-winning Angelo Pellegrini, who would go from the timber town to Seattle, where he eventually taught English at the University of Washington, wrote and cooked. His thought-ful books like *Immigrant's Return* (1951) remain well respected. His cookbooks, still in print a dozen years after his death, earned him enthusiastic reviews in the *New York Times*. A hundred or so miles south, another timber town had a young woman recognized for her journalistic efforts: Dorothy Anne Hobson, who as a nine-year-old began the monthly *Valsetz Star* newspaper. By the time she was thirteen, Dorothy Anne had traveled the ninety miles north to Oregon's largest city to be grand marshal of the Portland Rose Festival parade, she'd been written up in the *Christian Science Monitor* and the *New York Herald-Tribune*, and she'd made her first flight— a trip to Los Angeles for a guest spot on a national radio program. (Where she discovered, she reported, that no one had heard of Valsetz, and some people hadn't even heard of Portland.)[14]

Other company-owned communities had more fleeting relationships with those who had been or would become famous. Some people say that A. C. Gilbert, who invented the Erector set, spent part of his boyhood in an Oregon timber camp. The broadcaster Edward R. Murrow lived a few years in Blanchard, Washington, where his father, Roscoe, worked for the Samish Bay Logging Company. The film star Lana Turner was born in Wallace, Idaho, in the heart of the Panhandle's silver-mining communities. Seattle pioneer David Denny financed prospector James Holden's first trips to the North Cascades, but when the mining claims were filed, Holden conveniently left Denny's name off. The family name *was* on the factory that built most of Taylor, Washington: the Denny-Renton Clay & Coal Company.[15]

Some celebrities never saw the towns their relatives founded. Brookings was partly financed by John E. Brookings's cousin Robert, a St. Louis businessman better known for his longstanding support of the Brookings Institution. Beebe, Washington, an orchard camp on the Columbia River, was built by the family of Lucius Beebe, a writer and train aficionado. Samuel Clemens, better known as Mark Twain, was a distant relative of Carl and Hugh Clemans, the brothers who built Alpine. Carbonado, one of Washington's many coal-mining towns, was for several years owned by the "Big Four," the California rail barons Leland Stanford, Charles Crocker, Collis Huntington, and Mark Hopkins. None of them probably ever set foot in the town or in the nearby coal-mining hamlet named for Crocker alone, although Stanford's brother-in-law did bring his young daughter for a visit in the early 1900s.[16]

Others brought fame to company towns after the company influence had faded. Moulton Taylor, whose fanciful Aerocar could convert from a car to a plane in ten minutes, was an aeronautical engineer who ran his company from Longview, Washington. But R. A. Long was long dead and his company headed for acquisition by a corporate giant by the time Taylor's little vehicle flew across television screens on the popular 1950s *Bob Cummings Show* and onto the stage of the quiz show *I've Got A Secret.* Long, however, might have enjoyed knowing that Ford Motor Company executives finally made their way to Longview—even if the trip was to look over Taylor's invention, not Long's sawmill.

Today Taylor's Aerocars are museum pieces and so are the remnants of Northwest company-town life. The towns and their founders get an occasional sentence in travel guides and the remaining town sites are sometimes promoted as movie locations by government film offices, but seldom do you see any of the communities mentioned in headlines. They are no longer worthy of celebrity—now nothing more than curious anachronisms to the casual tourist and interesting footnotes to the history buff.

14 / The Paternalistic Company Town Boss

Hard-nosed businessmen determined to boost productivity and avoid unions; government bureaucrats pressured to meet wartime deadlines; entrepreneurs eager to test their theories about corporate welfare—they were all company-town bosses. Some were not ashamed to be regarded as dictators. Others considered themselves benevolent father figures, even fairy godfathers. Many were just doing a job, running massive construction projects and vital research projects, sewage treatment plants and movie houses.

The men who built corporate towns in the early 1900s styled themselves as latter-day George Pullmans, convinced they could avoid the mistakes made by the rail-car manufacturer in his Chicago suburb of the 1880s. Like Pullman, they wanted to create a better life for their employees: decent housing, good schools, and a "morally uplifting" society. In return, they expected stable, hard-working employees who would eschew the evils of drink and, most important, not fall prey to the blandishments of union organizers. The bureaucrats and government contractors who built communities like Coulee Dam and Richland three or four decades later had more realistic expectations. These town builders could legislate out prostitution and gambling and the gossip about war work, but they could no longer evict union members or fire every parent of a misbehaving school kid.

When you read histories of the early western Washington coal towns, you see control—control driven by greed. In the coal towns where the company owned everything, early managers were likely to demand that all shopping take place in town. If the company store didn't have it, nobody needed it, the boss believed. Those who wanted to work for the company lived in company housing and paid their rent to the company. Those who ran businesses operated in company-owned storefronts—and they sold only to those approved by the company. When the strikes came, as they always did, the grocers and butchers and saloonkeepers knew they had to close their doors to the strikers.

In towns like Potlatch, Idaho, and DuPont, Washington, built early in the twentieth century, drinking was a greater concern than greed. Like Pullman, the timbermen who founded Potlatch were determined to control liquor. They considered allowing a saloon where they could limit how much workers drank but finally decided to ban liquor completely—in town and for miles around. To keep opportunistic entrepreneurs from building taverns along the Potlatch Lumber Company's new railroad, the company kept its railway construction plans secret until it was too late for liquor licenses to be granted. In some communities, the company did allow one— but only one—tavern. When Alfred Anderson, a lumberman associate of Sol Simpson and the Bordeaux brothers, started construction of another Potlatch, his Phoenix Logging Company town on Hood Canal, he bought up miles of beach property to ensure that he could control when—and where—the only saloon was built. In company-owned coal towns, the company may not have run the tavern, but it owned all of the retail buildings; in towns like Roslyn, early leases stipulated that no business other than the company could sell liquor.[1]

Even after World War I, company towns and camps were typically dry. In Longview, the Washington city established (but not owned) by the Long-Bell Lumber Company founder, R. A. Long, the city eventually licensed beer sales, but the company-owned Ryderwood didn't have a tavern or sell beer in the grocery store. Holden, a central Washington copper-mining town built in the late 1930s, never had a tavern or a liquor store, although employees were free to carry in liquor—and many did return from trips outside with suitcases full of bottles. No liquor was sold in Grisdale, Washington, either, but little was said about the loggers who left community dances for quick nips from bottles left outside. In contrast, in the 1930s, Gilchrist, Oregon, was built with one retail space to be leased to a tavern, and the

Shevlin, Oregon, camp clerk operated a tavern in a company-owned building for years.[2]

Drinking wasn't the only aspect of employee behavior that many companies were determined to control. The Potlatch Lumber Company monitored the behavior of hotel maids and waitresses, immediately firing (and thus driving out of town) those suspected of "straying from the path of virtue." A teacher who became romantically involved with a student and a bachelor employee who fathered a high school student's child also were fired. To ensure that their workers weren't exposed to morally questionable entertainment, Potlatch managers, just like George Pullman, reviewed both the content of theater productions and the advertising for plays and movies. As late as 1940, they were objecting to movies with titles like *Sin*. In McCleary, although bootlegging, moonshining, and gambling drew little attention, the editors of the community newspaper were discouraged from running ads for the downtown brothel. Old-timers in Brookings, Oregon, claim that in the early 1900s, when prostitution flourished in the isolated timber community, the company owner, John Brookings, had his mess hall cook lace meals with saltpeter. (But business still boomed at the local bordello, noted a history written by the local Rotary Club.) In the mid-1920s, when one Longview matron wanted to hold her bridge luncheon at the company-built Community House, the manager insisted on writing Kansas City for permission from the town founder, R. A. Long. Long said no: cards were gambling and gambling was immoral. It took a direct appeal from the would-be hostess, explaining that no money exchanged hands at ladies' bridge games, before Long allowed the luncheon. At Valsetz, Oregon, loggers and mill hands couldn't buy beer in the company store in the 1950s, and sometimes they couldn't even find copies of girlie magazines; when the owner, Herbert Templeton, came to visit, the racier publications were hidden away.[3]

Keeping labor from organizing—or keeping unions subservient to the company—was the other most common aspect of company-town control. As the Tacoma daily paper wrote in 1918 about McKenna, Washington, executives were evaluated based on how distant they kept the union: "It is so far a successful experiment in keeping a Northwest mill running without labor troubles." In many logging camps and mill towns of that era, management fought off the Industrial Workers of the World (the organization known as the IWW or Wobblies) and then, to give workers a token union, introduced the Loyal Legion of Loggers and Lumbermen, the Four L. Several years before the Wobblies and the Four L, Potlatch Lumber Company employees who organized themselves into a group to present complaints of any kind to management were fired; a man who went to his boss alone was—according to early managers' comments—safe from punishment. Potlatch strikers were told to draw their pay, pack up, and leave; once they were no longer employees, they did not have the right to stay in town, especially for picketing. When the Wobblies became a threat across the Northwest, the Potlatch Lumber Company organized a citizen militia, supposedly to prepare workers who might soon be drafted for World War I. Some wondered, however, if the militia's frequent drills and their obvious weapons were intended as a deterrent to any Wobbly attacks.[4]

In 1921, when Washington coal-mine owners decided to cut employees' wages almost 25 percent, the miners went on strike and were ordered out of their homes. In some towns, when miners ignored the eviction demands, the mine managers went to court for a judge's help in forcing out workers. In 1939, when Howe Sound employees at Britannia, British Columbia, demanded safer working conditions and better food and lodging, the agitators were pulled from their beds one night and shipped out of camp. The same year workers at Howe Sound's Holden Mine struck for higher wages; later some residents questioned if that strike prompted the company's refusal to build a community swimming pool like those provided at the British Columbia mine.[5]

That the timber town owner Henry McCleary hated unions was well documented. Although Simpson Timber Company (which bought McCleary's town and company in the early 1940s) was tactful in its description of McCleary as "a flinty man" equal to the "demanding task of building a business," a 1930s union supporter screamed about the executive's treatment of union organizers. "Never a feudal baron of the dark ages ruled his land more despotically than the McCleary Timber Co. rules McCleary," claimed an article entitled "The Little Kingdom of M'Cleary." The author insisted that the McCleary saloon keeper who provided meeting space for union members was punished by having his lights and water turned off and then was harassed by the state police and liquor inspectors. Even gentle Angelo Pellegrini, who grew up in McCleary before and during World War I, pointed out the town had a well-established structure: one church, one school, and one boss.[6]

In some towns, that structure was very obvious. In Richland, Washington, built during World War II, government bureaucracy imposed rigid and far-reaching regulations, dictating where residents could park their cars and when they could water their lawns, when stores opened and closed, how churches were organized, and whether commercial buildings were identified by names or only numbers. Ted Goodwin, who pastored in the Long-Bell Lumber Company camp of Ryderwood, Washington, in the 1930s, recalled, "The company controlled the city, body and soul. If the preacher didn't shape up, he could be shipped out just like any gandy dancer or bull cook." Even when life was less formal and rules unwritten, every employee knew who the boss was—and he undoubtedly knew who each worker was. At Whites, Washington, not far from McCleary, the owners of the White Star Mill knew every employee by name. At DuPont, Washington, as late as the 1970s, the manager signed birthday cards for every employee. Especially in the most remote communities, it was typical for bosses to interview both prospective employees and their wives. Some women felt they were being inspected, but they also believed managers were trying to be honest in depicting the clique-ridden, sometimes claustrophobic society of isolated small towns.[7]

The dictates of the company often extended to government, both in elected and appointed positions. In towns like McCleary and Kinzua, relatives of the founder were appointed to the federal postmaster jobs; almost every school board was packed with company management. In Eatonville, Washington, where the community was for years dominated by the Eatonville Lumber Company, a school board candidate rallied his supporters as the 1932 election neared. "Let us demonstrate that ours is NOT a one-man community," George Moen's campaign ad exclaimed. "Vote to free our school district from despotism." His opponent, Moen pointed out, determined who got the town and school jobs and where the school district made its purchases: "He is The Boss." (Moen beat the lumber company president, John Galbraith, 392–296 for the school board seat, but Galbraith retained what was probably a greater political plum: his position as mayor.)[8]

When the company didn't own all the businesses in town, it often controlled them through land leases. Although there were sometimes legitimate reasons for not selling land (unwillingness to give up ownership of mineral rights under storefronts, for example), the company's retention of all land resulted in its ability to control both business owners and the kinds and numbers of businesses allowed. In modern Gilchrist, Oregon, the Gilchrist Timber Company provided space for only one business of a kind, ensuring monopolies for the grocery, restaurant, theater, tavern, and barber. In government towns, the number and kind of businesses also were limited. When the federal Bureau of Reclamation began work by the Grand Coulee Dam site, it received hundreds of applications from small business owners who wanted to open stores, but the government instead decided to control the atmosphere of its model town by limiting commercial ventures. Even traveling salespeople had to get permits when they came to town. In Richland, merchants were similarly controlled: until the late 1940s, no one could buy a business or the land on which to build one. When the *Tri-City Herald* publisher attempted to rent office space in Richland, he was told the community already had a newspaper—and one was enough. All the town needed, the Atomic Energy Commission decreed, was the little paper issued by a nonprofit organization—a weekly that focused on social, club, church, school, sports, and "dorm" news, with reports on electrical outages and the dog pound, but seldom a word on the government "plant."[9]

The bosses controlled who lived in company towns, too. In towns like Potlatch and Gilchrist and Richland, no one could buy a house. In most communities, only employees could rent. In Potlatch, Idaho, where the company preferred married workers, bachelors couldn't rent houses. If they didn't want to live in boarding houses, managers declared, the men could work elsewhere. Even if there had been other housing available within commuting distance, neither bachelors nor single women had the option to live outside town: in its early years, the Potlatch Lumber Company hired only residents. In Richland, homes were rented only to those who worked at the plant, or in what earlier company towns had been called the town site department: a business, school, church, or other local facility. As late as 1960, people who lost their jobs in Richland also lost their leases on their government-owned houses.[10]

In those towns where having a home was tied directly to having a job, bosses had a double weapon against infractions on the job, at home, and in school. In no case was this used more often than in union activism; western Washington coal companies made renters sign leases that prohibited the presence of union organizers—even as visitors—in company-owned houses. Home maintenance wasn't as serious an issue as activism, but many companies threatened to evict those who didn't keep up their yards. In Gilchrist, it was Frank W. Gilchrist himself who drove around town, upbraiding those whose yards weren't clean and tidy. In Potlatch, Idaho, early managers threatened to fire the fathers of children who misbehaved in school. This, an early visitor to town piously reported, "has the ideal advantage of throwing the responsibility of disciplining the child upon the parent." Forty years later, the bosses at Richland used a similar threat: if you couldn't control your kids, you might lose your security clearance—and your job. Up on the Skagit River, Seattle City Light managers didn't threaten to fire the parents of errant teenagers, but when kids kept pouring water in the school bus gas tank in 1959, the bosses were quick to point out that no one required them to provide transportation to school. To make its position on vandalism clear, City Light shut down the bus service for a few days, leaving Newhalem and Diablo students to get themselves the thirty to forty miles to Concrete High School.[11]

The requirement to rent from the boss, especially when the boss was an impersonal federal agency, sometimes led to a lack of community spirit. By the early 1950s, almost twenty years after work had started on Grand Coulee Dam, the Mason City and Coulee Dam settlements still hadn't developed the cohesiveness typical of company towns like Holden, Gilchrist, and Valsetz. It took a long time before townspeople could sustain clubs, church congregations, and civic projects, partly because of the transient atmosphere caused by the frequent turnover of construction workers and the general lack of job security. The Mason City neighborhood also suffered from changes in ownership: it was constructed by one dam contractor, sold to the second, and then reverted to federal control.[12]

In some towns, prices were low, jobs were good, houses were comfortable—but the paternalism was unavoidable. A few entrepreneurs ran their towns as if they were playing God. "His hobby is this company," a Tacoma newspaper wrote about the McKenna Lumber Company owner, R. W. Tweedy, in 1918. Because Tweedy ran both the company and the town, the lumberman "had all the fun of being logging camp, mill, railroad, store, land owner, dairyman, real estate dealer and a sort of fairy godfather capitalist." He was successful, Tweedy told the reporter, because he gave his laborers what they wanted before they knew they wanted it. Henry McCleary, who more than once declared, "A good kingdom is better than a poor democracy," was famous (or notorious) for bailing out favorite employees jailed after imbibing too much mountain dew. Some old-timers believe that McCleary, like other bosses of the era, maintained a bail fee account with the county sheriff for company mill workers. According to local legend, McCleary also rescued employees on other occasions; once he supposedly overheard the confrontation when a worker's car was being repossessed, strode over to the parking lot, and pulled out enough cash to cover the past-due payments. The federal government also was well known for its paternalism. In Richland, Washington, the Atomic Energy Commission provided plenty of police protection and so there were almost no crime or traffic problems. Medical care was free—and good. Rents were low, and the AEC paid for all utilities, so no one ever had to turn off their lights or their lawn sprinkler. But, especially after the war, residents resented the rigid control of the AEC and its contractor, the General Electric Company. The AEC-controlled weekly newspaper ran government edicts as front-page news: "Taking of Shrubs Must Stop," said one article, threatening "dire penalties" for "despoilers of government property" who transplanted government-planted shrubs to their own yards. Nor could local workers help themselves to the vegetables and fruit left in the fields by farmers when the government condemned the Richland area and seized everything: "Armed Forces to Get All Produce," announced another front-page article, emphasizing that "local pilfering . . . will not be tolerated."[13]

Some company mandates reflected corporate values or the managers' preferences. At Holden, Howe Sound financed the construction of many miner-built houses and regulated the sales price of all of them. To keep housing affordable and eliminate speculation, Howe Sound required that a house be sold for no more than its original cost plus the value of any improvements. At Cedar Falls, no one who worked for the City of Seattle power plant could have a dog. The barking would wake the men who worked night shifts and slept during the day, children were told—but some suspected that the longtime power plant superintendent simply didn't like dogs. In

Town founders and company managers often were lauded for
their business acumen and generosity by chambers of commerce
and company insiders. "Selleck is alive with industry," exclaimed
the publisher of a nearby newspaper in 1925, citing the "splendid"
labor conditions, the safe, modern mills, and the "sanitary" town
as evidence that the Pacific States Lumber Company manager
was "wide awake to the interests of the 250 people in the employ
of the company." In nearby Wilkeson, the publisher continued,
there was "complete harmony between employee and employer
and an entire absence of labor controversies" due to the "able
management and diplomacy" of the mill manager. Company
histories written by insiders are equally likely to portray town
founders as fairy godfathers. Ernest Teagle, whose family had
both business and personal ties to the founder of McCleary,
wrote, "Henry McCleary seemed to feel the obligation of man-
aging a 'one-man town.'. . . He was judge and jury in many
cases . . . and often aided a man when he got into trouble with
the law." Although many labeled McCleary a tightwad, Teagle
describes him only as "a prudent saver of small coin."

Others were direct in their condemnation of town-owner crit-
ics. In a 1924 special section devoted to Oregon's Pacific Spruce
Corporation, the Lumber World Review *wrote, "During the*
last ten years the American lumber manufacturer . . . has done
marvelous things for the comfort of the people who were associ-
ated with him, but we even yet hear a lot of loose talk from
anarchistic, bolshevistic-minded men concerning the attitude
of the logging and lumber-manufacturing fraternity toward the
care of its people; and so we have set out to show, with pictures
and pen, that the Pacific Spruce Corporation has not overlooked
an opportunity . . . to arrange for the comfort of its people."
(Sources: Louis Jacobis, "A Glimpse of the Charmed Land"
[1925], pp. 17, 20; Ernest C. Teagle, "An Informal Biography
of the Teagle Family" [1960], p. 11, and Out of the Woods: The
Story of McCleary *[1956], p. 9, Pacific Spruce Corporation*
and Subsidiaries *[1924], p. 82.)*

Potlatch, the company dictated where chickens could roam and what could be put into garbage cans. Other regulations, regardless of their intention, separated town residents into classes. At Cedar Falls, where the City of Seattle had built a swimming pool for its employees, families from the neighboring railroad and logging camps were resentful that they couldn't use the pool except as guests of city employees. At Coulee Dam, the government-built pool was reserved for Bureau of Reclamation employees (mostly engineering professionals and managers) and the children from Mason City, the community built for the dam contractors' skilled employees. If you worked on the dam but hadn't qualified for housing in either the USBR'S Government Town or Mason City, you weren't welcome at the pool.[14]

Some policies reflect the era. At Richland, the government and its contractors brought in thousands of people to work on wartime weaponry. Everyone was strictly forbidden to discuss their jobs. "Nobody knew what anyone else was working on," one local historian noted. Although the secrecy sometimes made sense, people didn't like the restrictions, especially when the Atomic Energy Commission dictates continued after the war. Even in the late 1940s, if anything somewhat newsworthy happened on the atomic project, it was kept secret until the AEC and General Electric had written, rewritten, and finally approved an official press release. Getting news from someone other than the AEC and GE was nearly impossible: the importance of secrecy was so deeply ingrained in Richland residents that few would risk talking to a reporter.[15]

The paternalism intended to protect children was easier to accept. At Holden and Grisdale, where the single workers were sometimes rough-talking, hard-drinking transient laborers, children couldn't enter the men's dorms. Paperboys could walk through the Holden bunkhouses to make their deliveries, but they didn't knock on doors to collect without the moral and physical support of their fathers. When Wellington Phillips was a Holden Mine manager, he also made sure paperboys didn't get stiffed by men who had quit their jobs; more than once Phillips collected subscription fees from a miner already aboard the outgoing bus. Children were sheltered in other ways. Although McCleary was notorious for its gambling and bootlegging, the prostitutes working above Roy and Ray Craft's newspaper office never invited the teenage journalists up—or, in fact, even discussed the nature of the upstairs business. "Gamblers, moonshiners and prostitutes respected

This 1945 paycheck stub for a Holden employee shows the deductions typical in company-owned towns: Board, Store, Club (the seventy-five cents due the recreational association), and, added by hand, "March of Dimes." (Courtesy of Gayle Rodgers Davidson)

young people whose parents were church-going," Roy Craft would later note. At Holden, teenagers had to be sixteen to participate in community-wide dances; younger children could attend, but only to watch the fun from the recreation hall balcony. The paternalism in some towns lasted long after the towns were sold off; in DuPont, when a trio of young children took a stroll down the railroad tracks one morning in the 1970s, the Burlington Northern crew whisked them into the caboose, gave them a lecture about venturing to the powder plant, and then slowly backed the train into town to return the kids to their frantic parents.

Many company owners also took care of the elderly and sick. For more than forty years starting in the 1920s, the Simpson Timber Company executive Mark Reed paid a barber to tend to hospitalized employees so that they'd look good when their families visited. Company executives or their wives sometimes sat with injured workers waiting for transportation to hospitals or accompanied the injured to medical facilities. When recession and depression forced companies to spread work around by employing only one member of each family, managers occasionally could find extra work for a family struggling with medical bills. Elderly loggers who couldn't afford to retire might find themselves gardening or making beds in a timber camp; even penny-pinching Henry McCleary is given credit for rescuing a former employee from the county poor farm.[16]

Making sure bills were paid was one example of company-town paternalism that benefited the local merchants. Occasionally, bosses also reviewed the prices in privately owned stores, to ensure that workers weren't being charged too much. Some managers monitored how much credit was being granted, to protect workers from becoming indebted. In Holden, as in many communities, the bosses determined how much scrip could be charged against future paychecks. In remote areas, one of the managers sometimes acted as a banker for the bachelors; in Oregon, during the 1930s and 1940s, the couple who managed the mess hall and bunkhouses also held on to paychecks for loggers determined to accumulate some savings.[17]

Company towns had a reputation for keeping employees indentured and trapped in low-paying, menial jobs, and that image is reinforced by the memories of some western Washington coal miners. The strikes that forced them out of the mines and into other occupations were their salvations, some said. In other industries, employees found that company-town living made it easy to save money. One Selleck, Washington, mill hand said he could send at least $80.00 a month home in the early 1920s, despite earning only $3.50 to $4.00 a day. When the Holden Mine opened in the late 1930s, the low cost of living allowed many to leave Holden with what one miner called a grubstake. No one needed a car because he could walk to work, housing was inexpensive, and stove wood was free for the cutting; all anyone really had to buy were clothes and groceries. At Grisdale, Washington, loggers didn't even have to buy many groceries; the local meat market wasn't well patronized because of the abundant game in the woods around the logging camp.[18]

Whether people lived in relative comfort and security or struggled to survive was determined by the company. Even those who cherish the memories of their company-town years acknowledge the paternalism. A job in a company town was more than employment, it was a way of life—the boss's way.

15 / When the Town Shut Down

Some company towns died almost overnight: the mine or mill shut its doors without notice at the end of a shift and never reopened. Other communities faded away slowly, as ore prices declined or timber supplies diminished, as the bosses cut back from three shifts to two and then to one, as the bunkhouses emptied, and the schools closed. Some towns didn't die, but they had to learn to make it on their own when the company decided it was getting out of the landlord business.

Across the United States, there were many different reasons that employers liquidated their towns. Some towns simply weren't needed: the mine or mill or factory had closed. Even when the employer was still in business, the operations may have been automated and the work site was no longer so remote: the few remaining workers could commute. Most corporate executives grew exasperated with maintaining town sites, especially as buildings and utility systems aged. Companies also found they could generate more income from their land through property sales or redevelopment; condominiums and marinas were more profitable than lime kilns and sawmills. Employees often didn't want to live in houses they couldn't own and in neighborhoods where everyone knew what everybody earned. In Washington, some towns were closed down by municipalities determined to protect their water supplies; watershed managers, anxious about pollution and sewage, forced out the logging camps, the clay mines, and the railroad roundhouses. Tragedy closed more than a few communities. When

When the Weyerhaeuser Company closed down its Snoqualmie Falls town site in 1958,
employees could buy houses for as little as $100 and have them moved across the river
to nearby Snoqualmie. One family moved the house it had lived in since 1923.
(Courtesy of the Weyerhaeuser Company Archives)

fires and floods and slides devastated mills and mines and railroads, many
employers had little choice but to liquidate. They (or their bankers) auc-
tioned off the equipment, pulled up the rails to sell for scrap and offered
houses for $25 or $50 to anyone who would move them. Many companies
and communities were one-man operations—and when that one man
retired or died, the business and the town died.

Some communities were built to be short-lived; although their closures
were mourned, they weren't unexpected. At logging camps like Shevlin,
Oregon, and Grisdale, Washington, houses were on "sleds" or skids so they

could be moved to new locations whenever the trees were gone. But the end came for villages like these when the company sold or took a new direction: Shevlin, the last of the Shevlin-Hixon Company camps, was closed soon after its owner sold to Brooks-Scanlon in 1950. Grisdale was razed after forty years, when Simpson Timber stopped logging high-elevation old-growth timber. Mowich, which always operated on a seasonal basis, shut down for good when the Deschutes Lumber Company moved from Oregon to northern California in 1944. But by then there were few loggers left in Mowich; many had already departed for better-paying defense-industry jobs. Wilark, a Columbia County, Oregon, camp named for the father-and-son team that owned it, closed in the early 1930s; all that remains of it are the few houses moved to nearby Vernonia during the late 1940s. The Western Cooperage camp near Olney, Oregon, that was memorialized in Sam Churchill's books was closed down about the same time; now there's nothing left of it and not much of Olney, either.

Towns like Holden, Washington, had what writers liked to call "an air of permanence," and some townspeople claimed to be shocked when closures were announced. Even when Holden was new, however, its owner predicted a short life, perhaps as brief as ten years. Starting in 1955, company managers had warned new hires that the mine might close in two or three years. Today volunteer guides at Holden's museum sometimes claim that miners were laid off with little notice, forced to leave their homes with dishes on the table and toys in the yard. The truth, however, is that Holden employees received several months of notice: the closure was announced in February 1957, and the mine continued to operate until the end of June. Many employees found new jobs before the closure; by the time newspaper photographers were in Holden recording "the last day of school forever," at least forty families were gone. After they'd sent their cars and moving vans downlake, miners could still return. They could even dismantle their houses and barge them out, if they wanted. Some made several visits back until winter storms closed the road to the village. A few former residents continued to make day trips to the abandoned village for years afterward. Janet Adams Westom, whose brother Nigel would later document the mine and town's history, was interviewed by a *National Geographic* crew during a return visit in 1960.

Although all of the Holden town site is located on Forest Service land

and the original government lease specified that the buildings were to be demolished when the mine closed, none of the miners' homes were razed until the early 1960s, after the community was given away. Revived as Holden Village, privately owned by the Lutheran church, the town is now a year-round home for about fifty people who live in the houses built for mining executives; their children attend school in the same building where miners' kids studied. Thousands of visitors arrive when the snow begins to melt, all still coming in via the *Lady of the Lake* and her successors or the same trails that prospectors traveled as much as a century ago. Every couple of years, the last of the Holden miners, now elderly, bring their children and grandchildren up the lake for a reunion.[1]

Several small western Washington towns were forced out of existence because of industrial and residential wastes that threatened to contaminate metropolitan water supplies. In Barneston, which the Kent Lumber Company sold to the City of Seattle in 1911 to avoid condemnation, workers had more than a decade of notice: the town wasn't vacated until 1923. Twenty-some years later, the people in Taylor, another town located in the City of Seattle watershed, also had ample warning. The local coal mines had closed in 1921, followed by the clay mines. Although tile and brick manufacturing continued, the Seattle city council voted in 1944 to acquire the town. The owner, Gladding, McBean & Company, was still negotiating in mid-1946, and when the clay works finally agreed to sell, fewer than a hundred people were left in town. Workers who owned their own homes (none of them owned the land) had at least a few months to move or dismantle the houses. Even those who lost their homes did not lose their jobs: Gladding, McBean moved Taylor workers to its two other local operations. The town of Lester shrunk after the Northern Pacific switched to diesel locomotives and no longer needed a station for the helper engines that had assisted steam trains over the Cascade Mountains, but Lester was forced out of existence by the City of Tacoma. Because Lester, like Nagrom and Baldi, was built within Tacoma's watershed, the city wanted the town demolished to prevent pollution. It began acquiring property in the area after World War II and in 1967 bought the Lester town site from the railroad. The city's control increased after a 1985 change in state school funding closed the school. Lester did not die quietly, however: the remaining handful of residents went to court for the right to stay. Even as the twentieth century ended, Gertrude Murphy, the community's last resident, was still providing local newspapers with colorful quotes about her differences with Tacoma officials.[2]

The last remnants of Manley-Moore, Melmont, and Fairfax were razed by the railroad. Built on Northern Pacific railroad land grants, these Washington villages faded away after their mines and mills closed in the 1920s and '30s; the few homeowners who stayed were forced out in 1991 by Burlington Northern, which controlled the land leases through its acquisition of the Northern Pacific. There's a gate across the road that used to lead to Valsetz, built high in the Oregon Coast Range early in the 1900s. When its final owner, Boise Cascade, closed the mill early in 1984, it let the school graduate one last class and then bulldozers took down the town. Today trees once again cover the site. It's the same at Kinzua, another Oregon mill town: their community razed in 1978, the old-timers meet in nearby Fossil for their annual picnic.

Many of Puget Sound's former company towns continue to shelter boats, but today the boats are yachts, not steamships and ferries. Roche Harbor, built because of lime mines and kilns, was sold by the founding family in the mid-1950s. The new owner fulfilled the few existing lime contracts and then converted the Victorian-era village to a resort. The former mill town of Port Ludlow is a resort, too, transformed by its longtime owners, Pope & Talbot. Port Blakely, sold after its founder's death and then sold again, is quiet now, with vacation homes and a dock near the site of the old sawmill and shipyard.

The transition to private ownership was made easier in those towns where the company continued to operate. In Potlatch, Idaho, the company took more than a decade to ease its way out of the town site business. The bank was sold in 1940 and the schools donated to a new consolidated district in 1948. By early 1952, several Potlatch Forests employees were working on the sale of nearly 300 homes and buildings. Tenants could buy their own homes, and to reassure townspeople that it wasn't looking for a quick profit, the company guaranteed that most of the purchase price would be refunded if the mill closed before the ten-year mortgages were paid off. The company gave the churches to their congregations and turned over the library and the fire hall, complete with fire truck, to the new village of Potlatch. Most workers did keep their jobs: the company-owned Potlatch Mercantile stayed open until it burned in 1963, and the mill ran until 1981.

In DuPont, Washington, built about the same time as Potlatch, the houses also were sold off in the early 1950s, but the company continued to allow widows and retirees to rent. The explosives plant operated for another quarter-century. By the time it closed, employment had gradually dwindled, so there were only a hundred or so to be laid off. Far more traumatic was the eventual development of the explosives site as a planned community for Fortune 500 firms; by the mid-1990s, quiet little DuPont found itself overwhelmed by thousands of new homes and commuters streaming into new office buildings and high-technology manufacturing facilities.

Henry McCleary sold his southwestern Washington town to Simpson Timber with little warning just as World War II started, but his door plant continued to operate without interruption, and the new owner gave McCleary workers more than a year to prepare for buying their homes and creating a local government. Simpson sold the houses for the equivalent of eighteen months of rent payments, which were then $6 to $12. In central Oregon, when the Gilchrist family sold its mill in 1991, the transition was just as gradual: no one lost a job, and a trio of Gilchrist grandsons operated, improved, and eventually began to sell off the town site.[3]

In federally supported towns like Coulee Dam and Richland, Washington, government subsidies eased the way to independence. Especially in Richland, where townspeople didn't even have to change their own light bulbs as late as 1946, the change was a shock. The government had hired a consultant in 1947 for help in selling Richland, but townspeople protested the loss of federal support. The actual incorporation didn't take place until 1958, after the Atomic Energy Commission promised partial funding for another ten years. Although Richland residents disliked the AEC's rigid control, they were astounded by the costs of self-government and private ownership, especially when they saw the high sales prices set by federal appraisers on local homes. People were unwilling to give up rents as low as $27 that included appliances and utilities.[4]

Towns like Brookings, Oregon, lost their payroll almost overnight, but the transition to private ownership took years. Established after World War I by a California lumberman who found himself overextended, the village was soon sold to the California & Oregon Lumber Company. With the company's help, the town had just built itself a new high school and church when the mill unexpectedly closed down in 1925. It never ran again. The company tried to sell off its houses and storefronts, but people were streaming out of town, heading for jobs in other Oregon timber communities. The population shrank from fifteen hundred to a few hundred. A chance discovery by a local gardener led to the farming of lily bulbs; eventually Brookings provided 90 percent of the Easter lily bulbs in the United States. After World War II, the timber industry was revived, and sawmills and plywood plants were built near John Brookings's original site.[5]

Strikes, compounded by the effects of the economic slump that followed World War I, sealed the destiny of many western Washington coal towns. In those communities where the company owned everything, striking workers were forced from their houses and the businesses operating on company-owned land were forbidden to serve strikers. As the first year of the strike turned to a second and then a third, miners drifted away to other jobs, and businesses shut down. Hampered by the inefficiency of the inexperienced strikebreakers they had hired and by frequent accidents, many mines closed and their towns shrunk. In Wilkeson, Washington, which had as many as 3,000 residents when World War I started, there were fewer than 400 in 1936. Unlike in most small towns, however, consolidation saved Wilkeson's school; as the twenty-first century began, children still attended class in the landmark building constructed in 1913 of locally quarried sandstone. Not far away, townspeople are baptized and married in two historic churches. Nearby is Carbonado, which the Pacific Coast Coal Company continued to control after it sold out in the late 1930s; covenants prohibited both commercial businesses and the excavation necessary for sewage systems, new construction, and home improvements. The constraints were finally lifted in the 1960s, and Carbonado ended the twentieth century with a little more than half the people it had had in 1920. Black Diamond, farther north, had almost 4,000 people in 2000; the best-known business is not a coal mine but an old-style bakery left from the mining days. In the Cascades, historic Roslyn is quiet again after the spurt of fame brought by the television series *Northern Exposure* in the 1990s.

A few Northwest towns are still employer-owned. They declined slowly, without the surprise and sadness and layoffs that accompanied the closure of some corporate towns. In Cedar Falls, as Seattle City Light automated its power plant, many employees left for retirement and were not replaced; by 1977, only three families remained. Today, although no one lives in Cedar

Falls, old-fashioned street lamps still brighten the town site, and the last of the Craftsman-style houses helps you imagine the pristine mountaintop neighborhood where kids played kick-the-can and begged treats from mess hall cooks. City watershed employees work in the few remaining buildings, and a new visitor center stands near the site of the Milwaukee Road sub-station. The railroad right-of-way is a trail, with hikers trekking where locomotives used to chug their way into the mountains. Newhalem and Diablo, Seattle City Light's two villages high in the North Cascades mountain range, are also historic landmarks, but they have a few dozen residents each. The illuminated gardens that J. D. Ross carefully landscaped just after World War I have been replanted. Each summer thousands of tourists walk the terraced paths, tour the power plants, and take boat tours of Ross Lake, just as their grandparents might have done in the 1920s and '30s.[6]

Seattle City Light logo, early 1900s

There are also communities that remain privately owned, although their employers have been gone for decades. Some can hardly be called towns: their schools were long ago consolidated and their few stores closed. In Selleck, Washington, the Pacific States Lumber Company went bankrupt in 1939, but two former employees bought the company town for $3,000 and kept it for twenty-six years. The sawmill never operated again; its machinery was sold for salvage. But the houses stayed; during World War II, when Seattle war workers were desperate for housing, many commuted the thirty-odd miles to rent in Selleck. The town sold again in 1966 and once more in 1970; some said it was the perfect site for a college, others wanted to build an alcohol-rehabilitation center. But none of those dreams ever came to fruition, and by the turn of the twenty-first century, Selleck was almost a museum; not a building had been added since 1930. "Among the best pre-served examples of a lumber company town," historians said when they drafted a landmark application.[7]

Ask former company-town residents what it was like when the town closed or when they had to leave, and you'll hear many different answers. In towns where those without jobs couldn't stay, people approaching retirement knew they would have to move. Where there were no high schools, many families set their own deadlines for leaving: they began looking for new jobs and new homes a year or so before their oldest children finished grade school. When towns closed completely, even when the company provided months of notice, some people were stunned. Many had spent twenty or thirty years working for the company; a few had even grown up in the same town. Especially in the timber towns that closed in the 1980s, most workers were middle-aged and knew no other industry; many had no place to look for new jobs. Now he knew, one Valsetz, Oregon, man said bitterly, how a woman feels when she's divorced after twenty years of marriage. Even those employees who were offered transfers to other company operations often called the closures traumatic: they were, after all, losing their homes—both the physical houses and their neighborhoods, their clubs and schools and friends.[8]

But much of what the longtime residents had treasured about their towns was fading—or already gone—long before the company shut down its operations or ended its subsidies. Many of the companies had been sold to huge corporations, for whose accountants the little town in Idaho or Oregon or Washington was just another entry on the balance sheet. The personal touch was gone; the owner didn't live in town, and sometimes the superintendent didn't, either. The community spirit was different, too. In Potlatch, Idaho, many local clubs had closed and activities ended during the Depression, when the company quit paying for recreational programs. In Valsetz, Oregon, the ritual of waiting for the mail train that Dorothy Anne Hobson had cherished was almost forgotten by the time the town closed. In Gilchrist, Oregon, the gaily painted theater and the community dances drew fewer and fewer people once mill workers could entertain themselves at home with television.

Today most company towns exist only in the memory of the people who lived in the communities, in the stories they share at occasional reunions and in alumni newsletters, in the memoirs they write and the memorabilia they donate to local museums. But those who lived in company towns, even for only a few years, are likely to remember them with joy and delight. Who would have thought, one woman said, that such a brief period would have been so important in her family's life. "An experience of a lifetime," she said. "Something you just never forget," added another.

16 / The Bottom Line

What was life really like in a company town? How much did it differ from life in any other small town of the era? Were these good places to live?

Sometimes it's hard to articulate what was unique about company towns. Some historians insist that these communities differed little from other small towns of the late nineteenth and early twentieth centuries. The American West was dotted with tiny communities dependent on a single employer or a single industry or dominated by a few powerful businesspeople or ranchers. Some of these villages were just as remote as company towns. Many had the same frenzy of church, school, lodge, club, and charitable activities, the same streets of lookalike houses, the same two-room schools. Company towns were not unique in inspiring tight-knit neighborhoods where friendships endured for decades; some towns have high school alumni associations and annual picnics that, much like company-town alumni groups, sponsor newsletters and periodic reunions.

The irrefutable difference is the issue of ownership. In communities that companies owned, every job could depend on the company—on the company's success and on the boss's dictates. In both the earliest company-owned settlements, the logging camps, and in some of the last, the war-worker communities, the employers literally owned almost everything except an employee's clothes and bedroll. It is easy to suggest that smaller companies made better owners than large ones, that life in timber towns was more

Everyone knew everything about everyone in Alpine, Washington, but if you some-how missed a birth, marriage, first snowfall, or the results of a War Bond drive, you could read about it at year's end, when the Alpine Lumber Company published a month-by-month report in the program for the annual banquet and dance. (Courtesy of Mary Daheim)

pleasant than that in coal towns, that the last communities to be founded offered the most freedom. But for every generalization, there are exceptions. Smaller companies often did foster better community life than huge corporations, but there were many more small companies than large ones. One of the prettiest towns in the Northwest was DuPont, Washington, built by what is now a Fortune 100 corporation. With 19,000 employees nationwide by 1919, DuPont was the largest company to own a town in the region. Picturesque Port Gamble, the longest-lived Washington company town, was run by a sawmill second only in size to that of another company-built community, nearby Port Blakely.

Ports Gamble and Blakely, like many other towns, were in their early years run by their owners. Some have said this made for better living conditions. When the boss lived in town, social and civic life reflected his (and occasionally her) values—and whims. How comfortable townspeople were with this influence depended on what the owner's biases were and whether the workers shared them. In Gilchrist, Oregon, the lumberman who subsidized his employees' rent was the same man who personally chastised workers who didn't maintain their yards to his satisfaction. The timber baron Henry McCleary and the quarry owner John McMillin were much maligned by the press of their eras, but both are remembered for make-work projects that kept at least a few men on the payroll during the Depression. By contrast, it is the coal mines' hired bosses, especially the managers of the mining subsidiaries of transcontinental railroads, who are most likely to be recalled as despots.

Almost all of the Pacific Northwest's company towns were built for extractive industries: for lumbermen and miners exploiting the natural resources. We look now at the neatly platted yards and streets, at the clapboard and shingles and shutters and are charmed by the quaintness of the few remaining company-built structures. But the earliest villages were seldom pretty: buildings were thrown up between stumps or on a site that had been clear-cut and then burned free of brush. The towns weren't clean, quiet, or safe. Lumber mill workers lived with the smoke from sawdust burners and the cinders and noise from steam locomotives. Fire—in the woods and in the mills—was a constant threat. Life in coal-mine towns was even grimmer. Miners and their families breathed the coal dust and the smoke from smoldering slag heaps. The dust and smoke dirtied the air, the houses, the gardens, the laundry hung out to dry—and the lungs of the miners.

Some residents of Pacific Northwest company towns considered themselves indentured. There's no question that company-town owners had extra leverage when they wanted to muscle out unions. Coal-mine bosses in the Northwest, like those elsewhere in the United States, were quick to evict workers who tried to organize. By the twentieth century, few timber companies were so blatant in their opposition. Perhaps because of the government pressure to ensure continuing lumber production during World War I, timbermen acquiesced to demands for a shorter workweek and sponsored an industry-approved union for loggers and mill workers. But even when companies cooperated with unions, wages remained low in many industries, and seasonal layoffs kept both loggers and coal miners from working year-round. Without fifty-two weeks of work to cover fifty-two weeks of rent and groceries, many employees did run up debts at the company store. When the selection in the store was limited or overpriced, however, families could turn to their gardens and berry patches; many also could hunt, fish, clam, and crab. Homes may have been small and some were shabby, but rent (unlike in George Pullman's infamous Illinois company town) was low and occasionally free. Coal miners' houses were heated with coal bought cheap from the company; loggers and millworkers remodeled their homes with reject lumber carried home free from the mill.

The communities that endured the longest are recalled with the most affection. Did towns like Port Gamble, Kinzua, Valsetz, Potlatch, DuPont, and Cedar Falls last longer because they were better run? Some had only one owner; none had more than a few over the course of a half-century. Perhaps workers were happier because of the stability of town ownership, of company policy, of employment, of population. The stability, especially during the Depression, also may have contributed to workers' loyalty: some of these towns had no work stoppages, and most had no ownership changes despite the economic crisis. Possibly the management qualities that kept these towns running for so many decades were the same qualities that made the communities desirable places to live. Maybe their owners could adapt to changing times, could accept that company towns were no longer personal fiefdoms. This also may be why the last company towns to be established—communities like Holden and Grisdale and Gilchrist—also are among those that prompt warm memories. By the time they were built, bosses still were paternalistic, but few were dictators. The law wouldn't let them be—and neither would the increasingly competitive labor market. The exceptions, of course, were the huge instant government communities of Coulee Dam, Vanport, and Richland, which struggled to get past the camp transiency, to develop the cohesiveness common in private-sector towns. All three were run by bureaucrats and all three swelled and shrank depending on federal dictates.

The most unusual characteristic of many company towns is that they no longer exist in any form. Some aren't even dots on a map. These towns didn't fade away quietly, as did some other early settlements, or find themselves absorbed into larger communities. With a company-owned town, someone had the right to declare the community obsolete, no different than when the boss surplussed an outdated piece of equipment. But these company towns were more than saws and warehouses, mine shafts and mills. When these company towns were shut down or sold off, a unique way of life ended.

GAZETTEER

Algoma, Klamath County, Oregon
This town, supported by the Algoma Lumber Company, was ten miles north of Klamath Falls. It had a population of 400 in 1919 and almost 600 by 1931. The post office closed in 1943.

Alpine, Snohomish County, Washington
Founded as Nippon in the early 1900s (perhaps because of Japanese railroad workers), Alpine was located just west of the Stevens Pass ski area. The Alpine Lumber Company was owned by Carl Clemans, the first football coach at Stanford University, and his brother Hugh. Both were distant relatives of Samuel Clemens, better known as Mark Twain. The town, which once had more than 200 residents, was razed in 1929, but was revived—in fiction—as the setting of Mary Daheim's mysteries, introduced in 1992 with *The Alpine Advocate.*

Barneston, King County, Washington
Concerned about pollution in its watershed, the City of Seattle bought Barneston from the Kent Lumber Company in 1911 and forced operations to close in the early 1920s. The town was razed in 1924. Built in 1898, Barneston had a significant Japanese population. By 1920, when the census showed a total of 231 residents, 74 were Japanese.

Beebe, Douglas County, Washington
Established by the William Beebe Orchard Company early in the 1900s, this fruit orchard labor camp was located seven miles east of Chelan on the Columbia River. Even in the 1950s, it was accessible only by a company-owned bridge. Mail was delivered via rowboat or motor launch for several years. The community once had its own store and school, although the population was usually less than 100.

Black Diamond, King County, Washington
Established in the 1880s by the California-based Black Diamond Mining Company, this coal-mining town thirty miles southeast of Seattle eventually had some privately owned homes and businesses. Most buildings, however, were on property leased from the company. The Pacific Coast Coal Company owned Black Diamond from 1904 to 1937. The population was 1,033 when the town incorporated in 1959 and 3,600 in the late 1990s.

Bordeaux, Thurston County, Washington
Established by the Bordeaux brothers' Mason County Logging Company in the late 1890s, this timber town a dozen miles southwest of Olympia once had a population of more than 400. At its peak, the sawmill and logging operations employed 700. The town was also the site of the Mumby Lumber & Shingle Mill, which the Bordeaux family had purchased from Joseph Vance in 1924. The company began selling logged-off land to Washington state in 1933. The Mumby operation was closed in 1939. In 1941, the mill shut down, and the town began to die. The post office closed in 1942. Most of the Mason County Logging land became part of the state-owned Capitol Forest.

Britannia Beach, British Columbia, Canada
Now the location of the British Columbia Museum of Mining, this community is thirty-two miles north of Vancouver, B.C., on Howe Sound. It and the adjacent village of Townsite (Mount Sheer) were accessible only by boat until the 1950s. Once the largest producer of copper in the British Empire, the mine closed in 1974. The Howe Sound Company also built Holden, a nonferrous mine in a similarly remote area of Washington, and operated a mine at Cobalt, Idaho.

Brookings, Curry County, Oregon

When this community was established in 1912, it could be reached only by coastal steamers. Until about 1920, when a wharf was built, everything from railway locomotives to groceries was lightered to small boats or rafts or swung in via a cable suspended between boat and shore. The original town design was by the noted California architect Bernard Maybeck, but few of his structures were built before John E. Brookings was forced to sell out to the California & Oregon Lumber Company. It closed the mill in 1925. By 1931, there were only 275 people left. During World War II, Brookings was the only spot in the continental United States bombed; in September 1942, a Japanese flyer dropped an incendiary bomb near Mount Emily. The town founder was a cousin of Robert Brookings, a wealthy St. Louis business-man who helped finance the sawmill and also gave his name and support to the Brookings Institution in Washington, D.C.

Burnett, Pierce County, Washington

About thirty miles from Tacoma, this South Prairie Coal Company com-munity had about 400 residents when it was taken over in 1906 by the Pacific Coast Coal Company. The population had dropped sharply by the time workers struck in 1921; after the lengthy national coal strike ended, the mine ran only until 1927. The school consolidated with Buckley's in 1928. As the community died, many of the company-owned houses were moved to Carbonado, another Pacific Coast Coal Company town.

Carbonado, Pierce County, Washington

This "model mining camp," as a local newspaper described it in 1925, was established about thirty-five miles from Tacoma after a mine was opened in 1880. Except for those few merchants to whom the Pacific Coast Coal Company agreed to lease land, all houses and businesses were company owned. The mine officially closed in 1937. When houses were sold, covenants in the sales agreements prohibited commercial businesses and digging, which meant no septic systems could be installed and no new homes or businesses could be constructed; partly as a result, the population dropped to as few as 75. The covenants were finally removed in 1966. By 2000, the community had almost 700 residents.

Carlsborg, Clallam County, Washington

Established in 1915, this community east of Port Angeles had a post office, butcher shop, general store, cookhouse, bunkhouses, and about a dozen homes for married workers. By 1919, it had 300 residents. There were several privately owned businesses and structures, including a grange hall, school, and homes. After several ownership changes, the sawmill was closed in the late 1960s. A two-room elementary and high school operated as late as the early 1950s. One former owner's son said mill management maintained a charge account with the local sheriff for bailing out workers after weekend binges.

Cedar Falls, King County, Washington

A few of the original employee houses continue to be used as offices, and a new visitor center now stands near the site of Cedar Falls. The community was established by the City of Seattle in the early 1900s for the employees who built and then operated the city's first power plant in the Cascade Mountain foothills, almost fifty miles east of Seattle. Near Moncton, an earlier community that was flooded by Rattlesnake Lake, Cedar Falls also was the location of Milwaukee Road and Pacific States Lumber Company camps. The elementary school was established in 1910 and consolidated in 1944 with North Bend's to become the Snoqualmie Valley district.

Cherry Valley, King County, Washington

The Cherry Valley Lumber Company, located near Duvall, shut down its operations in 1930, sold the remnants of its holdings to the Weyerhaeuser Company, and was formally disincorporated in 1947. Its school, one of the few company-town districts to offer twelve grades, had had 199 students by 1920. In 1943, the school was consolidated with what became the Riverview School District, where the Cherry Valley name lives on in an elementary school.

Clay City, Pierce County, Washington

In 1907, the Far West Clay Company built a brickyard and town at Clay City, about seventeen miles from Tacoma, on the Tacoma Eastern Railway line between Lake Kapowsin and Ohop Lake. The town had 150 people in 1915, but the post office closed in 1922. The school eventually consolidated with Eatonville's, four miles toward Mount Rainier. A 1950 fire destroyed everything that wasn't constructed of brick, but the factory was still operating in the late 1970s.

Clear Lake, Skagit County, Washington
Built two miles south of Sedro-Woolley, Clear Lake (sometimes Clearlake) was company dominated rather than company built. The Day brothers, who also dominated nearby Big Lake, built mills in town in the 1890s. Later it was the Clear Lake Lumber Company that developed most of the community, including a boarding house, the company store, and a recreation center. During the community's peak in the mid-1920s, eight passenger trains traveled through town daily. The company went into receivership in the mid-1920s, was sold, closed again by 1935, and was dismantled in 1938. Never incorporated, Clear Lake today is a quiet neighborhood of about 1,100.

Cobalt, Lemhi County, Idaho
The Howe Sound Company took over cobalt-mining claims after World War II, moving some staff from Holden as production at that mine diminished. Although Howe Sound built some town site facilities such as housing and a recreation hall, the community was near such towns as Salmon and so did not experience the isolation (or community spirit) of other Howe Sound locations. The population peaked at 1,500. Howe Sound's contract with the U.S. government ended in 1959, closing down the operation. The Blackbird mine, also the site of a copper mine, is the only known large deposit of high-grade cobalt in the United States.

Concrete, Skagit County, Washington
Concrete was established in the late 1800s and incorporated in 1909 after the construction of a Superior Portland Cement Company plant. Although Concrete was not a company-built town, the cement works provided worker housing, ran the Superior Mercantile, and was important in the community, funding such programs as adult education. As a market center for both cement companies and logging camps in the period before World War I, Concrete boasted fourteen saloons on its Main Street alone. It had one of the largest regional concentrations of Italian immigrants outside

Seattle because of the unskilled laborers recruited by the concrete plant. The community boomed again in the mid-1920s with the construction of the City of Seattle's Skagit River dams and power plants, which are reached via Concrete and neighboring Rockport.

Conda, Caribou County, Idaho
Established in the 1920s by the Anaconda Copper Mining Company, this phosphate-mining and-processing operation in Idaho's southeast corner was sold in 1950 to the J. R. Simplot Company for fertilizer production. The community was accessible only by train until 1936. Simplot shut down most mining operations in 1992.

Coulee Dam, Douglas, Grant, and Okanogan Counties, Washington
Established in the mid-1930s, Coulee Dam was originally two communities that housed those who worked on the construction and operation of Grand Coulee Dam. On one side of the Columbia River, the original dam contractor, MWAK (Mason-Walsh-Atkinson-Kier), built Mason City for its skilled laborers; on the other river bank, the federal Bureau of Reclamation constructed Engineers' Town, or Coulee Dam, for government engineers and professional staff. In the early years, the communities together housed thousands; the population had decreased to 1,317 when they were incorporated jointly as Coulee Dam in 1959.

Crocker, Pierce County, Washington
Named for Charles Crocker, one of the "Big Four" railroad barons of California (along with Leland Stanford, Collis Huntington, and Mark Hopkins), this little coal-mining town was about twenty miles from Tacoma, on the Northern Pacific.

Cumberland, King County, Washington
Another of the coal towns in the line that stretched from the Canadian border south through western Washington to the Carbon River, Cumberland was seven miles from Black Diamond. Once dominated by the National Coal Company, it had 800 residents in 1919 but only 150 by 1931. Its elementary school enrollment peaked about 1920 with 100 students.

Dalkena, Pend Oreille County, Washington
Named for founders Dalton and Kennedy, this sawmill town was built in 1902. It had a school, store, post office, bunkhouses and cookhouse, pool hall, and train depot. The population was 400 in 1919 and 500 as the Depression began. Daily passenger train service continued until the early 1940s, even though the mill burned in the mid-1930s and was not rebuilt. The post office closed in 1942. The store continued to serve the community for years after the company was gone.

Dee, Hood River County, Oregon
Built in the early 1900s by the Oregon Lumber Company, Dee had 200 residents in 1919. It was sold about 1958 to the Edward Hines Lumber Company, which dismantled the town. The post office closed in 1959 after fifty years of service.

Diablo, Whatcom County, Washington
Built by Seattle City Light in the 1920s for construction workers on a Skagit River dam and power plant, this is the most remote of the City Light communities. Located seven miles farther into the mountains than Newhalem, Diablo is still sometimes isolated by winter avalanches. The community was dependent on the city's own railroad until 1954; the completion of the North Cascades Highway in 1972 brought the first good highway. In 2000, Diablo had a population of 40.

Dryad, Lewis County, Washington
Built seventeen miles west of Chehalis, Dryad had 500 people in 1910 and 600 about the time the Schafer Bros. Logging Company bought the Lendinghaus Lumber Company and the Dryad town site in 1929. The operation was shut down in 1939, and the Schafer family sold the company to the Simpson Timber Company in 1955.

DuPont, Pierce County, Washington
Established in 1906 to manufacture explosives for E. I. du Pont de Nemours, this historic site was once the local outpost for the Hudson's Bay Company and, before that, an important gathering place for Nisqually Indians. DuPont residents could buy their homes starting in 1951, but the company

owned the surrounding land until 1976, when the site was sold to the Weyerhaeuser Company, itself a former owner of company towns. Eventually
Weyerhaeuser transformed the location into Northwest Landing, a corporate campus and residential community. Now consolidated with a neighboring suburban district, the DuPont school had enrolled as many as 626
elementary and junior high students in 1950. The original village of DuPont,
about sixteen miles south of Tacoma, is on the National Register of Historic
Districts.

Eatonville, Pierce County, Washington

Although not a company town, this community thirty miles south of
Tacoma was dominated by the Eatonville Lumber Company for decades.
Founded in 1907, the lumber company by 1923 claimed that it paid more
than two-thirds of the town's taxes. The company president once served
simultaneously as mayor and a director of the school board. The company
ran several retail operations, including a company store. During the
Depression, Eatonville Lumber acquired and briefly ran Manley-Moore near
Fairfax. The Eatonville mill, often closed in its last years, was sold in 1953.

Elk River, Clearwater County, Idaho

Although not established by the Potlatch Lumber Company, this community was dominated by the company's mill, which was constructed early
in the twentieth century. Housing and many services were provided by the
lumber company. At its peak, Elk River had 1,200 people. The lumber company closed its operations in 1930 and deeded its property to the town in
1936. Today the community has a few hundred people.

Engineers' Town

See "Coulee Dam."

Fairfax, Pierce County, Washington

Fairfax was a Northern Pacific community that remained accessible only
by foot or train until 1921. Like many western Washington coal towns, it
was almost entirely owned by the company. Mining started in 1898 and
ended in 1929, after the 1925 sale of the mine to the Wilkeson Coal & Coke

Company. The town was also supported by the logging operations of the Manley-Moore Lumber Company. The population was 500 in 1915 when the mine employed more than 80 people. School enrollment reached 86 in grades one through ten in 1920 and then declined. By 1940 there were only a dozen children left. Ironically, in 1925, the local newspaper editor had proclaimed, "Fairfax has a future. . . . She not only has sufficient timber to keep her big lumber and shingle mills running for many years to come, but she has one of the richest coal deposits in the state." The town was razed in 1991 by Burlington Northern, successor to the Northern Pacific.

Franklin, King County, Washington
This coal-mining town thirty-five miles southeast of Seattle was established by Henry Villard's Oregon Improvement Company, a unit of the Northern Pacific. Franklin was taken over by the Pacific Coast Coal Company after Villard went broke. The town has been well publicized for its labor problems, which resulted in black strikebreakers being imported in 1891. The population peaked at about 1,000; by 1919 the mine employed only about 75.

Gilchrist, Klamath County, Oregon
Established in 1938 by the Gilchrist Timber Company, which moved many of its employees from an existing operation in Mississippi, Gilchrist has had a population of about 600 for most of its existence. In 1991, the Gilchrist family sold the mill to Crown Pacific; three Gilchrist grandsons formed a land development company to manage and sell the houses and town-site buildings.

Government Town
See "Coulee Dam."

Grande Ronde, Polk County, Oregon
A logging headquarters for the Long-Bell Lumber Company. Grande Ronde once had about 150 company-owned houses and a company store. Along with Long-Bell, it was acquired by International Paper; the settlement had a couple of dozen houses and a total population of 75 when IP sold it in the early 1960s.

Grisdale, Grays Harbor County, Washington

Operated by the Simpson Timber Company from 1946 to 1985, this community received national acclaim for being the last logging camp in the Lower 48. It included about fifty family houses, bunkhouses, a recreation hall, a two-room school, and for part of its life, a branch of the Lumbermen's Mercantile. Some loggers came to Grisdale as newlyweds and stayed until the camp closed.

Hanford, Benton County, Washington

One of three villages settled in the early 1900s through a government-sponsored development program, Hanford (along with White Bluffs and Richland) was condemned by the federal government during World War II for use in the Manhattan Project. A camp, with housing and minimal services for workers, was built by the government during the war. See "Richland."

Harding, Pierce County, Washington

Located about sixteen miles south of Tacoma, near Graham, this railroad stop and small sawmill community was established about 1905. The mill closed in 1923.

Headquarters, Clearwater County, Idaho

Established in the late 1920s by the Potlatch Lumber Company, this timber community served as a hub for several logging camps, with a roundhouse in the railroad logging days, heavy equipment maintenance shops, a small general store and post office, school, recreation hall, and swimming pool. In 1960, it still had bunkhouses and about 100 company-owned houses for employees. The last of the company-owned houses were sold to their occupants or dismantled in the mid-1990s.

Hines, Harney County, Oregon

Located near Burns, this sawmill town was established in 1928 by the Edward Hines Lumber Co. It had about 300 residents when it incorporated in 1930.

Hobart, King County, Washington

Dominated by the Wood & Iverson Lumber Company, Hobart peaked in the 1920s; by 1920, the school enrolled 131 in grades one through nine. By 1931, there were only 150 people total. Today the area has become a suburb of Seattle, which is twenty-seven miles to the northwest.

Holden, Chelan County, Washington
Never accessible except by boat, this mining community was established on United States Forest Service land in the 1930s by the Howe Sound Company. The source of most of the copper used by the U.S. military in World War II, Holden had a peak population of about 600. After the mine closed in 1957, the town sat empty until the early 1960s. The original town site, with recreation hall, school, management housing, and bunkhouses, continues to be used today as Holden Village, a Christian retreat center that attracts thousands of visitors each summer. The permanent population is about fifty.

Irondale, Jefferson County, Washington
Now on the National Register of Historic Districts, Irondale was established about 1879. The Irondale Steel Company built houses for its workers about 1902. Employment ranged from 100 to 300. The population reached 300, and the community was served by daily steamers until the steel operation shut down in 1919.

Kanaskat, King County, Washington
This little coal town was near Black Diamond and Lester, about thirty-five miles southeast of Seattle.

Kerriston, King County, Washington
About fifty miles from Seattle, near North Bend, this shingle-mill town once had 500 residents. It was founded in the early 1900s by Albert S. Kerry, who had come to Seattle in 1886 to work in an Oregon Improvement Company sawmill; he later owned part of the Roslyn (Washington) Coal Mine. After Kerry sold Kerriston, the shingle mill operated until the early 1940s. The school enrolled twenty or thirty students. The community declined in the Depression, and by 1931 there were only 150 people left; the school was consolidated in 1936 with Taylor's.

Kinzua, Wheeler County, Oregon

Established in 1927 by E. D. Wetmore, this logging and sawmill community once had as many as 800 residents, making it for many years the largest town in sparsely populated Wheeler County. The Kinzua Pine Mills also ran logging camps, including Camp 5, or Wetmore, which had its own post office until 1948. The town, camp, and company were acquired by the Biles-Coleman Lumber Company of Omak, Washington. In the mid-1960s, the elementary school closed. Kinzua itself was closed in 1978 and razed; a tree farm now covers the site.

Klaber, Lewis County, Washington

The town was established about 1906 approximately thirteen miles southwest of Chehalis by Herman Klaber, a Tacoma and Portland hops broker and grower. Although the permanent population was only 80 in 1910, seasonal employment reportedly swelled the community to as many as 2,000. There were several privately owned businesses. Klaber drowned on the *Titanic* in 1912, and the town faded. The post office closed in 1958 after the store burned.

Klickitat, Klickitat County, Washington

The sawmill and most of the Klickitat town site were taken over in the early 1920s by Julius Neils, who closed his lumber operations in Minnesota and moved his family and many of his employees west. (In the Midwest, Neils was a business partner of Thomas Shevlin, whose son established the Shevlin-Hixon Company that later built Shevlin, Oregon.) Neils set up headquarters for the J. Neils Lumber Company in Portland, Oregon, 110 miles from the Klickitat site. Neils's son-in-law, Hugo A. Schmidt, ran the Klickitat mill until he retired, a few years after the family sold to the St. Regis Paper Company in 1957. The population peaked at about 800 in the late 1930s. The company owned the general store and the employee housing, but there were several privately owned stores, a hotel, restaurant, and gas station. A Lutheran church, the first church in town, was established by the Neils family, and the congregation met for many years in a company house converted into a chapel. Later, a few employees organized a Mormon congregation, which met in homes and finally in a room rented at the community gym. After St. Regis sold Klickitat, the town site was liquidated. A subsequent owner, Champion International, closed the mill.

Kosmos, Lewis County, Washington

In 1935, the Kosmos Timber Company started building two logging camps south of Morton. The Kosmos operations once employed more than 400 men. Those who worked at Camp 2 went to camp each Sunday on railroad speeders and stayed in bunkhouses until Friday night. Located at an elevation of about 3,000 feet, this camp closed each winter when the snow was too deep for logging. It burned in the early 1950s, about the time the Kosmos Timber Company was purchased by U.S. Plywood (later Champion International). The main camp and the neighboring community were flooded in 1969 when the City of Tacoma completed Mossyrock Dam on the Cowlitz River, creating Riffe Lake.

Ladd, Lewis County, Washington

A coal mine built by the William Ladd Coal Company in 1906 prompted the development of this little town a few miles west of Mineral. By 1910 it had 150 residents. Originally it provided fuel for the Tacoma Eastern Railway, which became the Milwaukee Road's National Park Branch. A later investor was the Skinner & Eddy Corporation, the Seattle firm that had bought the Port Blakely mill from William Renton's heirs (see "Port Blakely"). It used the coal for its steamships. The mine closed in 1919 after a flood and fire devastated the community.

Lawson, King County, Washington

A predominantly Finnish community built by Eugene Lawson in 1895, the town was sold to the Pacific Coast Coal Company in 1898. After an explosion in 1910, the coal mine remained closed until the 1940s.

Lester, King County, Washington

Established as a Northern Pacific helper station in 1891 for steam locomotives heading over Stampede Pass, this community sixty miles southeast of Seattle also had logging camps. The railroad owned most of the land. A school opened in 1919; in 1936, it officially absorbed the neighboring

Nagrom school, but together the communities never enrolled more than about sixty students or offered more than grades one through ten. Accessible only by rail for most of its life, Lester began to decline after World War II when the NP began using diesel locomotives. When Washington state eliminated support for tiny districts, the school closed. The City of Tacoma bought the area to protect its watershed and pressured residents to leave; by 2000, there was only one woman still living in Lester.

Lindberg, Lewis County, Washington

This community was built about two miles north of Morton by Gustaf Lindberg, owner of the Taylor Logging and Lumber Company. The company operated from the early 1900s until the Depression. Most of the settlement burned after the mill closed, but several brick houses built for company managers still stood along the west side of Highway 7 in 2000, their exteriors only slightly modified from their company-town years.

Longview, Cowlitz County, Washington

Although designed by the Long-Bell Lumber Company and its founder, R. A. Long, this small city was never intended to be a company town. Long-Bell developed the community and worked hard to sell residential, commercial, and industrial sites. Within a few years of its founding in the early 1920s, Longview had incorporated and attracted such other employers as Weyerhaeuser and Longview Fibre. As gifts to the community, Long-Bell and Long himself built many of the parks and public buildings, including the YMCA, the high school, and the library. The founders also financed the establishment of the *Longview Daily News.*

Malone, Grays Harbor County, Washington

Named for Hector J. Malone, who built a shingle mill in 1897, this town was later owned by Joseph Vance and then sold in 1924 to the Bordeaux brothers of the Mason County Logging Company. The population was as high as 500 in 1915.

Manley-Moore, Pierce County, Washington

The community began as a logging and sawmill camp operated on Northern Pacific land by the Manley-Moore Lumber Company starting in 1909. After the 1929 stock market crash it was bought by the Eatonville Lumber Company, which closed the mill in the early 1930s. Before 1923, the only access was by train from Tacoma to Fairfax and then via railroad speeder. Groceries for the cookhouse, including quarters of fresh beef wrapped in burlap, were sent to Fairfax by train and then up the tracks to Manley-Moore. The main village included fifty houses, a hotel, a doctor's office, a schoolhouse that was converted to a silent movie theater on weekends, and a community hall. The company's logging camp three miles away was reached by an incline railway. In 1917, the mill employed 100 and the logging operations, 100 to 125. The mill was one of the largest inland sawmills in the state.

Mason City
See "Coulee Dam."

McCleary, Grays Harbor County, Washington
The town was founded in the early 1900s by the Henry McCleary Timber Company, which operated what was once the world's largest fir door manufacturing plant as well as a plywood mill. All of the retail businesses and some homes were privately owned. The population was 1,000 in 1919 and 2,000 as the Depression started. The entire company, including timberlands and town, was purchased on the last day of 1941 by the Simpson Timber Company, which sold off the town site to residents starting in 1943. As the twenty-first century began, Simpson was still the major employer in the community.

McKenna, Pierce County, Washington
The McKenna Lumber Company started out owning almost everything in this timber town, but the owner's original intention was to convert the store to a co-op and sell the houses to workers for cost plus 6 percent. Soon after it was founded, the company had divided land outside town into farms of seven to ten acres, which it sold to employees on credit with no down payment. By 1918, it employed 300 people in its logging camps and mill; the town had a population of 600. The mill and camps closed about 1932, but the company continued to operate some facilities, including the water system, for decades. The population began to decline in the 1930s; by the 1940s,

there were only about 200 people left in the town, which is located about twenty miles south of Tacoma.

McMillin, Pierce County, Washington
McMillin, about fifteen miles south of Tacoma, was founded in the late 1800s by John McMillin, who established lime quarries and mills. Later, after McMillin abandoned these quarries and moved to Roche Harbor, the community turned to farming.

Melmont, Pierce County, Washington
This was a Northern Pacific coal town, located two miles from Fairfax and some forty miles from Tacoma, that could be reached only via the train from Carbonado or a horse trail. NP's Northwestern Improvement Company built the miners' cottages, a hotel with store, butcher shop, and post office, a saloon, a depot, and a school. The mines operated from 1902 until the early 1920s, when the town burned.

Mineral, Lewis County, Washington
Named for minerals like arsenic that were once mined here, Mineral was never a company town. It was the site of several shingle and lumber mills and near the Ladd coal mine. The West Fork Logging Company, owned by L. T. Murray, ran two logging camps in the area and owned the Mineral Lake Lodge until 1943, when the operations (but not the land or timber) were sold to the St. Regis Paper Company. Murray's properties became part of his family's Murray Pacific Corporation, now also known as West Fork Timber Company, still a Tacoma-based company.

Mowich, Klamath County, Oregon
Established eight miles north of Pauniana in 1926 as a Southern Pacific railroad siding, this outpost became a logging camp in 1934 when W. E. Lamm (who also owned the Lamm Lumber Company) and the Deschutes Lumber Company set up seasonal operations. In 1944, the company relocated to northern California, abandoning the site. The camp briefly operated a one-room school, but children usually attended school in Crescent and later in Gilchrist.

Nagrom, King County, Washington

Located in the City of Tacoma's Green River watershed and on Northern Pacific land, this community was named for its founder, the Morgan Lumber Company (Nagrom is simply Morgan spelled in reverse). It had 200 people in 1919 but only a couple of dozen by the time the Depression started.

National, Pierce County, Washington

This logging camp's name came from its location just west of the Nisqually entrance to Mount Rainier National Park. Built in the early 1900s, it once had 350 people. Originally the community had both a shingle mill and a lumber company. By the time it was sold in 1944, the only employer was the original sawmill, Pacific National Lumber Company. The next owner, Harbor Plywood, dismantled the sawmill but continued the logging operation. In 1957, when the town had a permanent population of thirty-three families, the town and property were purchased by Weyerhaeuser, which shut down the town site. The school became part of the Eatonville district in 1949. The post office, opened in 1910, closed in 1957.

Neverstill, Columbia County, Oregon

Between 1915 and 1925, A. S. Kerry's Columbia & Newhalem River Railroad (the Kerry Line) ran twenty-five miles east from the Columbia River to Neverstill, serving several logging camps en route. The Neverstill post office closed in 1919. Soon after, Kerry returned to Seattle and became president of the Community Hotel Corporation, which in 1924 constructed what is now the Four Seasons Olympic Hotel. Kerry's name endures in a park that overlooks downtown Seattle. His nearby mansion was designed by Carl F. Gould. (Also see "Kerriston" and "Pysht.")

Newcastle, King County, Washington

"Here was once a booming coal-mining town," reported *Washington, a Guide to the Evergreen State*, first published in 1941. "Now cattle graze in the yard of the abandoned schoolhouse, and a cluster of shabby little dwellings clings to the side of a bare hill." Also known as Coal Creek, this community was established in the 1800s and had 800 people at the turn of the century. It faded before World War I and then boomed again when war increased the demand for coal. The population surged to 1,000 in 1919, but by the late 1920s, the mines were closed. A 1931 city directory shows only 160 residents.

Newhalem, Whatcom County, Washington

One of the last employer-owned communities in the United States, Newhalem was built by Seattle City Light starting in 1920. For at least its first twenty years, it could be reached only by the city's own Skagit River Railway, which ran twenty-three miles to connect to the Great Northern at Rockport. Construction of the first road, described as appropriate for bold drivers, was begun in the 1930s by the Civilian Conservation Corps. Despite Newhalem's remoteness, J. D. Ross, the legendary City Light director, marketed the village and the Skagit River operations as tourist destinations starting in the early 1920s. Today, the community, shrunk to a few dozen residents as a result of power plant automation, continues to welcome visitors on City Light–sponsored tours. Both it and nearby Diablo are listed on historic registers.

Olney, Clatsop County, Oregon

Several logging camps were located near this tiny community south of Astoria. Many were originally accessible only by gas launch up Young's River and by the Kerry Line (see "Neverstill"). The Western Cooperage Headquarters camp established in 1910 and operated by the Tidewater Timber Company from 1923 to 1943 was the setting of Sam Churchill's memoirs about life in a remote camp between 1911 and 1922.

Onalaska, Lewis County, Washington

Built by the Carlisle Lumber Company, which became the largest mill in Lewis County, this community grew from 900 in 1919 to 1,500 in 1931. The mill closed in 1938, but there was still a population of about 1,200 in the 1940s.

Ostrander, Cowlitz County, Washington

Just a few miles outside Longview, this town was not founded by the Ostrander Timber Company, but it was dominated by the Company's mill in the late 1800s and early 1900s. The mill closed in 1939. The community was never larger than a few hundred people.

Perry, Union County, Oregon
Just a few miles west of LaGrande, this community was once owned by the Grande Ronde Lumber Company. In 1919 it had 200 people.

Pilchuck, Snohomish County, Washington
Several daily trains once ran through this community, built in 1900 by the Parker-Bell Lumber Company. In 1919, it had a population of 350, but a massive slide closed the railroad in 1921; in 1922 the town was sold off, with houses priced from $25 to $50.

Pine Ridge, Klamath County, Oregon
In 1939, a fire demolished this town, most of which was then owned by the Forest Lumber Company. Dozens of company-owned structures burned, including forty employee houses, the hotel where single men lived, the office, company store, gas station, box factory, planer, and sawmill, and 62 million board feet of lumber. Because the fire jumped the Williamson River and burned all the way to Highway 97, it also destroyed many other homes and several farms. The company did not rebuild, and many of the 300 employees sought work at Gilchrist.

Pittsburg
See "Spiketon."

Pondosa, Union County, Oregon
Built by the Stoddard Lumber Company in the mid-1920s, this community about thirty miles southeast of LaGrande was later owned by the Mount Emily Lumber Company, a division of the Valsetz Lumber Company. It was sold at auction in 1953.

Port Blakely, Kitsap County, Washington
This Bainbridge Island village was founded in 1863 by William Renton (for whom Renton, Washington, is named). By the 1880s, it claimed to have the largest sawmill in the world. Renton built the mill, dormitories, and houses for families, but some employees also owned their own homes. An entire neighborhood was built with mill rejects by Japanese workers. Renton also built four houses for ship captains to stay in while their ships were being

loaded. The mill was not the only employer; Renton encouraged the Hall brothers to move their shipyard from Port Ludlow to Port Blakely in 1880. A school was founded in 1876. The company store, described as a major profit center for the company, served employees as well as nearby loggers and farmers. In 1903 Renton's heirs sold the mill to David E. Skinner and John W. Eddy, lumbermen from Michigan. (See "Ladd.") The mill shut down in 1922. Later most of the community was demolished; during the Depression, the owners tried to market Port Blakely lots for vacation homes. Today the company name lives on in the real estate business, as a developer of subdivisions.

Port Gamble, Kitsap County, Washington
Established in 1853 by the Puget Mill Company, the company that became Pope & Talbot, Port Gamble was Washington state's last company-owned timber town, not closing its mill until 1995. The entire community is still owned by a Pope & Talbot subsidiary. Never incorporated, it is a historic district. Several buildings have been carefully restored, including an 1870s church similar to the church in East Machias, Maine, Andrew J. Pope and Captain William C. Talbot's hometown. Some of the buildings were designed by Bebb & Mendel, a leading Seattle architecture firm of the early 1900s. Bebb was later a partner of Carl F. Gould (see "Pysht").

Port Ludlow, Kitsap County, Washington
This timber community got its start in 1852 with the construction of a sawmill. The mill was purchased in the late 1870s by the Puget Mill Company. The timber company, later Pope & Talbot, was not the only employer in the community, which was never incorporated. The Pope & Talbot mill shut down permanently in 1936; in 1966, the company redeveloped the area as a resort and marina.

Potlatch, Latah County, Idaho
Started in 1905 by the Potlatch Lumber Company, now the Spokane-based Potlatch Forests, Inc., this community is one of the best examples of a Northwest company town. Built by a group of timbermen (including the Weyerhaeuser family) who were inspired by George Pullman's model town, Potlatch was controlled—and supported—by the company for most

of its first fifty years. Almost all buildings and businesses were company owned, and many school and civic programs and organizations received significant company funding. The town site, including the houses, was sold beginning in the early 1950s, but the company store operated until it burned in 1963. The mill was closed in 1981. Two decades later, privately owned sawmills continued to operate nearby, providing forest-products jobs in the community.

Potlatch, Mason County, Washington

A Phoenix Logging Company village, Potlatch was established about 1900 by Alfred Anderson, a lumberman colleague of Sol Simpson and the Bordeaux brothers. Located sixteen miles north of Shelton and three miles from Hoodsport, near the current Lake Cushman golf course, the community and several camps endured for four decades. It had about 100 residents between World War I and the beginning of the Depression. It closed in 1940, after the timber had been cut and the mill closed.

Powers, Coos County, Oregon

Established in 1915 by Al Powers of the Smith-Powers Logging Company, this sawmill community had many privately owned structures and businesses. By 1919 it had 1,200 residents. It was sold a few years later. The successor company, the Coos Bay Lumber Company, sold out to Georgia-Pacific in the 1950s.

Preston, King County, Washington

Twenty-two miles east of Seattle was the site of the Preston Mill Company, which built a shingle mill in 1892 and a lumber mill in 1897. August Lovegren built houses, a store, and some recreational facilities for the community, which had two neighborhoods: Preston and, two miles away, Upper Preston. He sold out in 1910 to C. J. Erickson, whose family operated Upper Preston until the 1930s and the Preston planing mill for decades afterward; even in 1964, the mill still employed 35. The mill at its peak employed 200; the community had a population of 500 in 1919 and 800 in the late 1920s. Erickson's daughter and her family retained much of the property until the 1970s.

Gazetteer
Pysht, Jefferson County, Washington
This was the site of a Merrill & Ring logging camp that operated between 1916 and 1944. Before roads were built on the Olympic Peninsula, visitors from Seattle reached the camp only by climbing from idling steamships to camp skiffs in the Strait of Juan de Fuca. The camp had a school and weekly movies soon after it was established. As the twentieth century ended, a Merrill & Ring tree farm was headquartered in one of the original logging camp buildings designed by Carl F. Gould, a noted Seattle architect. (Also see "Neverstill.")

Ravensdale, King County, Washington
The Northern Pacific owned the homes, hotel, and stores in this coal-mining town southeast of Seattle, but a mine explosion in 1915 ended most operations. The community still had about 450 residents in 1926, when it was sold to a Seattle coal-mining company. The school, which enrolled 216 in a five-room school in 1908, had 63 students (in grades one through ten) in 1920. In 1943, its school, along with those of Hobart and Taylor, consolidated to create the Tahoma district.

Richland, Benton County, Washington
This community had just a few hundred people when it was condemned by the federal government during World War II for plutonium production. Expanded by DuPont, the original Manhattan Project contractor, the town was later taken over by General Electric. The number and kind of businesses were controlled, and for years, no buildings or property could be privately owned. When the federal government did decide to sell off the town, residents protested the price of the town site and the projected cost of self-government, delaying incorporation until 1959, when Richland had a population of 22,000.

Roche Harbor, San Juan County, Washington
John S. McMillin established a lime quarry and mill here in the late 1800s after moving from McMillin, Pierce County. An important component in brick mortar, wall plaster, steel, cement, and glass, lime was shipped out on McMillin's own boats. Never incorporated, the San Juan Island community was entirely owned by McMillin, who was active in politics and

Gazetteer

hosted such guests as President Teddy Roosevelt. At the beginning of the Depression, Roche Harbor had about 200 residents. Reuben Tarte purchased the operation in the late 1950s from the McMillin heirs and converted the site to a resort and marina.

Ronald, Kittitas County, Washington

A mile from Roslyn is the coal village of Ronald, which was established in the late 1800s by the Northern Pacific railroad. Its population reached 700 in the peak coal-mining years, but dropped significantly after the mine closed. The railroad sold the houses to area residents in the mid-1960s.

Roslyn, Kittitas County, Washington

The Northern Pacific railroad, which needed coal to fuel its steam locomotives, started developing Roslyn in 1886. The first businesses included a general store and saloon operated by the Northern Pacific Coal Company (later the Northwestern Improvement Company), but there were also many private businesses and homes. The area was also home to several smaller coal-mining companies. Because of strikes, the Northern Pacific imported black miners from Illinois in the late 1800s; many stayed, giving Roslyn and neighboring Ronald an unusually large minority population for decades. The peak coal production came in 1920, when the town had a population of 4,000.

Ryderwood, Cowlitz County, Washington

Called one of Washington state's earliest model logging camps, Ryderwood was built about 1922 by the Long-Bell Lumber Company to supply the company's mills in Longview. The community, completely owned by Long-Bell, once had a population of 2,000, a church, and an elementary and high school. By 1952, however, the timber was cut and there were only 500 people left. The school closed, and the entire village was sold for $90,000 to be redeveloped as a senior-citizen community.

Selleck, King County, Washington

Like Holden and Port Gamble, this former company town was still privately owned at the end of the twentieth century. It has not had an employer since 1939, however. Built a dozen miles northeast of Enumclaw in 1908 by the

Pacific States Lumber Company, it has been described by historians as one of the best-preserved examples of a western Washington lumber town. After Pacific States went bankrupt in 1939, the entire town was purchased by two former employees for $3,000. After salvaging the mill equipment and running the town as a rental housing project, they sold it in 1966; it was sold again in 1970 to the family that still owned it in 1999. While the mill operated, the town had a significant Japanese population, with its own baseball team, fine arts club, clubhouse, bathhouse, samurai movies, and Japanese language school.

Shevlin, Klamath and Deschutes Counties, Oregon

Like many timber companies of its era, the Shevlin-Hixon Company had logging camps with relocatable buildings. Shevlin attracted notice because it, unlike many camps known only by numbers, had a name and, even more unusual, a post office that moved with it. It had a peak population of 600 and, between 1916 and 1951, several locations in central Oregon. Post office records show the Shevlin name was first assigned in 1931. Shevlin houses were known for their design and construction, which facilitated relocation. After Shevlin-Hixon was acquired by the Brooks-Scanlon Company in 1950, some camp buildings made one final move, to the new owner's Timbers camp seven miles north of Gilchrist. Most houses, however, were sold and the community name was changed.

Snoqualmie Falls, King County, Washington

This was another model timber town, established just before World War I by the Snoqualmie Falls Lumber Company, which was owned by the Weyerhaeusers and the Fishers. O. D. Fisher, a Lake States timberman like the Weyerhaeusers, was a longtime director of the Weyerhaeuser Timber Company and the founder of Seattle's Fisher Mills and Fisher Broadcasting (KOMO-TV). The lumber company eventually merged with Weyerhaeuser. The town site included a school, store, hospital, recreation center, and hundreds of houses. Before the town was razed in 1958, employees could buy houses for $100 to $175 and move them to nearby Snoqualmie.

Spiketon, Pierce County, Washington

Located just south of Buckley, this coal-mining community included a company-owned store, hotel, and saloon but no company-owned housing. The American Coal Company acquired an existing mine from the South Willis Coal Company between 1909 and 1911. The mines were sold in 1919 and closed in 1927. By 1919, there were only about 100 residents. The school was consolidated with Buckley's in 1921. Also called Pittsburg and Morristown.

Starkey, Union County, Oregon
Once the Mount Emily Lumber Company headquarters, this town thirty miles southwest of LaGrande was liquidated by the Valsetz Lumber Company in 1955. It had fifty residents in 1919 and seventy-five in 1931.

Stibnite, Valley County, Idaho
Because of its isolation, this community developed slowly. Gold and other mining and smelting operations started in the 1930s; tungsten mining began during World War II. Most operations shut down after the war, and the town was razed.

Taylor, King County, Washington
Located six miles east of Maple Valley in the City of Seattle's watershed, this coal- and clay-mining community was founded in 1893 and named for an official of the Denny-Renton Clay & Coal Company. One investor was a member of Seattle's pioneer Denny family. Most of the coal was used to fire the kilns for the clay pipe, tile, and brick works. Between 1927 and the time it closed, the clay works supplied almost all of the clay sewer pipe for western Washington and more than half of the region's flue lining and chimney pipe. Its bricks were used in several prominent Seattle buildings, including St. James Cathedral and many University of Washington structures. Taylor was condemned by the City of Seattle because of the pollution it created in the watershed. The Taylor school, established in 1904, served 139 children in grades one through nine by 1920, when the population was about 800. By 1930 the town had only 300 people left, and school enrollment had declined to 49 children. Before the clay plant was dismantled starting in 1946, the school had been consolidated with those in Hobart and Ravensdale, and all the stores had closed.

Tono, Thurston County, Washington
Eleven miles northeast of Centralia, this coal-mining village was developed about 1907 by the Union Pacific Coal Company; it eventually had 600 residents. By 1932, however, there were only 350 left, and operations were being run by the Bucoda Coal Mining Company. The name comes from "ton of" coal.

Trinity, Chelan County, Washington
Built about twenty miles north of Leavenworth, just five miles from the crest of the Cascade Mountains, this copper-mining community was developed starting in the late 1920s. It was extremely isolated; for as many as six months of the year, the only access was via sled or snowshoes. The Royal Development Company experienced financial difficulties for years, was forced into receivership in the early 1940s, and finally dissolved in 1948. The site remains privately owned.

Vail, Thurston County, Washington
The Weyerhaeuser Timber Company built this community in 1927 about sixteen miles southeast of Olympia. At one time, it had 600 residents, about sixty houses, bunkhouses, a dining hall and meeting hall, tennis courts, a ballpark, and a company store that operated until 1952. By 1969 there were only ten houses left.

Valsetz, Polk County, Oregon
Now a tree farm, this remote community in the Coast Range was razed in 1984 by Boise Cascade after almost sixty years. Built by Cobbs & Mitchell during World War I, Valsetz won notoriety for its record rainfalls and national publicity for the *Valsetz Star*, a community newspaper started in the late 1930s by the nine-year-old daughter of the cookhouse managers. Cobbs & Mitchell sold the town in 1947 to its sales agent, Herbert Templeton, who operated it as the Valsetz Lumber Company until 1959, when he sold to Boise Cascade. The community once had more than a thousand residents, an elementary and high school, and championship high school basketball teams.

Vanport, Multnomah County, Oregon
Like a company town, this community near Portland had no city govern-

ment, no property taxes, and not a single homeowner. Founded during World War II as a private housing project by Henry Kaiser, who operated the Oregon Shipbuilding Corporation, Vanport was named for nearby Vancouver, Washington, and Portland. It was run by the Housing Authority of Portland in conjunction with the federal government. Built on 650 acres along the Columbia River, it had a population estimated at 39,000 by late 1943. Besides apartment buildings, the project included elementary and nursery schools, fire stations, a theater, post office, library, infirmary, police station, and shopping centers. Its town site staff of 850, larger than the population of most true company towns, handled all maintenance, even repair of the apartment furniture. Originally, renters had to be employed in a certified war industry; as many as two-thirds worked in Kaiser's shipyards. Because of the nationwide recruiting for the shipyards, thousands of blacks moved to Vanport, giving Portland a significant nonwhite population for the first time. The entire community floated down the Columbia River after dikes broke in a 1948 storm. The site is now within the city limits of Portland.

Vaughn, Lane County, Oregon

Established in the 1920s by the Snellstrom Brothers Lumber Company, this timber community was later owned by the Long-Bell Lumber Company, which was sold to International Paper in the mid-1950s.

Wauna, Clatsop County, Oregon

Built on the Columbia River across from Cathlamet, Washington, this mill town was run by the Wauna Lumber Company from 1912 until the company was sold to Crown Zellerbach. In 1919 it had a population of 400, and as the Depression was starting, 700 people. Crown Zellerbach liquidated the town site, demolished the sawmill, and by the mid-1960s was operating a paper mill where houses once stood. This last mill was closed in the late 1990s by the Fort James Corporation.

Wendling, Lane County, Oregon

Wendling was developed in the 1890s and bought just before the turn of the century by the Booth-Kelly Lumber Company. In 1910 a fire destroyed most of the town, but it was rebuilt within months with larger houses and indoor plumbing. The community boomed during World War I; the population peaked at 900. When the Depression began, many residents stayed despite the sawmill's closure. The mill closed permanently in 1945 and the post office in 1952. Today the town site is a Georgia-Pacific tree farm.

Westfir, Lane County, Oregon
The Western Logging Company established this community thirty-five miles south of Eugene about 1923. By 1931 it had 500 people. The mill was later sold to the Westfir Lumber Company and then in 1946 to the Edward Hines Lumber Company. A series of fires closed the mill in 1984. Today the population is about 300.

Wheeler, Tillamook County, Oregon
Established in 1913 by the Coleman Wheeler family, the Wheeler Lumber Company sawmill once employed 450, and the town had a peak population of 1,200. The community started to fade in 1932. Today there are about 300 people. The son of the town founder later went into business with Fred Powers, the son of the founder of Powers, Oregon; their timber firm was acquired by a forerunner of Willamette Industries, itself acquired by Weyerhaeuser in 2002.

Whites, Grays Harbor County, Washington
Also known as White Star, this community of about 100 was established by the White Star Lumber Company after an earlier mill was destroyed in the Yacolt Burn of 1902. The mill operated until after World War II, with the company owning a store, bunkhouses, a cookhouse, and cottages for married workers.

Wilark, Columbia County, Oregon
This logging camp was founded by the Clark & Wilson Lumber Company, a father-and-son firm based in Linnton, Oregon. The post office opened in 1924. Once employing several hundred, Wilark was closed in the early 1930s. Clark & Wilson was liquidated during World War II, and the Clark family became increasingly active in the Willamette Valley Lumber Company (later Willamette Industries), in which it had invested in 1920. After World War II, Wilark was the site of an Oregon state forestry fire camp.

Wilkeson, Pierce County, Washington

The Northern Pacific ran tracks into Wilkeson in 1877 when it began construction of a coal mine to supply fuel for the steam locomotives operating out of its Tacoma terminus thirty miles away. The company built a boardinghouse, school, store, and miners' cottages and opened a post office in the depot. Because Wilkeson's downtown was built on land that wasn't part of the Northern Pacific land grant, all of the other businesses, many homes, a sawmill, and a clay mine were privately owned. In 1883 Henry Villard's Oregon Improvement Company took over the mine; in 1886 a privately owned stone quarry opened. Population peaked at 2,200 in 1917 but dropped dramatically after the coal miners' extended strike in the early 1920s. By 1936, there were only 386 people left in town. Today the town has a few more people; its landmark school and Greek Orthodox and Catholic churches still stand.

NOTES

1 / WHEN THE BOSS BUILT THE TOWN

1. Norman Porter, *McCleary Stimulator*, Dec. 4, 1958, clipping, McCleary Museum.

2 / BUNKHOUSES, TENTHOUSES, AND SILK STOCKING ROW

1. May G. Munyan, *DuPont: The Story of a Company Town* (1972), p. 58; Robert Stafford, "The Reality of an Atomic Utopia: The Town with a Past," *Intellect* (1975), p. 226; Michael Brogan to the author, Aug. 14, 1999.

2. Nancy Irene Hall, *Carbon River Coal Country* (1980), pp. 93–94, 150.

3. Paul C. Pitzer, *Grand Coulee: Harnessing a Dream* (1994), p. 180; David W. James, *Grisdale: Last of the Logging Camps* (1986), p. 63; Patricia Erigero, "Skagit River Hydroelectric Project FERC No. 553" (1991), Sec. 7, pp. 18–19, and Sec. 8, p. 30.

4. McCleary (Wash.) Museum files; anecdotes in the revived *Holden Miner* newsletter, an annual publication by Patty Haddon Tappan for former employees of the Holden Mine.

5. Harriet Wilbour to the author, July 7, 1999.

6. Gertrude Murphy oral history, June 24, 1992, p. 2.

7. Brenda Getty Clark to the author, Nov. 3, 1999; *Holden Miner*.

8. Impie (Marian) Hanga Sipila, "My Remembrances of Taylor, Washington,"

in *Hobart Area Recollections* (1988), p. 22; Dorothy Anne Hobson, *The Valsetz Star* (1942), p. 43.

9. Barbara J. Kubik, *Richland: Celebrating the Heritage* (1994), p. 39; Ted Van Arsdol, *Tri-Cities: The Mid-Columbia Hub* (1990), p. 56; Richard H. Syring, "Turning an Atom City Over to Private Owners Is No Simple Matter," *Wall Street Journal*, Aug. 2, 1952, p. 1.

10. Keith C. Petersen, *Company Town: Potlatch, Idaho, and the Potlatch Lumber Co.* (1987), pp. 91, 98; Samuel A. Schrager, "The Early Days: Logging in the Inland Northwest" (Ph.D. dissertation, University of Pennsylvania, 1983), p. 280.

11. Florence K. Lentz, National Register Nomination for Seattle City Light (1996), Cedar Falls, Sec. 8, p. 6; "Big Improvements at Mines Finished," *Tacoma Daily Ledger*, Dec. 30, 1917.

12. Bill Buchanan, "Bernard Maybeck and Brookings, Oregon," oregoncoast.net/maybeck.html (1998); T. William Booth, "Design for a Lumber Town by Bebb and Gould, Architects," *Pacific Northwest Quarterly* (1991), pp. 132–134.

13. G. W. Hitchcock, "The World's First All-Electric City: Mason City," *Pacific Builder & Engineer*, Jan. 19, 1935, p. 4; Ted Van Arsdol, "Atomic Richland Builds for Tomorrow's Future," *Spokane Spokesman-Review*, Jan. 30, 1955; Paul Beardsley, *The Long Road to Self-Government: The History of Richland, Washington, 1943–1968* (c. 1968), pp. 15, 19.

14. Manly Maben, *Vanport* (1987), pp. 9, 30, 33, 44–45, 58.

15. "The housing policy, frequently revised and increasingly complex over the years, was to become a major source of dissatisfaction for workers on the Skagit, exacerbated by the growing emphasis on facilities for tourism." Erigero, "Skagit River," Sec. 7, p. 16. Ross was critical of those employees who complained that he built structures primarily for tourists: "Some of our people have said that we should have facilities for them instead of building for those making up the tours. They forget that the tourist pays his way." Ibid., Sec. 8, pp. 26–27.

16. Ronald L. Gregory, "Life in Railroad Logging Camps of the Shevlin-Hixon Co., 1916–1950" (M.A. thesis, Oregon State University, 1977), pp. 63–65; Lee Maker to the author, Aug. 3, 1999; Lyle Compton Sears, *Sampler of the Early Years*, vol. 2 (1986), p. 206; Lois Maker Gumpert and Dorothy Cale, "Shevlin Camp," in *A History of the Deschutes Country in Oregon* (1985), pp. 94–95.

17. Marian Thompson Arlin, oral history, Nov. 3, 1993. Because power plant employees, like City of Seattle employees on the Skagit projects, didn't pay for their electricity, they seldom turned lights off. Marian Thompson Arlin and Dorothy

Graybael Scott, eds., *Cedar Falls: As Remembered by Some of Those Who Lived There* (1989).

18. John S. Ott and Dick Malloy, *The Tacoma Public Utilities Story: The First 100 Years* (1993), pp. 79–80; Ernest C. Teagle, "An Informal Biography of the Teagle Family" (1960).

19. Mary McWilliams, *Seattle Water Department History* (1955), p. 136.

20. Gregory, "Life in Railroad Logging Camps," pp. 53–55; 1940 U.S. Census data.

21. Donald Denno to the author, Jan. 6, 2000.

22. Bruce O. Schneider, "The Historic Mining Landscape of Taylor, Washington" (paper for REM 598, Central Washington University, n.d.), p. 23; Petersen, *Company Town*, p. 147; Maben, *Vanport*, p. 36.

23. Art Sherman to the author, April 29, 1999; Charles Hale to the author, June 3, 1999; James, *Grisdale*, p. 62.

24. Jan M. Eakins, "Historic American Engineering Record, Port Gamble" (1997), p. 3; "All Flags Join in U.S. War Work," *Tacoma Daily Ledger*, Nov. 20, 1918; Pitzer, *Grand Coulee*, p. 104; Tom Hallman, "Valsetz, 1919–1984," *Sunday Oregonian*, July 1, 1984, p. 14; Mike Thoele, "Brothers Ensure Gilchrist Remains a Survivor," *Eugene (Ore.) Register-Guard*, Oct. 10, 1991, pp. 1, 6A.

25. Landmark application drafts for Cedar Falls and Selleck; Louise Schmidt Robertson to the author, April 10, 2000; Patty Haddon Tappan to the author and author's tour of the former Curzon, Wilbour, and Phillips residences at Holden Village, Wash., July 1999.

26. Steve Willis to the author, Jan. 22, 2000; Lee Maker to the author, Aug. 3, 1999; "Simpson Archives: Timber Company Roots," *Simpson Magazine*, November 1977, pp. 2–3.

27. Lou and Ann Messmer to the author, Jan. 8, 2000; Petersen, *Company Town*, p. 123; Tappan to the author, 1999; Elmer Smith to the author, 1999.

28. Hall, *Carbon River*, p. 75; Jennifer A. Meisner, "The Future of Roslyn, Washington: Preservation of a Vernacular Town" (Master's thesis, University of Washington, 1994), p. 95; *Olympia (Wash.) Recorder*, Sept. 10, 1910; Angelo M. Pellegrini, *Immigrant's Return* (1951), p. 45; Grace Brandt Martin, *An Oregon Schoolma'am*, Book 2: *The Depression Years* (1981), p. 64.

29. Tappan to the author, April–November, 1999; Harriet Wilbour to the author, April–November 1999; Holden Portal Museum files.

30. Edward Gray, *Roughing It on the Little Deschutes River, 1934–44* (1986), p. 139.

31. Petersen, *Company Town,* p. 120; Pitzer, *Grand Coulee,* pp. 179–180.

32. Maben, *Vanport,* p. 25; Stuart McElderry, "Vanport Conspiracy Rumors and Social Relations in Portland, 1940–50," *Oregon Historical Quarterly* (1988), p. 154.

33. Wilbour, Tappan, Bill Phillips, and Janet Adams Westom to the author, all April–November 1999.

34. Mary Gilchrist Ernst to the author, July 20, 1999; Gregory, "Life in Railroad Logging Camps," pp. 58–59; Richard H. Syring, "Turning an Atom City Over" (1952), pp. 1–2.

35. Petersen, *Company Town,* p. 137; *Mason City (Wash.) Columbian,* June 16, 1938; Kubik, *Richland,* p. 48; Beardsley, *Long Road,* pp. 11, 21; Marilyn Garcia to the author, Feb. 16, 2000; Maben, *Vanport,* p. 34; Erigero, "Skagit River," Sec. 7, pp. 17.

36. Chris Brown and John Schroeder, "An Investigation of Place and Community through Photographs, Maps, and Oral Histories" (University of Washington class project, 1996); "Old Sawmill Town Remembered," *Northwest Nikkei* (1994), pp. 7, 15.

37. Jan M. Eakins, "Port Gamble Historic Landmark, HAER No. WA-135" (1997), p. 28; James, *Grisdale,* p. 62; Wilbour to the author, Jan. 19, 2001; Gregory, "Life in Railroad Logging Camps," pp. 71–73.

38. Petersen, *Company Town,* p. 138; James, *Grisdale,* p. 63; Stafford, "Reality," p. 226.

39. Maben, *Vanport,* p. 24; Kubik, *Richland,* p. 58; Gray, *Roughing It,* pp. 112, 117; Joye Hamm Malmstrom to the author, Sept. 18, 1999.

40. Malmstrom to the author; Tappan to the author, Sept. 8, 1999.

3 / WHO LIVED IN COMPANY TOWNS?

1. Andrew Prouty, "More Deadly Than War: Pacific Coast Logging, 1827–1981" (Ph.D. dissertation, University of Washington, 1982), p. 99, claims that a total of 74 women worked in forestry in Washington state in the early 1900s (in contrast to more than 20,000 men). In 1923, when Estella Dodge graduated from the University of Washington, the *Timberman* reported ("Girl Graduates in Forestry") that she was the only known woman graduate of an American forestry school. U.S. Census data for 1920 show a handful of women working in mining—a tenth of 1 percent of the total employed. By 1940, things hadn't changed much: of the 2,620 people working in coal mining in Washington state, only 26 were women. In Other Mining and Quarrying, the census category that included the Holden copper mines

and the Roche Harbor lime quarries, there was a total of 2,736 employed; 50 were women, but 35 were described as urban employees, probably workers in metropolitan offices. Similarly, of the 35,000 who worked in sawmills in Washington in 1940, there were 974 women, 767 of whom were described as urban.

2. Prouty, "More Deadly," p. 60. *Chelan Valley Minor,* Dec. 4, 1941. Among some immigrant groups, the men significantly outnumbered the women; for example, in 1910, Washington state had 11,000 Italian-born residents, but only 2,000 were women or girls. David L. Nicandri, *Italians in Washington State Emigration, 1853–1924* (1978), p. 31.

3. George A. Shipman, *The Grand Coulee Dam Area: A Preliminary Report* (1953), p. 14; Beardsley, *Long Road,* p. 11.

4. Hall, *Carbon River,* p. 149; Diane Olson and Cory Olson, *Black Diamond: Mining the Memories* (1988), p. 76.

5. Olson and Olson, *Black Diamond,* p. 154; Harriet Wilbour to the author, June 23, 1999.

6. Ted Goodwin, *Stories of Western Loggers* (1977), p. 43; Bob Paasch audiotape; Gregory, "Life in Railroad Logging Camps," p. 80; Dave Parker to the author, Oct. 20, 1999; retired Kosmos Timber Company employees to the author at the Kosmos Korner reunion, Glenoma, Wash., Aug. 15, 1999.

7. Tappan to the author, April–November, 1999.

8. Pitzer, *Grand Coulee,* pp. 111–112, 200.

9. Bill Phillips to the author, Sept. 13, 1999.

10. Gregory, "Life in Railroad Logging Camps," p. 121; *Holden Miner,* 1948–54.

11. Phillips, letter to the author; Mary Gilchrist Ernst to the author, June 22, 1999; "A Town Called DuPont," *Steilacoom Historical Museum Quarterly* (1994), pp. 1, 4–8; Denno to the author.

12. Pellegrini, *Immigrant's Return,* p. 82; McCleary Museum files; "Biggest Logging Camp in the World," *Cowlitz Historical Quarterly* (1988), p. 21; Gary Poole to Charles Hale, spring 1999.

13. Murray Morgan, *The Dam* (1954), p. 132; Hobson, *Valsetz Star,* various references; Arlin and Scott, *Cedar Falls.* Even after World War II, children and adults in Washington peeled cascara. Sherwood Forest Farms, Seattle, was one of the largest U.S. wholesalers of cascara bark between 1903 and the 1980s, when synthetic cascara was developed. Scott Tretheway to the author, Sept. 20, 1999.

14. Tappan, letter to the author; *Holden Miner,* 1948–54; *Wenatchee Daily World,* March 1, 1958; Ernest C. Teagle, *Out of the Woods: The Story of McCleary*

Notes to Chapter 3

(1956), p. 42; *Simpson Lookout,* 1950–53; "Grisdale Is an Old Logger's Dream of Life in Big Woods," *Seattle Times,* Dec. 6, 1947; Dave Parker to the author, Oct. 20, 1999.

15. U.S. Census data; figures for Hispanics are included with whites.

16. Petersen, *Company Town,* p. 119; John Driscoll, "Gilchrist," *Oregon Historical Quarterly* (1984), p. 139; Tappan to the author.

17. Isabelle Fletcher Anderson to Charles Hale, spring 1999; "Old Sawmill Town Remembered," pp. 7, 15.

18. Tappan to the author; Doran Curzon Gordon to the author, Sept. 7, 1999.

19. Petersen, *Company Town,* p. 119; Pellegrini, *Immigrant's Return,* p. 63; Nicandri, *Italians,* pp. 29, 34, 63; Freda A. Adams, "The Port Blakely I Knew," in *Kitsap County History* (1977).

20. Employers across the U.S. took advantage of the deteriorating race relations in the latter part of the nineteenth century to keep employees from organizing. Robert A. Campbell, "Blacks and the Coal Mines of Western Washington, 1888–1896," *Pacific Northwest Quarterly* (1982), pp. 146–155.

21. Campbell, "Blacks and the Coal Mines," pp. 146–155. In 1904 the Roslyn population was approximately 4,000, mainly Slavs, blacks, Italians, and Germans, according to Mary Ann Petrich and Barbara Roje, "The Slavs in the Coal Mining Communities of Central Washington," in *The Yugoslav in Washington State: Among the Early Settlers* (1984), pp. 47–52. The comment regarding black workers appeared on page 252 of *An Illustrated History of Klickitat, Yakima and Kittitas Counties,* first published by the Interstate Publishing Company (Chicago) in 1904 and later reproduced by the Yakima Valley (Wash.) Genealogical Society; the comment was repeated without attribution in the volunteer-written *Spawn of Coal Dust: History of Roslyn, 1886–1955* (1955), p. 208.

22. Pitzer, *Grand Coulee,* pp. 141–142. Of the three counties whose residents had priority for jobs on the dam under the Works Progress Administration, Douglas Country reported twenty-three black men and women, Okanogan one man, and Grant no men or women. Nearby Lincoln County, where some of the Mason City buildings were prefabricated, reported two black men in its 1930 census.

23. John Hanscom, "Franklin and the Oregon Improvement Company," *Columbia Magazine* (Spring 1994) pp. 13–18; Pitzer, *Grand Coulee,* pp. 200–201; Schrager, "Early Days," p. 276; Pellegrini, *Immigrant's Return,* p. 44.

24. "Old Sawmill Town Remembered," pp. 7, 15; Mary Woodman and Richard Gilbert, "Barneston's Japanese Community" (1995), p. 15.

25. Pellegrini, *Immigrant's Return,* pp. 68–69.

26. Driscoll, "Gilchrist," p. 139; Arlin, oral history, p. 62; L. Vaughn Downs, *The Mightiest of Them All: Memories of Grand Coulee Dam*, rev. ed. (1993), pp. 41–42; Angelo M. Pellegrini, *Americans by Choice* (1956), p. 23.

27. Gordon to the author; Nigel Adams audiotape (1979); Tappan to the author, May 4, 1999; Marge Haddon Stansfield to the author, Sept. 8, 1999.

28. Pitzer, *Grand Coulee*, p. 89; Kubik, *Richland*, p. 44; "Okay! So You Want to Work in the Logging Camp," *The Timberman* (1948), pp. 82, 84.

29. Maude Nelson, "Muckers' Special, or I Taught at Holden," typescript in Holden Portal Museum, c. 1961.

4 / WHEN THE DINNER BELL CLANGED

1. Catherine Baldwin, *Making the Most of the Best: Willamette Industries' Seventy-Five Years* (1982), pp. 74–75; Paul Hosmer, *Now We're Loggin'* (1930), p. 176; *History of Spruce Production Division* (c. 1919), p. 77; Joann Roe, *The North Cascadians* (1980), p. 134. Food preoccupied men, said Joseph Conlin in "Old Boy, Did You Get Enough Pie?" (*Journal of Forest History* [1979], p. 176). He wrote, "It is interesting to compare the loggers' attitude toward food and their indifference to the weather, lice, filth, and even relatively, to wages." Some historians suggest that employers were similarly obsessed; as Ronald L. Gregory wrote about the Shevlin-Hixon Company, the corporate philosophy was "a full stomach meant a happy employee." "Life in Railroad Logging Camps," p. 77.

2. James, *Grisdale*, p. 69; Gray, *Roughing It*, pp. 32, 105.

3. A 1914 survey showed that loggers were fed 8,000 calories a day while the U.S. Army provided a soldier 5,000 calories. Prouty, "More Deadly Than War," p. 157; *History of Spruce Production Division*, introduction, p. 18; Doug Welch, "Chamber Tourists Visit Coulee Dam," *Seattle Post-Intelligencer,* April 18, 1939, p. 1; James, *Grisdale*, p. 69; Gregory, "Life in Railroad Logging Camps," p. 77; Don Duncan, "Life on a Limb," *Seattle Times,* July 25, 1982, mag. sec., p. 15; *Lakewood (Wash.) Log,* March 25, 1949.

4. Sam Churchill, "Christmas in Camp," *Timberbeast* (Winter 1984), p. 10; *Simpson Lookout,* January 1951; "Loggers Enjoy Annual Dinner," *Polk County (Ore.) Itemizer-Observer,* Dec. 1, 1938, p. 8.

5. Merle Savery, "Northwest Wonderland: Washington State," *National Geographic* (1960), p. 472.

6. H. A. (Andy) Solberg to the author, November 1999.

Notes to Chapter 5

7. James, *Grisdale,* p. 64; Margaret Elley Felt, *The Enterprising Mister Murray* (1978), p. 34; *Lakewood Log.*

8. *West Coast Timberman* (1943); Mike Bolinger, "Old Time Logging and the Cookhouse," *Timberbeast* (Spring 1985), pp. 8–11; newspaper clipping, c. 1943, in the files of the Holden Portal Museum, Holden Village, Wash.

9. Hogs have been called one of the "less agreeable realities" of company-town life. A former Port Gamble, Washington, resident commented on the risk of walking near the cookhouse when the mill whistle blew because the hogs raced from all over town for the kitchen scraps. Eakins, "Port Gamble," p. 29. Gray, *Roughing It,* p. 104; "Howe Sound Mine Has Million Dollar Payroll," *Chelan Valley Mirror,* Dec. 4, 1941. The $1.20 paid by Holden miners in 1941 had the buying power of $14.51 in 2001.

5 / EDUCATION IN THE COMPANY TOWN

1. Petersen, *Company Town,* pp. 122, 200; "Biggest Logging Camp," p. 17; Stuart D. Brandes, *American Welfare Capitalism* (1970), p. 57.

2. Jim Fisher, *Gilchrist: The First Fifty Years* (1988), p. 23; John M. McClelland Jr., *R. A. Long's Planned City: The Story of Longview* (1976), pp. 81, 83; Annual Reports, Kitsap County, Wash., Superintendent of Schools.

3. John Fahey, *The Inland Empire: Unfolding Years, 1879–1929* (1986), p. 74; Barneston files, Cedar River Watershed City of Seattle Archives; Martin, *Oregon Schoolma'am,* p. 64; Hall, *Carbon River,* p. 159; Mary Young McDivitt to the author, June 5, 1999; Lentz, National Register Nomination, Sec. 8, p. 38; Cheryl Cronander, National Register registration form for Selleck, Wash. (1989), Sec. 7, and Cronander's notes for the application.

4. James, *Grisdale,* p. 64.

5. Annual Reports, King and Pierce Counties, Wash., Superintendent of Schools, show that by 1940 King County had ten one-room schools left, including a few company-town schools. Louise Schmidt Robertson to the author, April 10, 2000; Petersen, *Company Town,* p. 150; *Spawn of Coal Dust,* pp. 43–44.

6. U.S. Census, 1910; Fahey, *Inland Empire,* p. 75. Ads in January 1931 issues of the Portland *Oregonian* promised boarders home-cooked meals, a short walk to school, and motherly supervision for $5 a week.

7. Olson and Olson, *Black Diamond,* pp. 139–140.

8. Clarence Bagley, *History of King County* (1929), p. 506; Gregory, "Life in Railroad Logging Camps," pp. 85–88.

9. *Holden Miner,* March 1990, quoting the *Chelan Valley Mirror* issue of Dec. 20, 1989; Erigero, "Skagit River," Sec. 8, p. 25; Mary Ellen Field Lacy to the author, Nov. 15, 1999.

10. Janet Adams Westom to the author, April 19, 1999; Stansfield to the author; "500 Holden Miners Get Pay Increase," *Chelan Valley Mirror,* July 1941.

11. Gordon to the author; Stansfield and Patty Haddon Tappan to the author, Sept. 8, 1999.

12. Arlin and Scott, *Cedar Falls,* several references to Emmett Jackson; Lou Messmer to the author.

13. James, *Grisdale,* p. 71; Lou Messmer to the author; Arlin, *Cedar Falls; Simpson Lookout,* spring 1952; *Holden Miner,* spring 1948; Brenda Getty Clark to the author, Nov. 3, 1999; Parker to the author; Hallman, "Valsetz, 1919–1984," p. 26.

14. Olson and Olson, *Black Diamond,* p. 78; Arlin, *Cedar Falls.*

15. McClelland, pp. 64, 65; Maben, *Vanport,* pp. 24–25; Pitzer, *Grand Coulee,* p. 44.

16. Woodman, "Barneston's Japanese Community." In *Women in Pacific Northwest History: An Anthology* (1988), pp. 225, 229, Gail M. Nomura notes that Congress in 1924 prohibited the immigration of "aliens ineligible to citizenship." This act meant that Japanese men already in the U.S. could no longer return to Japan, marry, and bring their new wives to the U.S., and it ended the immigration of other Japanese men and women.

17. Petersen, *Company Town,* p. 122; Martin, *Oregon Schoolma'am,* p. 103; Annual Reports, Kitsap and King Counties, Wash., Superintendent of Schools.

18. Annual Reports, King County, Superintendent of Schools.

19. Nelson, "Muckers' Special"; Parker to the author.

20. Arlin and Scott, *Cedar Falls;* Tappan, Westom, Phillips to the author; Max Woods to the author, Feb. 20, 2000; Denno to the author.

21. Wendell B. Laughbon reminiscence in the *DuPont Villager,* Sept. 16, 1966; Sandy Wigbers Adam to the author, Sept. 20, 1999; "So You Think You Had Snow," *Life* (1956), p. 76; Nelson, "Muckers' Special"; undated clipping from a 1927 issue of the *Olympia (Wash.) Morning Olympian,* McCleary Museum.

22. Bagley, *History of King Country,* p. 504; Petersen, *Company Town,* p. 120;

Notes to Chapter 6

Spawn of Coal Dust, pp. 188, 229; Brown, "An Investigation of Place"; Kubik, *Richland,* p. 76.

6 / RELIGION IN THE COMPANY TOWN

1. Brandes, *American Welfare Capitalism,* p. 68.

2. Kubik, *Richland,* p. 48; "Richland Grows Like a Boom Town," *Spokane Spokesman-Review,* June 17, 1951.

3. Louise Schmidt Robertson to the author, April 10, 2000; Lester and Joan Lockhart Snider to Charles Hale, June 1999; "Richland Church System Is Revolutionary," *Tri-City Herald,* Oct. 11, 1953; Synod of Alaska Northwest, Presbyterian Church (U.S.A.) *Annual Report* (1944), p. 25.

4. Olson and Olson, *Black Diamond,* pp. 161–165; Bruce Ramsey, *Britannia: The Story of a Mine* (1967), p. 147.

5. Port Gamble historical supplement, *Bremerton (Wash.) Sun,* Nov. 19, 1966; *More Than 100 Years of Ministry* (1988); "Roche Harbor Resort," rocheharbor.com (2002).

6. Driscoll, "Gilchrist," p. 139; DuPont files in the Tacoma Public Library's Northwest Room and Special Collections; Petersen, *Company Town,* p. 95. For years this Lutheran church was the only building in town not owned by the Potlatch Lumber Company. Edward G. Olsen, ed., *Then Till Now in Brookings-Harbor: A Social History of the Chetco Community Area* (1979), pp. 139–140.

7. Ernest C. Teagle, *A Brief History of the McCleary Methodist Church, 1910–1960* (1960); Goodwin, *Stories,* p. 37; Munyan, *DuPont,* p. 58; Don Duncan, "Town's Sale Doesn't Upset National," *Tacoma News Tribune,* April 7, 1957.

8. Olson and Olson; *Black Diamond,* pp. 161–165.

9. *Holden Miner,* June 14, 1948; Nigel Adams audiotape (1979); Janet Adams Westom to the author, Oct. 20, 1999.

10. Frank A. Reed, *Lumberjack Sky Pilot* (1965), p. 5; Roe, *North Cascadians,* p. 120; "Evangelistic Services at Presbyterian Church," *Concrete Herald,* Feb. 2, 1924, p. 1; George Redden, *From Bootblack to Pastor of the Pines and Twenty-two Thousand Miles through the Pines of the Northwest with the Lumber-Jack* (c. 1932), and "The 'Pastor of the Pines: A Modern Circuit Rider,'" *ABC* (c. 1932).

11. "Biggest Logging Camp," pp. 23, 26; Goodwin, *Stories,* p. 37; "Sky Pilot," *Weyerhaeuser Magazine,* November 1954, p. 8.

12. George C. F. Pringle, *Adventures in Service* (1929), pp. 12–13; "The 'Pastor of the Pines'"; Goodwin, *Stories,* p. 49.

13. "Old Sawmill Town Remembered," pp. 7, 15; *Spawn of Coal Dust*, p. 35; Lars E. Carlsson, *Port Blakely Mills and Milltown: Historic Buildings/Cultural Resources Survey for Port Blakely Mill Co.* (1992), p. 23.

14. The only couple wed in Holden during mining years was Roy and Marge Shoeppach, who married in a friend's home.

7 / BASEBALL, BOWLING, BANDS,

AND BRIDGE TOURNAMENTS

1. Richard L. Neuberger, *Our Promised Land* (1938), p. 376.

2. Petersen, *Company Town;* Munyan, *DuPont;* Nigel B. Adams, *The Holden Mine: Discovery to Production, 1896–1938* (1981); Arlin and Scott, *Cedar Falls;* Felt, *Enterprising Mister Murray.* The description of Kinzua's Jeffmore Hall was provided by Marilyn Garcia in an interview on Feb. 16, 2000. The communities that offered no recreation positioned themselves for failure, Manley Maben noted in *Vanport* (1987), pp. 45–46: "World War II shipyard workers moved in—and out—of the community at an almost unbelievable pace despite the difficulty in finding housing in Portland during wartime. One reason was that Vanport offered almost no commercial adult recreation. Other than a single theater which could seat only a fraction of the project's 40,000 residents, Vanport had no place to relax: no pool hall, no bowling alley, no card room, no tavern or bar."

3. Movies were an antidote for grumbling and their "hypnotic powers were soon recognized" by employers, Stuart Brandes wrote in *American Welfare Capitalism,* p. 77. One boss showed movies daily at noon "to keep [workers] from getting together in little groups and talking about their troubles." Regarding movies in Northwest company towns, see "Equipment for Camp Movies," *The Timberman* (December 1923), p. 160; the Works Progress Administration manuscripts on Ryderwood; Stafford, "Reality of an Atomic Utopia," p. 226; *Richland Villager,* 1945–50; *Holden Miner,* March 15 and 22, 1948.

4. "Old Sawmill Town Remembered," pp. 7, 15.

5. Jim Fisher, "Gilchrist, Oregon: Last Timber Company Town," *Forest World* (1989), pp. 26–29; Joan Lockhart Snider to Charles Hale, spring 1999; Gregory, "Life in Railroad Logging Camps," pp. 59, 111–112, 126.

6. LaVonne Sparkman, *From Homestead to Lakebed* (1994), pp. 144–145; Schneider, "The Historic Mining Landscape," pp. 19–20; Munyan, *DuPont,* p. 80; "Kinzua News," *Fossil (Ore.) Journal,* December 1954 issues.

7. Olson and Olson, *Black Diamond.*

8. The importance of baseball is noted by Brandes, *American Welfare Capitalism;* Petersen, *Company Town;* Olson and Olson, *Black Diamond;* and Hall, *Carbon River.* Other sources: the 1948–54 issues of the *Holden Miner* and a program for Holden's 1944 Independence Day celebration, Holden Portal Museum; John Bley to the author, Oct. 24, 1999; Munyan, *DuPont,* p. 137; the June 16 and Aug. 25, 1938, issues of the *Mason City Columbian,* and a *Polk County Itemizer-Observer* story, "Valsetz Ball Team to Open Sunday," April 18, 1940, p. 1.

9. *Spawn of Coal Dust,* pp. 54–55; *Holden Miner,* 1945–54, and March 1995; *Mason City Columbian,* 1938.

10. *Wenatchee Daily World,* Feb. 10, 1940; "A Town Called DuPont," pp. 1, 4–8; bowling tournament reports in the *Tacoma Daily Ledger,* December 1917; Munyan, *DuPont,* p. 64.

11. Teagle, *Out of the Woods,* pp. 37–38; Gregory, "Life in Railroad Logging Camps," p. 105.

12. Gregory, "Life in Railroad Logging Camps," p. 117; R. L. Polk *Gazetteers,* 1931–32; *Holden Miner,* 1948–54; Elmer Smith to the author, Aug. 28, 1999; Arlin and Scott, *Cedar Falls,* various references to dance and 4-H orchestras; Victor Stevens, *The Powers Story* (1979), p. 33; Beardsley, *Long Road,* pp. 6, 10.

13. Ramsey, *Britannia Beach,* p. 153.

14. Van Arsdol, "Atomic Richland"; Petersen, *Company Town,* pp. 148–149; *Holden Miner,* 1948–54; Beardsley, *Long Road,* p. 27.

15. Van Arsdol, "Atomic Richland"; *Richland Villager,* 1945–49; *Holden Miner,* 1948–54.

16. Petersen, *Company Town,* pp. 148–149; Teagle, *Brief History; DuPont Villager,* Dec. 20, 1968.

17. *Mason City Columbian,* 1938–39; *Simpson Lookout,* March 1953; *Holden Miner,* Nov. 11, 1948, and spring 1951.

18. Petersen, *Company Town,* p. 144; Tappan and Stansfield to the author, Sept. 8, 1999; Margaret Elley Felt, *Capitol Forest: The Forest That Came Back* (1975), p. 29.

19. Gordon and Phillips to the author; Petersen, *Company Town,* pp. 1, 143, 144.

20. Hall, *Carbon River,* p. 26.

21. Neuberger in *Our Promised Land* (p. 247): "Years ago . . . collection boxes

in various Western cities solicited old books and magazines for 'the men in our forests.'" Petersen, *Company Town,* pp. 128–129; "Library Popular: State Meets Need of Rural Communities," *Olympia Morning Olympian,* April 30, 1909, pp. 1, 4; "Kinzua News," *Fossil (Ore.) Journal,* April, 1942; Arlin and Scott, *Cedar Falls.*

22. "Formally Open New Puget Hotel," *Seattle Post-Intelligencer,* Sept. 27, 1903, p. 11; Petersen, *Company Town,* p. 154; Gray, *Roughing It,* pp. 160–161; program for Holden Independence Day celebration; *Wenatchee Daily World,* April 29, 1940.

23. Gregory, "Life in Railroad Logging Camps," pp. 94–105; Petersen, *Company Town,* p. 151.

24. *Holden Miner,* 1948–54; *Mason City Columbian,* June 16, 1938.

25. *Mason City Columbian,* June 30 and Aug. 25, 1938; Arlin and Scott, *Cedar Falls.*

26. Grace Sherman Brooks, oral history, April 1977; Petersen, *Company Town,* p. 149.

27. Sipila, "My Remembrances," p. 22; Wilbour, letter to the author.

28. Elmer Smith to the author, May 22, 1999; Hallman, "Valsetz, 1919–1984," p. 11; Arlin and Scott, *Cedar Falls;* Gregory, "Life in Railroad Logging Camps," pp. 122–124; "Biggest Logging Camp," p. 18.

29. Myrtle Beckwith Alexander to the author regarding Kosmos Timber Company closures for fishing for smelt and hunting, Aug. 15, 1999, and *The Timberman,* Oct. 10, 1938, p. 85, reporting the Booth-Kelly Lumber Company closing "to accommodate the hunting yen of the crew." The Selleck berry-picking trip is recorded in Cheryl Cronander's notes.

30. Smith, letter to the author; Betty Bickford Christianson to the author, Feb. 5, 2000; Arlin and Scott, *Cedar Falls.*

31. "Dolfay's Dolphin," *Holden Miner,* October 1990; Morgan, *The Dam,* p. 70.

32. Edgemont sources include September 1999 correspondence between the author and Elbert Hubbard Sr., who purchased the site in the late 1940s, and a Sept. 7, 1999, conversation with Wilma Johnson, who in the 1920s worked across Lake Chelan from Edgemont. Roy Craft discussed "Big Betty" in a column in the Nov. 20, 1959, *Skamania County Pioneer.*

33. Gregory, "Life in Railroad Logging Camps," p. 82.

34. Teagle, *Out of the Woods,* p. 35; McCleary Museum files; Joann Roe, *Stevens Pass* (1995), p. 44; Hall, *Carbon River,* pp. 52–53; Gertrude Murphy, oral history, June 24, 1992, p. 3.

35. Goodwin, *Stories,* p. 24.

Notes to Chapter 8

8 / THE IMPORTANCE OF THE COMPANY STORE

1. James B. Allen, *The Company Town In the American West* (1966), discusses company stores in general. The scrip system typical in Appalachian coal-mining towns is described in "Fire in the Hole," *The Kentucky Cycle*, by Robert Schenkkan (1993), pp. 221–222: "We on the scrip system here, Company money only," a new employee is told. Some company stores continued to operate even after they became cash drains; Simpson Timber Company archives indicate that by the 1950s, the McCleary branch of the Lumbermen's Mercantile was not profitable. Sally A. Maddocks, *Guide to the Historical Archives of the Simpson Timber Co.*, 2d ed. (1985).

2. Petersen, *Company Town*, pp. 132, 135, 153; Clifford Lewis Imus, "A Social History of Potlatch, Idaho" (B.A. thesis, Washington State College, 1910), p. 13; Lumbermen's Mercantile scrapbooks and photos; James, *Grisdale*, p. 32; *Camp & Mill News*, January 1929, p. 7; Marilyn Garcia to the author, Feb. 16, 2000. Many companies issued paper scrip, often in coupon books; some, like Howe Sound and Kinzua Pine Mills, minted lightweight coins.

3. Hall, *Carbon River*, pp. 76, 90; Pitzer, *Grand Coulee*, p. 181.

4. Torger Birkeland, *Echoes of Puget Sound* (1960), pp. 80–81; Elmer Smith to the author, May 22 and Aug. 28, 1999.

5. Willis to the author, Aug. 14, 1999; R. L. Polk *Gazetteers*, 1931–32; Art Sherman to the author, April 29, 1999; Gregory, "Life in Railroad Logging Camps," pp. 88, 121; Harriet Wilbour to the author, Aug. 14, 1999. Erickson's, the Bend, Oregon, grocer that for a few years maintained a branch store at Shevlin, also ran a delivery route the sixty-three miles to Mowich, a seasonal logging camp.

6. Elmer Smith to the author; Wigbers Adam to the author.

7. Petersen, *Company Town*, p. 135; Goodwin, *Stories*, p. 31; Elmer Smith, letter to the author.

8. Arlin and Scott, *Cedar Falls*; Gray, *Roughing It*, p. 153; Denno to the author; "Valsetz News," *Polk County Itemizer-Observer*, Feb. 14, 1935, p. 4.

9. Arlin, oral history, p. 54; Ruth Bley audiotape (1981).

10. "Old Sawmill Town Remembered," pp. 7, 15; "Kinzua News," *Fossil (Ore.) Journal*, Oct. 26, 1928; Elmer Smith to the author.

11. "Summer Comes to Holden Camp," *Wenatchee Daily World*, June 20, 1956; *Holden Miner*, March 22 and Nov. 22, 1948.

12. *Spawn of Coal Dust*, p. 12; Goodwin, *Stories*, p. 17; *Mason City Columbian*, June 16, 1938; McCleary Museum newsletter, spring 1995.

13. Wigbers Adam to the author.

14. *Spawn of Coal Dust,* p. 12; McCleary Museum files; *Camp & Mill News,* December 1930, p. 6; Brown, "An Investigation of Place"; Elmer Smith to the author; Wilbour to the author.

9 / 40 MILES FROM NOWHERE

1. "Ore Tug Operator Soon Will Finish 20-Year Haul on Lake Chelan," *Chelan Valley Mirror,* spring 1957, pp. 1, 3; John Bley to the author, Oct. 24, 1999; Brenda Getty Clark to the author, Nov. 3, 1999; Janet Adams Westom to the author, Oct. 20, 1999.

2. Wigbers Adam to the author; *Holden Miner,* 1948–1954; Wilbour to the author, Oct. 22, 1999.

3. "Daily Life in Mining Days" audiotape; Wilbour to the author; Christine Leigh Plimpton, "An Ethnoarchaeological Study of Honeymoon Heights: The Original Camp of the Holden Mine, Holden, Washington" (Master's thesis, Washington State University, 1984), p. 1. The difficulty in "getting out" from Honeymoon Heights was similar to that at another Howe Sound community. While those who lived at Britannia Beach, the mining company's waterfront village in British Columbia, simply walked to the dock for the 7 A.M. boat to Vancouver, miners' families who lived in the Townsite community up the mountain had a much more complicated trip. They walked to an electric railway for a thirty-minute trip and then transferred to an incline railway for a fifteen- or twenty-minute ride down a steep grade standing in an open flatcar. The final leg of the journey—just to get to the waterfront for the half-day-long boat ride—was 347 uncovered steps between the incline railway stop and the dock. Ramsey, *Britannia,* pp. 151–153.

4. *Holden Miner,* Feb. 13, 1951.

5. Paul C. Pitzer, *Building the Skagit: A Century of Upper Skagit History, 1870–1970* (1978), pp. 86, 90; *North Cascadians,* pp. 138, 185; *Concrete Herald,* Sept. 8, 1949.

6. "Newhalem Train Blocked by Slide," *Concrete Herald,* Feb. 25, 1937, p. 1; Roe, *Stevens Pass,* p. 44.

7. Kramer A. Adams, *Logging Railroads of the West* (1961), pp. 22–23 and appendix; Felt, *Capitol Forest,* p. 23; Frank C. Beeson, "Kinzua—Profile of a Company Town," *Crow's Forest Products Digest* (1968).

8. Hall, *Carbon River,* pp. 151, 164.

Notes to Chapter 9

9. Kenneth J. Watson, "If I Had Known, I Might Have Turned and Fled," *Snoqualmie Valley Reporter*, Nov. 24, 1993, p. 7; "Biggest Logging Camp," pp. 12, 27; Denno to the author; "Valsetz Road Conditions Now Best in Years; Repairs Made," *Polk County Itemizer-Observer*, Feb. 27, 1941, p. 1.

10. H. A. Durfey, Pacific Coast R.R. Company brochure (1958); Arlin and Scott, *Cedar Falls*.

11. "A Brief History of the Washington, Idaho & Montana Railway Company," University of Idaho Library, Special Collections. In retirement, the Potlatcher served as the concession stand for a local 4-H club. Kramer Adams, *Logging Railroads*, p. 129, and "W.I. & M. Ry. Co.," *Potlatch Story* [1960], p. 9.

12. Peter J. Replinger to the author, Aug. 18, 1999.

13. John T. Labbe and Peter J. Replinger, *Logging to the Salt Chuck, 1885–1989* (1990), pp. 158–159; Replinger to the author; James, *Grisdale*, p. 31; Ann Messmer; *Simpson Lookout*, January 1949, p. 2. The Grisdale speeder was nicknamed Kalakala because its shape was vaguely reminiscent of the ferry of that name that served Puget Sound cities starting in the 1930s.

14. Felt, *Enterprising Mister Murray*, p. 54; K. Adams, *Logging Railroads*, p. 101; Prouty, "More Deadly Than War," p. 298; Dennis Blake Thompson, *Logging Railroads in Skagit County* (1989), p. 171; *Pacific Spruce Corporation and Subsidiaries* (1924), p. 27.

15. Because every 1-foot rise in a distance of 100 feet represents a 1 percent increase in grade, an incline railway with a 48 percent grade would gain 48 feet of elevation in 100 feet of distance. Thompson, *Logging Railroads*, p. 171. See also, K. Adams, *Logging Railroads*, p. 59; Erigero, "Skagit River," Sec. 7, pp. 34–35; Ramsey, *Brittania*, pp. 151–153; N. Adams, *Holden Mine*, pp. 53, 55.

16. *Holden Miner*, May 1988; Plimpton, "An Ethnoarchaeological Study," p. 66; Ramsey, *Britannia*, p. 55.

17. Hobson, *Valsetz Star*, p. 108.

18. *Simpson Lookout*, March 1949; *Holden Miner*, Nov. 8, 1948, and April, 1996; former Holden residents Bill Phillips, Doran Curzon Gordon, and Harriet Wilbour to the author, 1999.

19. Lentz, National Register Nomination, Sec. 8, p. 38; Duncan, "Life on a Limb," p. 10; Bill Lindstrom, "Grisdale's Last Boss Reminisces: 'We walked out of there with our heads held high,' He Recalls," unidentified newspaper (c. 1986).

20. *Spawn of Coal Dust*, p. 298; "Great Northern Railway Has Been 'Empire

Builder' in Skagit Valley, Too," *Concrete Herald,* June 21, 1951, Sec. 5, p. 5; Charles Dwelley, *So They Called the Town "Concrete"* (1980), p. 65.

21. Arlin and Scott, *Cedar Falls;* Parker, Christianson, and Gordon to the author.

10 / GETTING THE NEWS IN COMPANY TOWNS

1. *McCleary Builder* (1943); McCleary Museum brochure.

2. *Holden Miner,* Spring 1948 and July 1994.

3. *Richland Villager,* 1945–1950; "Carlton Fitchett, Seattle Newsman, Visits Village," *Richland Villager,* Sept. 27, 1945, p. 4.

4. *DuPont Villager,* 1966–1976.

5. Donald A. Black, "Path to Editor's Door," *Christian Science Monitor,* Oct. 25, 1939, p. 2; Hobson, *Valsetz Star.*

6. Marilyn Garcia to the author, Feb. 16, 2000.

7. Fahey, *Inland Empire,* p. 160; Petersen, *Company Town,* p. 136; Lou Messmer and Ann Messmer to the author; *Proceedings, McCleary Community Study* (1955–56), p. 39; Michael Brogan to the author, Aug. 14, 1999.

8. Hallman, "Valsetz, 1919–1984," p. 11; Bob Paasch audiotape.

9. Gumpert and Cale, "Shevlin Camp," pp. 94–95.

10. "'No Letter Today' Theme at Grisdale," *McCleary Stimulator,* Feb. 7, 1957.

11 / WHEN THE "DEAD WHISTLE" BLEW

1. Robert E. Ficken, *The Forested Land* (1987), pp. 132–133; *History of Spruce Production Division;* "Accident Prevention," *Timberman,* November, 1923, p. 90; Arlin and Scott, *Cedar Falls;* Pearl Engel and Jeannette Hlavin, eds., *History of Tacoma Eastern Area* (1954), p. 103. Prouty, "More Deadly Than War," p. 375, said that in a 68-year period, there were more accidents and more serious accidents in the timber industry than in any other. In 1911, of the 279 work-related fatalities in the region, 157 occurred in forest products; the next most dangerous industry, railroad construction, had 23.

2. Sam Churchill, *Big Sam* (1965), pp. 143–144; James, *Grisdale,* p. 32.

3. Stevens, *Powers Story,* p. 102; Teagle, *Out of the Woods,* p. 42.

4. "Rolling Stone Paralyzes Camp Fire Fighter," *Polk County Itemizer-Observer,*

Sept. 22, 1927, p. 1; "Slide at Ruby Creek Kills Two—Injures Four," *Concrete Herald*, Feb. 19, 1948, p. 1.

   5. Roy E. Stier, *Down the Hill: A True Story of Early Logging in the Pacific Northwest* (1995), pp. 170–171; Hall, *Carbon River*, p. 159.

   6. K. Adams, *Logging Railroads*, pp. 111, 115. Another railway historian, George Abdill, notes in *This Was Railroading* (1958), p. 185, that not all logging railroads were poorly constructed. Large timber companies such as Weyerhaeuser, Simpson, and Long-Bell built high-quality railroad lines that were equal in safety to—or better than—some short-line common carriers.

   7. Louis T. Corsaletti, "Newcastle Area's Mining Industry Helped Region Coalesce in 1860s, '70s," *Seattle Times*, Jan. 15, 1998; Olson and Olson, *Black Diamond*, p. 76.

   8. N. Adams, *Holden Mine*, p. 55; Harriet Wilbour to the author, June 23, 1999.

   9. Mary Ellen Field Lacy to the author, Nov. 15, 1999; Sandy Wigbers Adam to the author, Sept. 20, 1999; Getty Clark.

   10. Arlin and Scott, *Cedar Falls*; Munyan, *DuPont*, pp. 70–71; *DuPont Villager*, Oct 10, 1969.

   11. Thompson, *Logging Railroads*, pp. 56–66; typescript of 1986 interview with Theodora Thompson, about life in Cedar Falls from 1927 to 1956.

   12. Petersen, *Company Town*, p. 125; *Spawn of Coal Dust*, p. 187; Munyan, *DuPont*, p. 29.

   13. Roe, *North Cascadians*, p. 130; Plimpton, "Ethnoarchaeological Study," pp. 66–67; Wilbour to the author, March 14, 2000.

   14. Pitzer, *Grand Coulee*, p. 152; Wilbour to the author.

   15. Plimpton, "An Ethnoarchaeological Study," pp. 14–19; Mary Young McDivitt questionnaire, 1987; Arlin, oral history, pp. 22, 69; Wilbour to the author.

   16. "Partially Solved Mystery," *Holden Miner*, October 1990; Roe, *North Cascadians*, p. 132.

   17. Denno to the author; "Phil Moran Injured on Ruby Creek Job," *Concrete Herald*, Jan. 14, 1937, p. 1.

   18. Wilbour, letter to the author; Gray, *Roughing It*, pp. 110, 143.

   19. Nelson, "Muckers' Special"; Lou and Ann Messmer to the author; *Holden Miner*, November 1988; Linda Powell Jensen to the author, October 2000.

   20. Powell Jensen to the author.

   21. Wilbour to the author, Nov. 2 1999; Hall, *Carbon River*, p. 164.

   22. Wigbers Adam to the author; *Wenatchee Daily World*, March 1, 1957; Ernest

Bertolsen, "Living Memories in a Ghost Town," *Seattle Times,* Oct. 26, 1947; Frances Stone, "Six Families Face Sad Christmas as Work of Mine Rescue Stops," *Tacoma Sunday News-Ledger,* Dec. 23, 1917, p. 6.

23. *Deschutes Pine Echoes,* Vol. 27, No. 10.

12 / DEPRESSION AND WORLD WARS

1. *History of Spruce Production Division,* introduction and p. 16; Ralph W. Hidy, Frank Ernest Hall, and Allan Nevins, *Timber and Men* (1963), p. 336; files of the McCleary branch, Timberland Regional Library; Petersen, *Company Town,* p. 158.

2. The U.S. government spent $45.5 million on the Spruce Production Division, $15 million of it on railroads and mills not completed prior to the armistice. *History of Spruce Production Division,* introduction and pp. 23–24.

3. "DuPont News," *Tacoma Daily Ledger,* Feb. 16, 1919; "Reception Tendered Sidney and Glenn Hill," *Friday Harbor Journal,* Nov. 7, 1918, p. 1.

4. *Tacoma Daily Ledger,* 1918–1919.

5. Mary Daheim, "An Alpine Memoir," *Pacific Search* (1974), p. 12; McCleary (Wash.) Museum newsletter, 1992; "DuPont News," *Tacoma Sunday Ledger,* Feb. 9, 1919.

6. Shannon Kracht, "Wendling: A Company Town," *Lane County Historian* (Spring 1975), p. 2. Denno to the author. *Polk County Itemizer-Observer,* 1930–36. City directories for the early 1930s show the Valsetz population as low as 22, compared to several hundred in the 1920s, and the Wendling population at 400, about half what it had been prior to the stock market crash.

7. A 1933 paycheck of $21 was worth less than $300 in 2001 dollars. David Richardson, *Pig Wars Islands* (1971), p. 334.

8. Sam Churchill, *Don't Call Me Ma* (1977), pp. 191–192.

9. Jack Young to the author, May 30, 1999; Arlin and Scott, *Cedar Falls;* "Mill at Kinzua Resumes Work after Shutdown," *Fossil (Ore.) Journal,* Jan. 28, 1938; Louise Schmidt Robertson to the author, April 10, 2000; Dario Bulgarelli, oral history, March 10, 1985.

10. McClelland, *R. A. Long's Planned City,* p. 201.

11. Goodwin, *Stories,* p. 24; *Mason City Columbian,* Nov. 17, 1938, Dec. 15, 1938, and Nov. 30, 1939.

12. Clark I. Cross, "Factors Influencing the Abandonment of Lumber Mill Towns in the Puget Sound Region" (Master's thesis, University of Washington, 1946), p. 52.

13. Stewart Holbrook, *Wildmen, Wobblies, and Whistle Punks* (1992), p. 288.

14. By July 1942, the average weekly wage in mills and logging operations in western Washington and Oregon was $38.83, compared to $55.32 in Washington State shipyards. "Labor Situation in Western Lumber Industry," *Monthly Labor Review* (1942), pp. 1126, 1129. *West Coast Timberman,* January 1943; Driscoll, "Gilchrist," p. 144.

15. "Furlough to Mines," *Business Week,* Aug. 7, 1943, pp. 64–68; John Bley to the author, Oct. 24, 1999. According to the *Chelan Valley Mirror,* April 29, 1943, Holden Mine was sent sixty GIs starting in November 1942.

16. Marilyn Garcia to the author, Feb. 16, 2000.

17. Carlos Arnaldo Schwantes, *Hard Traveling: A Portrait of Work Life in the New Northwest* (1994), p. 136; Charles Hale to the author; Sparkman, *From Homestead,* p. 134; *Fossil (Ore.) Journal,* August 1942.

18. *Fossil Journal,* 1942–44; Petersen, *Company Town,* p. 182; Mary Ellen Field Lacy to the author, Nov. 15, 1999; Mary Young McDivitt to the author, June 9, 1999; "Valsetz to Form as Sharpshooters," *Polk County Itemizer-Observer,* March 26, 1942, p. 6.

19. Arlin and Scott, *Cedar Falls;* Gordon to the author; Betty Bickford Christianson to the author, Feb. 15, 2000; Hobson, *Valsetz Star,* p. 141.

20. McDivitt to the author, Jan. 21, 2000; "Books" by Lewis Gannett, in *While You Were Gone* (1946), pp. 448–449.

21. Christianson, letter to the author. Victory gardens were encouraged to keep Americans well fed despite food rationing. But, according to an early 1942 story, "Victory Garden Program Started," in the *Fossil Journal,* growing and preserving food at home also saved tin, which was in limited supply; reduced the need for shipping when trains were carrying war materials; and freed up commercially canned food for shipment to Great Britain and to U.S. troops overseas.

22. Christianson to the author.

13 / FAME—EVEN IF FLEETING

1. Ben Bothian, "Riches Pour from Holden Mine," *Wenatchee (Wash.) Daily World,* April 26, 1939, Sec. 3, pp. 1, 26, 30; William Galbraith, "The Law Comes to the Town of Holden," Spokane *Spokesman-Review,* March 21, 1948, p. 6; "So You Think You Had Snow," p. 76.

2. "Skyscraper Country: Here is Sunset's Guide to the Fabulous North Cascades,"

Sunset (August 1958), p. 44; Nathaniel T. Kenney, "The Spectacular North Cascades," *National Geographic* (1968), pp. 651, 655.

3. James, *Grisdale*, p. 69; *Simpson Lookout*, December 1950; Savery, "Northwest Wonderland," p. 477; Bill Richards, "The Olympic Peninsula," *National Geographic* (1984), p. 668; Byron Fish, *Seattle Times*, Nov. 21, 1948; "Valsetz Still Holds Oregon Rain Record," *Polk County (Ore.) Itemizer-Observer*, Feb. 15, 1940, p. 1; Hal Boyle, "Must Be 6 Feet Tall or Drown in Valsetz," *Seattle Times*, May 4, 1950, p. 43.

4. Edward Parks, "Washington Wilderness, the North Cascades," *National Geographic* (1961), pp. 366; Savery, "Northwest Wonderland," p. 457.

5. Mary Daheim to the author, March 12, 2000.

6. "Grand Coulee," *Fortune* (July 1937), p. 160; "Biggest Thing on Earth," *Harper's* (February 1937), pp. 242–258; "8th World Wonder," *Saturday Evening Post* (July 1935), p. 23; Hitchcock, "The World's First All-Electric City," pp. 3–4; Maynard Owen Williams, "The Columbia Turns on the Power," *National Geographic* (June 1941), p. 771.

7. Thomas R. Horner, "The Mountains Light a City: Seattle's Ambitious River Power Development," *Scientific American* (August 1925), pp. 112–133; Jim Marshall, "It Can't Be Done, Can't It?" *Collier's* (March 1936), p. 36; Carl Dreher, "J. D. Ross, Public Power Magnate," *Harper's* (June 1940).

8. "The Warrior's Promise," *Time* (July 1985), p. 45; "War Workers' City," *Business Week* (June 1943), p. 18; Syring, "Turning An Atom City Over," p. 1; "All American Cities," *Look* (April 1961), p. 95.

9. Russell Bookout, "Sitting on Dynamite," *Atlantic Monthly* (June 1929).

10. Munyan, *DuPont*, p. 71; Felt, *Enterprising Mister Murray*, p. 77; *Holden Miner*, November 1998, p. 3; Tappan to the author, April 28, 1999; Malmstrom to the author, Nov. 16, 1999.

11. Baldwin, *Making the Most*, pp. 20–21; K. Adams, *Logging Railroads*, p. 119; McClelland, *R. A. Long's Planned City*, pp. 149–151; *Simpson Diamond*, May 1961, p. 5, and June 1963, pp. 2–3.

12. State film offices, Washington and Oregon.

13. Willis to the author, Oct. 5, 1999.

14. Pellegrini discussed McCleary in *Immigrant's Return* (1951) and *Americans by Choice* (1956); Hobson's monthly newspapers were compiled in *The Valsetz Star* (1942).

15. Thompson, *Logging Railroads*, p. 124; N. Adams, *The Holden Mine*, pp. 2–3.

16. The Alpine Lumber Company founders' relationship to Samuel Clemens, whose branch of the family had modernized its surname's spelling, is described in Daheim, "An Alpine Memoir," p. 13. Nancy Irene Hall, "Carbonado Centennial, 1880–1980" (1980), p. 2, and *Carbon River,* p. 87.

14 / THE PATERNALISTIC COMPANY TOWN BOSS

1. New liquor licenses were prohibited within five miles of common-carrier railroads, but license renewals were permitted for any saloon that had opened at least six months prior to railroad construction. Peterson, *Company Town,* p. 83.

2. Ironically, bachelors in dry Ryderwood lived in what was called the Tavern. "Biggest Logging Camp," p. 8. Although the author of one Holden history claims that the community once had a package liquor store, Washington State Liquor Control Board records show that no liquor stores were ever authorized for Holden, Lucerne, Stehekin, or other uplake communities. Susan Peterschick to the author, Nov. 3, 1999. Lou and Ann Messmer to the author; Gregory, "Life in Railroad Logging Camps," p. 59.

3. Petersen, *Company Town,* pp. 136, 146; McClelland, *R. A. Long's Planned City,* p. 83; Hallman, "Valsetz, 1919–1984," p. 11; Gordon to the author.

4. "This Town Has Idea Behind It," *Tacoma Daily Ledger,* Nov. 17, 1918; Schrager, "The Early Days," p. 275; Imus, "A Social History," pp. 35, 38.

5. Nancy Irene Hall, *Dateline: Wilkeson* (1984), p. 15; Ramsey, *Britannia,* p. 98; Tappan and Stansfield to the author; *Chelan Valley Mirror,* July 13, 1939.

6. Bert Dietz, "The Little Kingdom of M'Cleary," *Timber Worker,* Sept. 18, 1936; Pellegrini, *Immigrant's Return,* p. 44. Decades after McCleary's death, the timber baron's desk was still in use—but in the office of his town's top union official, at the Western Council of Industrial Workers, Local 2761.

7. Goodwin, *Stories,* p. 31; Ted Rakoski to the author, Aug. 14, 1999; John Marshall, "Loggers' Dream Town Turns to Sawdust," *Seattle Post-Intelligencer,* June 27, 1985, p. D-1.

8. "Who Runs Our School District?" advertisement, *Eatonville Dispatch.*

9. Pitzer, *Grand Coulee,* pp. 103–104; "Year-old City Proves Its Maturity," *Seattle Times,* May 8, 1960; D. McManman and K. Bradford, "Herald Leaders Were Bullish on Tri-Cities," *Tri-City Herald,* Nov. 13, 1997.

10. "Richland Unique among American Cities," *Tacoma Sunday Ledger-News Tribune,* Dec. 14, 1952; "Year-Old City Proves . . . "

11. Imus, "A Social History," p. 20; Hall, *Dateline: Wilkeson*, p. 26; *Concrete Herald*, December 1959.

12. Shipman, *Grand Coulee Dam Area*, p. 13.

13. "This Town Has Idea Behind It"; Willis, Oct. 24, 2000; *Richland Villager*, 1945.

14. Wilbour to the author, July 7, 1999; Arlin and Scott, *Cedar Falls;* Imus, "A Social History," p. 73; *Mason City Columbian*, July 14, 1938.

15. Kubik, *Richland*, p. 49; Beardsley, *Long Road*, pp. 5, 6; McManman, "Herald Leaders Were Bullish."

16. *Simpson Diamond*, January 1963. In "Bringing the Past to Life in McCleary," the July 9, 1998, *Montesano (Wash.) Vidette* reported that historians working near McCleary had found an old light bulb stamped "Stolen from the Henry McCleary Timber Co."

17. Elmer Smith to the author, Aug. 28, 1999; Stacey Graham to the author, Dec. 17, 1999.

18. Six-day workweeks were typical in this period. "Old Sawmill Town Remembered," pp. 7, 15. Gordon to the author; Wilbour to the author, June 23, 1999; Messmer to the author.

15 / WHEN THE TOWN SHUT DOWN

1. Harriet Wilbour to Rudy Edmunds, Oct. 26, 1988, regarding inaccuracies in his speech on the Holden Mine closure, and Wilbour to the author, June 5, 1999; Parks, "Washington Wilderness," pp. 366–367.

2. Woodman, "Barneston's Japanese Community"; Douglass Welch, "Taylor Residents Resigned to Fate," *Seattle Post-Intelligencer*, Nov. 22, 1944, p. HH-13; F. B. Ortman, president, Gladding, McBean & Co., to Seattle City Council, May 20, 1946; Dario Bulgarelli, oral history, March 10, 1985; Ott, *Tacoma Public Utilities Story*, p. 201; Lily Eng, "Gathering the Memories of a Town Called Lester," *Seattle Times*, June 14, 1998.

3. Petersen, *Company Town*, pp. 200–201; Munyan, *DuPont*, p. 80; Thoele, "Brothers Ensure," pp. 1, 6A; Mike Freeman, "For Sale: Gilchrist, Body and Soul," *Bend (Ore.) Bulletin*, undated.

4. Kubik, *Richland*, pp. 62, 67, 71; Syring, "Turning an Atom City Over," pp. 1–2.

5. Olsen, *Then Till Now in Brookings-Harbor*, pp. 52, 75.

6. Marie Ruby, public programs supervisor, Cedar River Watershed, and two former Cedar Falls residents, Jack Young and Mary Young McDivitt, to the author, 1999; Erigero, "Skagit River," several references.

7. Cheryl Cronander, National Register of Historic Places registration form (1989), Sec. 8, p. 7, and Lentz, National Register Nomination, Sec. 8, p. 39.

8. Hallman, "Valsetz, 1919–1984," p. 21.

BIBLIOGRAPHY

ARTICLES, BOOKS, THESES, AND WEBSITES

"A Brief History of the Washington, Idaho, & Montana Railway," in University of Idaho Special Collections, lib.idaho.edu/specialcollections/Manuscripts/ mg139.htm (July 1997).

Abdill, George B. *This Was Railroading.* Seattle: Superior Publishing, 1958.

Adams, Freda A. "The Port Blakely I Knew," in *Kitsap County History.* Silverdale, Wash.: Kitsap County Historical Society, 1977.

Adams, Kramer A. *Logging Railroads of the West.* Seattle: Superior Publishing, 1961.

Adams, Nigel B. *The Holden Mine: Discovery to Production, 1896–1938.* Wenatchee, Wash.: Washington State Historical Society, 1981.

Allen, James B. *The Company Town in the American West.* Norman: University of Oklahoma Press, 1966.

Arlin, Marian Thompson, and Dorothy Graybael Scott. *Cedar Falls: As Remembered by Some of Those Who Lived There.* North Bend, Wash.: Snoqualmie Valley Historical Museum, 1989.

Bagley, Clarence. *History of King County.* Seattle and Chicago: S. J. Clarke Publishing, 1929.

Baldwin, Catherine. *Making the Most of the Best: Willamette Industries' Seventy-Five Years.* Portland, Ore.: Willamette Industries, 1982.

Beardsley, Paul. *The Long Road to Self-Government: The History of Richland, Washington, 1943–1968.* Richland; City of Richland, c. 1968.

Bibliography

Beeson, Frank C. "Kinzua—Profile of a Company Town," *Crow's Forest Products Digest,* October 1968.

"Biggest Logging Camp in the World," *Cowlitz Historical Quarterly,* Vol. 30, No. 1, 1988.

Birkeland, Torger. *Echoes of Puget Sound.* Caldwell, Idaho: Caxton Printers, 1960.

Bolinger, Mike. "Old Time Logging and Cookhouse," *The Timberbeast,* Spring 1985.

Booth, T. William. "Design for a Lumber Town by Bebb and Gould, Architects," *Pacific Northwest Quarterly,* October 1991.

Brandes, Stuart D. *American Welfare Capitalism.* Chicago: University of Chicago Press, 1970.

Buchanan, Bill. "Bernard Maybeck and Brookings, Oregon," a Harbor Construction site, www.oregoncoast.net/maybeck.html (January 2003).

Buder, Stanley. *Pullman: An Experiment in Industrial Order and Community Planning, 1880–1930.* New York: Oxford University Press, 1967.

Campbell, Robert A. "Blacks and the Coal Mines of Western Washington, 1888–1896," *Pacific Northwest Quarterly,* October 1982.

Carlsson, Lars E. *Port Blakely Mills and Milltown: Historic Buildings/Cultural Resources Survey for Port Blakely Mill Co.* Olympia, Wash., 1992.

Churchill, Sam. *Big Sam.* Garden City, N.Y.: Doubleday & Co., 1965.

————— *Don't Call Me Ma.* Garden City, N.Y.: Doubleday & Co., 1977.

————— "Christmas in Camp," *Timberbeast,* Winter 1984.

Conlin, Joseph. "Old Boy, Did You Get Enough Pie?" *Journal of Forest History,* October 1979.

Cross, Clark I. "Factors Influencing the Abandonment of Lumber Mill Towns in the Puget Sound Region." M.A. thesis, University of Washington, 1946.

Daheim, Mary. "An Alpine Memoir," *Pacific Search,* April 1974.

Downs, L. Vaughn. *The Mightiest of Them All: Memories of Grand Coulee Dam,* rev. ed. New York: ASCE Press, 1993.

Driscoll, John. "Gilchrist," *Oregon Historical Quarterly,* Summer 1984.

Dwelley, Charles. *So They Called the Town "Concrete."* 1980.

Eakins, Jan M. "Port Gamble Historic Landmark, Historic American Engineering Record (HAER) No. WA-135." Seattle: Columbia Cascade Support Office, National Park Service, 1997.

Engel, Pearl, and Jeannette Hlavin, eds. *History of Tacoma Eastern Area.* Eatonville, Wash.: Operation Bootstrap, Southern Pierce County Study Group, 1954.

Bibliography

Erigero, Patricia. "Skagit River Hydroelectric Project FERC No. 553, Survey and Documentation for the Historic American Building Survey and Historic American Engineering Record and National Register Nomination Form." Seattle: City of Seattle, City Light Department, 1991.

Fahey, John. *The Inland Empire: Unfolding Years, 1879–1929*. Seattle: University of Washington Press, 1986.

Felt, Margaret Elley. *Capitol Forest: The Forest That Came Back*. Olympia: Washington State Department of Natural Resources, 1975.

———— *The Enterprising Mister Murray*. Weiser, Idaho: Caxton Printers, 1978.

Ficken, Robert E. *The Forested Land: A History of Lumbering in Western Washington*. Seattle and Durham, N.C.: University of Washington Press and Forest History Society, 1987.

Fisher, Jim. *Gilchrist: The First Fifty Years*. Gilchrist, Ore.: Gilchrist Timber, 1988.

"Gilchrist, Oregon: Last Timber Company Town," *Forest World*, Fall 1989.

Goodwin, Ted. *Stories of Western Loggers*. Chehalis, Wash.: Loggers World, 1977.

Gray, Edward. *Roughing It on the Little Deschutes River, 1934–44*. Eugene, Ore.: 1986.

Gregory, Ronald L. "Life in Railroad Logging Camps of the Shevlin-Hixon Co., 1916–1950." Master's thesis, Oregon State University, 1997.

Gumpert, Lois Maker, and Dorothy Cale. "Shevlin Camp," in *A History of the Deschutes Country in Oregon*. Bend, Ore.: Deschutes County Historical Society, 1985.

Hall, Nancy Irene. *Carbon River Coal Country*. Enumclaw, Wash.: Courier-Herald Publishing, 1980.

———— *Carbonado Centennial, 1880–1980*. 1980.

———— *Dateline: Wilkeson*. South Prairie, Wash.: Washington State Genealogical and Historical Review, 1984.

Hanscom, John. "Franklin and the Oregon Improvement Company," *Columbia Magazine*, Spring 1994.

The Henry McCleary Timber Co. Tacoma: Plywood Pioneers Association, 1968.

Hidy, Ralph W., Frank Ernest Hall, and Allan Nevins. *Timber and Men: The Weyerhaeuser Story*. New York: MacMillan, 1963.

History of Spruce Production Division. Portland, Ore.: U.S. Army and United States Spruce Production Corp., c. 1919.

Hitchcock, G.W. "The World's First All-Electric City: Mason City," *Pacific Builder & Engineer*, January 19, 1935.

Bibliography

Hobson, Dorothy Anne. *The Valsetz Star*. Portland, Ore.: Creation House, 1942.

Holbrook, Stewart. *Wildmen, Wobblies, and Whistle Punks*, edited by Brian Booth. Corvallis: Oregon State University Press, 1992.

Hosmer, Paul. *Now We're Loggin'*. Portland, Ore.: Metropolitan Press, 1930.

Imus, Clifford Lewis. "A Social History of Potlatch, Idaho." B.A. thesis, Washington State College, 1910.

James, David W. *Grisdale: Last of the Logging Camps*. Belfair, Wash.: Mason County Historical Society, 1986.

Journals of the Diocese of Olympia, Annual Meetings of the Convention. Seattle: Diocese of Olympia, 1951–1970.

Kracht, Shannon. "Wendling: A Company Town," *Lane County Historian*, Spring 1975.

Kubik, Barbara J. *Richland: Celebrating the Heritage*. Richland: City of Richland, 1994.

Labbe, John T., and Peter J. Replinger. *Logging to the Salt Chuck, 1885–1989*. Seattle: Northwest Short Line, 1990.

Lentz, Florence K. *National Register Nomination for Seattle City Light*, Cedar Falls, Wash., 1996.

"Library Popular: State Meets Need of Rural Communities," *Morning Olympian* (Olympia, Wash.), April 30, 1909.

"Logging a Million Feet of Timber Daily at Vail," *West Coast Lumberman*, October 1929.

Maben, Manly. *Vanport*. Portland: Oregon Historical Society Press, 1987.

Martin, Grace Brandt. *An Oregon Schoolma'am*, Book 2: *The Depression Years*. Brownsville, Ore.: Calapooia Publications, 1981.

McCleary Community Study. *Proceedings, McCleary Community Study, McCleary, Washington 1955–1956*. Part 4 of 4. McCleary, 1955–56.

McClelland, John M., Jr. *R. A. Long's Planned City: The Story of Longview*. Longview, Wash.: Longview Publishing, 1976.

McElderry, Stuart. "Vanport Conspiracy Rumors and Social Relations in Portland, 1940–50," *Oregon Historical Quarterly*, Summer 1998.

McWilliams, Mary. *Seattle Water Department History*. Seattle: City of Seattle, 1955.

Meisner, Jennifer A. "The Future of Roslyn, Washington: Preservation of a Vernacular Town." Master's thesis, University of Washington, 1994.

Morgan, Murray. *The Dam*. New York: Viking Press, 1954.

More Than 100 Years of Ministry. Seattle: Diocese of Olympia, 1988.

Bibliography

Munyan, May G. *DuPont: The Story of a Company Town*. Puyallup, Wash.: Valley Press, 1972.

Neuberger, Richard L. *Our Promised Land*. New York: Macmillan, 1938.

Nicandri, David L. *Italians in Washington State Emigration, 1853–1924*. Tacoma: Washington State American Revolution Bicentennial Commission, 1978.

Nomura, Gail M. "Tsugiki, a Grafting: A History of a Japanese Pioneer Woman in Washington State," in *Women in Pacific Northwest History: An Anthology*, edited by Karen J. Blair. Seattle: University of Washington Press, 1988.

"Old Sawmill Town Remembered," *Northwest Nikkei*, May 1994.

Olsen, Edward G., ed. *Then Till Now in Brookings-Harbor: A Social History of the Chetco Community Area*. Brookings, Ore.: Rotary Club of Brookings, 1979.

Olson, Diane, and Cory Olson. *Black Diamond: Mining the Memories*. Seattle: Black Diamond Historical Society, 1988.

Ott, John S., and Dick Malloy. *The Tacoma Public Utilities Story: The First 100 Years*. Tacoma, Wash.: Tacoma Public Utilities, 1993.

Pacific Spruce Corporation and Subsidiaries: C. D. Johnson Lumber Company, Manary Logging Company, Pacific Spruce Northern Railway Co., a supplement to *Lumber World Review*, Feb. 10, 1924.

Parks, Edward. "Washington Wilderness, the North Cascades," *National Geographic*, March 1961.

Pellegrini, Angelo M. *Immigrant's Return*. New York: Macmillan, 1951.

——— *Americans by Choice*. New York: Macmillan, 1956.

Petersen, Keith C. *Company Town: Potlatch, Idaho, and the Potlatch Lumber Company* Pullman, Wash.: Washington State University Press, 1987.

Petrich, Mary Ann, and Barbara Roje. "The Slavs in the Coal Mining Communities of Central Washington," in *The Yugoslav in Washington State: Among the Early Settlers*. Tacoma: Washington State Historical Society, 1984.

Pitzer, Paul C. *Building the Skagit: A Century of Upper Skagit History, 1870–1970*. Portland, Ore.: Galley Press, 1978.

——— *Grand Coulee: Harnessing a Dream*. Pullman: Washington State University Press, 1994.

Plimpton, Christine Leigh. "An Ethnoarchaeological Study of Honeymoon Heights: The Original Camp of the Holden Mine, Holden, Washington." Master's thesis, Washington State University, 1984.

Price, Andrew, Jr. *Port Blakely: The Community Captain Renton Built*. Seattle: Port Blakely Books, 1989.

Bibliography

Pringle, George C. F. *Adventures in Service.* Toronto: McClelland & Stewart, 1929.

Prouty, Andrew. "More Deadly Than War: Pacific Coast Logging, 1827–1981." Ph.D. dissertation, University of Washington, 1982.

Ramsey, Bruce. *Britannia: The Story of a Mine.* Britannia Beach, B.C.: Britannia Beach Community Club, 1967.

Redden, George. *From Bootblack to Pastor of the Pines and Twenty-two Thousand Miles through the Pines of the Northwest with the Lumber-Jack.* Bend, Ore. [c. 1932].

Reed, Frank A. *Lumberjack Sky Pilot.* Old Forge, N.Y.: North County Books, 1965.

Richardson, David. *Pig War Islands.* Eastsound, Wash.: Orcas Publishing, 1971.

Roe, Joann. *The North Cascadians.* Seattle: Madrona Publishers, 1980.

———— *Stevens Pass.* Seattle: Mountaineers, 1995.

Russell, Jervis, ed. *Jimmy-Come-Lately History of Clallam County.* Port Angeles, Wash.: Clallam County Historical Society, 1971.

Savery, Merle. "Northwest Wonderland: Washington State," *National Geographic,* April 1960.

Schenkkan, Robert. "Fire in the Hole," in *The Kentucky Cycle.* New York: Plume, 1993.

Schrager, Samuel A. "The Early Days: Logging in the Inland Northwest." Ph.D. dissertation, University of Pennsylvania, 1983.

Schwantes, Carlos Arnaldo. *Hard Traveling: A Portrait of Work Life in the New Northwest.* Lincoln: University of Nebraska Press, 1994.

Sears, Lyle Compton. *Sampler of the Early Years,* vol. 2. Washington, D.C.: Forestry Wives Club of Washington, D.C., 1986.

Shipman, George A. *The Grand Coulee Dam Area: A Preliminary Report.* Ephrata, Wash.: U.S. Department of the Interior, Bureau of Reclamation, 1953.

Sipila, Impie (Marian) Hanga. "My Remembrances of Taylor, Washington," in *Hobart Area Recollections.* Maple Valley, Wash.: Maple Valley Historical Society, 1988.

"So You Think You Had Snow," *Life,* April 9, 1956.

Sparkman, LaVonne. *From Homestead to Lakebed.* Bend, Ore.: Maverick Publications, 1994.

Spawn of Coal Dust: History of Roslyn, 1886–1955. Roslyn, Wash.: Community Uplift, 1955.

Stafford, Robert. "The Reality of an Atomic Utopia: The Town with a Past," *Intellect,* December 1975.

Stevens, Victor. *The Powers Story.* 1979.

Bibliography

Stier, Roy E. *Down the Hill: A True Story of Early Logging in the Pacific Northwest.* Wilsonville, Ore.: BookPartners, 1995.

Teagle, Ernest C. *Out of the Woods: The Story of McCleary.* Shelton: Wash.: Simpson Logging, 1956.

———*A Brief History of the McCleary Methodist Church, 1910–1960.* 1960.

———"An Informal Biography of the Teagle Family." Typescript, 1960.

Thompson, Dennis Blake. *Logging Railroads in Skagit County.* Seattle: Northwest Short Line, 1989.

Van Arsdol, Ted. *Tri-Cities: The Mid-Columbia Hub.* Chatsworth, Calif.: Windsor Publications, 1990.

Van Sickle, Edwin. *They Tried to Cut It All.* Seattle: Pacific Search Press, 1980.

Washington, a Guide to the Evergreen State, rev. ed. Portland: Binford & Mort and the Washington State Historical Society, 1950.

ADDITIONAL NEWSPAPERS

Daily life in company-owned and company-dominated communities has been documented in such local, company, and industry publications as the *Chelan (Wash.) Valley Mirror; Concrete (Wash.) Herald; DuPont (Wash.) Villager; Fossil (Ore.) Journal; Holden (Wash.) Miner; Mason City (Coulee Dam, Wash.) Columbian; Polk County (Dallas, Ore.) Itemizer-Observer; Richland (Wash.) Villager; Tacoma (Wash.) Daily Ledger; Wilkeson (Wash.) Record;* Brooks-Scanlon Deschutes *Pine Echoes; Potlatch Story; Shevlin-Hixon Equalizer; Simpson Lookout, Simpson Diamond,* and *Simpson Magazine; Weyerhaeuser Magazine; Camp & Mill News; 4 L Lumber News;* and *The Timberman.*

INTERVIEWS AND OTHER SOURCES

Cited audiotapes and the Nelson and Wilbour typescripts regarding the Holden School have been available in the Holden Village tape library or the Holden Portal Museum. Some Holden historical materials are being sent to Pacific Lutheran University, Tacoma, Wash., for archiving.

All landmark application materials for the Cedar River watershed communities of Cedar Falls and Selleck and the transcripts of oral histories and interviews with Marian Thompson Arlin, Theodora Thompson, and Dario Bulgarelli are in the Cedar Falls archives, as are the results of three class projects: Mary Woodman

Bibliography

and Richard Gilbert's "Barneston's Japanese Community" and Chris Brown and John Schroeder's "An Investigation of Place and Community through Photographs, Maps and Oral Histories," both written for University of Washington internships, and Bruce O. Schneider's "The Historic Mining Landscape of Taylor, Wash.," written for a Central Washington University class.

Landmark application materials for the Skagit River communities of Newhalem and Diablo are on file with the City of Seattle, and for Port Gamble, at the Columbia Cascade Support Office of the National Park Service in Seattle. The Gertrude Murphy oral history transcript is available from Tacoma Public Utilities.

The Works Progress Administration manuscripts cited are in the files of the Washington State Historical Society, Tacoma. Annual reports filed by school superintendents in King, Pierce and Kitsap Counties are available in the Puget Sound Regional Archives.

INDEX

Pages with illustrations are indicated in boldface type.

Index

tinctions in, 48, 90, 96; during
Depression, 165; hazards in, 147,
150, 152, 153; housing in, 17, 26;
library privileges for residents, 91;
as movie location, 184; orchestra,
63, 88; recreational facilities of, 80,
196; school in, 43, 59, 63, 64, 65, 67;
shopping from, 108–9, 113; social
life in, 94, 95; transportation to,
123, 124; during World War II,
171, 172. *See also* Diablo, Wash.;
Jackson, Emmett; Newhalem,
Wash.
Celebrations, 90–94, 95, 96
Celebrities: company-town residents
as, 184; visiting, 180, 182–83, 184
Cherry Valley, Wash., 60, **128**, 216
Children: of bosses, 44, 47–48; Christmas parties for, 37, 77, 89–90, 93,
166; misbehavior of, 193; paid and
volunteer work for, 41–42, 136–37,
139–41, 150–51, 161, 185; protecting,
69, 152–53, 196–97; recreation for,
95–96, 97–98; during World War II,
169, 171
Church activities: buildings for, 60,
70–72, **72**; create communities, 78;
financial support for, 73–74, 77; and
ministers, 70, 72, 74, 75; for minorities, 77; as social events, 88, 89, 163;
United Protestant, 71–72
Church by Mail, 73
Churchill, Sam, 53, 147, 164, 183
Clay City, Wash., 124, 216–17
Clear Lake (Clearlake), Wash., 217
Clemans, Carl and Hugh, **179**, 185, 213

Clemens, Samuel (Mark Twain), 185,
213
Closure of towns, 163, 166, 199–205;
Holden, 42–43; media attention
to, 178, 181; Pine Ridge, 43–44;
Pullman, 10; reasons for, 35, 132,
166, 174
Clubs, 88–91, 171, 174, 193
Coal Creek, Wash., 32, 61, 124, 163, 229
Cobalt, Idaho, 43, 217. *See also* Holden,
Wash.; Howe Sound Company
Cobbs & Mitchell, 23, **97**, **103**, 139–41,
164. *See also* Hobson, Dorothy
Anne; Valsetz, Ore.; *Valsetz Star*
Company store, 101–8; company con-
trol of, 188, 189; during Depression,
49, 102, 164; monopolistic, 12; paymaster located in, 104–5; post office
in, 136, **144**, 144–45; prices, 107;
Santa Claus at, 80, 93
Concrete, Wash., 44–45, 184, 217–18
Conda, Idaho, 218
Cookhouses, 40, 50–51, 54; bull cooks
for, 42; in "car camps," 56; dining
hall in Bordeaux, 52; prices in, 51,
55; provisions for, 39, 51, 54–55, 152;
in Valsetz, 140
Coulee Dam, Wash., 218; age of population in, 38; community cohesiveness in, 193; and the Depression,
166, 174; discrimination against
blacks and women in, 40, 46, 65;
housing in, 18, 25, 32; media attention for, 180; recreation in, 84, 85,
93–94, 98, 196; and shopping, 104,
110–11, 192

LIBRARY OF CONGRESS CATALOGING-IN-PUBLICATION DATA

Carlson, Linda.
Company towns of the Pacific Northwest / Linda Carlson.
p. cm.
Includes bibliographical references and index.
ISBN 0-295-98332-9 (acid-free paper)
1. Company towns—Pacific States—History.
2. City and town life—Pacific States—History.
3. Pacific States—Social conditions.
4. Pacific States—Economic conditions.
5. Pacific States—History, Local.
6. Company towns—Northwest, Pacific—History.
7. Northwest, Pacific—History, Local.
I. Title.
F851.C277 2003   307.76'7'09795—dc21   2003046766